Suzanne S. G.

READABLE, DOABLE
AND
DELICIOUS

READABLE, DOABLE AND DELICIOUS

Requested Recipes and
Stories from the Past to the Present

Suzanne S. Jones

Copyright © 2011 by Suzanne S. Jones.

Library of Congress Control Number: 2011911359
ISBN:
    Hardcover   978-1-4628-4570-5
    Softcover   978-1-4628-4569-9
    Ebook   978-1-4628-4571-2

All rights reserved. No part of this book may be reproduced or transmitted in any form or by any means, electronic or mechanical, including photocopying, recording, or by any information storage and retrieval system, without permission in writing from the copyright owner.

This book was printed in the United States of America.

To order additional copies of this book, contact:
Xlibris Corporation
1-888-795-4274
www.Xlibris.com
Orders@Xlibris.com
96530

CONTENTS

APPETIZERS

AMERICAN CAFÉ HOMEMADE KETCHUP 17
BAKED CHICKEN NUGGETS WITH HOT AND
    SWEET MUSTARD SAUCE 18
BLUE CHEESE COOKIES 19
CHEESE AND CHIVE SPREAD 20
CHICKEN PATE WITH ALMONDS 21
CORNED BEEF PATE 22
CREAM CHEESE AND VEGETABLE SPREAD 23
FAVORITE CHOPPED CHICKEN LIVERS 24
FROGGIES LA TARTE AU TOMATES ET FROMAGES CHEVRES 25
HOLIDAY (OR OTHER) HAM BALLS 27
HOT CHEESE AND CRAB DIP 29
JACQUES PEPIN'S SALMON TARTARE 30
LOBSTER FRITTERS WITH LEMON SAUCE 31
LOW-FAT (HOLIDAY) TERRINE 33
MAX'S GRILLE SPINACH ARTICHOKE DIP 35
MELITZANOSALATA (GREEK EGGPLANT DIP) 37
PISTACHIO BRIE WITH RASPBERRY SAUCE 39
ROASTED SWEET POTATO DIP 41
SEAFOOD WORLD STUFFED MUSHROOMS 43
SESAME CHEESE BREAD STICKS WITH
    SUN-DRIED TOMATO HUMMUS 44
SWISS ONION SQUARES 46
TWO GEORGES CRAB DIP 47

SOUPS

BAKED POTATO SOUP 51
BUTTERNUT SQUASH SOUP WITH PEARS 53
CABBAGE BORSCHT 54
CHICKEN AND ESCAROLE SOUP 56
CHICKEN "POZOLE" 58
CHILLED APPLE VICHYSSOISE 60
COUNTRY-STYLE TOMATO SOUP 61
CREAM OF BROCCOLI SOUP 63
CREAM OF GARLIC SOUP 65
CREAM OF MUSHROOM SOUP 67
CUCUMBER AND DILL SOUP 69
HORSERADISH SOUP 71
NICK'S MINESTRONE SOUP 73
PRIEST'S SOUP (OR LENTIL SOUP OR ESAU'S POTAGE) 75
PUMPKIN BISQUE 77
PUREE CRECY (A COLD CARRO/POTATO SOUP) 78
SALMON-TOMATO BISQUE 79
THE REAL GULASCHSUPPE 81
TOMATO BLEU CHEESE SOUP 83
VEGETARIAN PUMPKIN SOUP 85
WATERCRESS SOUP 86

SALADS

BARLEY AND SAUSAGE SALAD 89
CHICKEN PASTA SALAD 91
CHICKEN SALAD WITH GRAPES 95
COLD LAMB SALAD 96
COUSCOUS SALAD 97
EGG WHITE ONLY AND NO-EGG MAYONNAISE 99
FRESH CUCUMBER MOUSSE 101
GRILLED CHICKEN COBB SALAD WITH KEY LIME
    VINAIGRETTE 103

HAM AND MACARONI SALAD	105
MANGO SALAD DRESSING	106
MARTHA'S VINEYARD SALAD WITH RASPBERRY-MAPLE DRESSING	107
MOLDED POTATO AND HAM SALAD (A.K.A. CAKE)	109
ORIENTAL RICE SALAD	111
PATRICK'S CAESAR SALAD	113
ROASTED THREE-POTATO SALAD	115
SHANGHAI CHICKEN SALAD WITH SPICY HONEY MUSTARD DRESSING	117
STRAWBERRY-PRETZEL SALAD	119
TRISH'S HOT CHICKEN SALAD	120
WALNUT AND WATERCRESS SALAD	122
WILD RICE SALAD	123
WHO'S ON FIRST FRESH TUNA SALAD	125

BREADS

APPLE CREAM COFFEE CAKE	131
BOURBON-PECAN BREAD	132
BUTTERY CARAMEL QUICKS	133
CEREAL BRUNCH COFFEE CAKE	134
CHILI BREAD	137
CHOCOLATE CHIP COFFEE CAKE	139
CHOCOLATE STICKY BUNS	141
DRIED CRANBERRY/NUT MUFFINS	143
EASY ONION CASSEROLE BREAD	145
ENGLISH MUFFIN BREAD	147
HERBED OATMEAL PAN BREAD	149
HERO BREAD	151
HOLLY'S MYSTERY MUFFINS	153
HONEY GRAHAM CRACKERS	155
MAYBURN'S PEPPER CHEESE BREAD	157
ORANGE JUICE MUFFINS WITH HONEY SPREAD	158
RISEN BISCUITS	159

RIVERSIDE HOTEL BROWN BREAD 161
STOUFFER'S COFFEE CAKE 163
STUFFING BREAD 165
SWEET TOMATOES TANGY LEMON MUFFINS 167
WHOLE WHEAT BISCOTTI 169

VEGETABLES

BAHAMIAN PEAS AND RICE 173
BEER BATTER FRIED ASPARAGUS 175
BROCCOLI CUSTARD BAKE 176
CAULIFLOWER AU GRATIN 177
CURTIS' BROCCOLI SOUFFLE 179
HENRY'S SWEET POTATO GRATIN 181
HIMMEL UND ERDE (HEAVEN AND EARTH) 183
LIGHT CORN FRITTERS 184
MASHED POTATO PUFFS FOR TWO 185
NUTTY BAKED CABBAGE 186
ORANGE GLAZED CARROTS 187
RATATOUILLE 189
ROASTED GARLIC BREAD PUDDING 191
SAUTEED BRUSSELS SPROUTS WITH NUTS 193
SPINACH ROSEMARY CAKES 195
SWEET POTATO MASH 197
ZUCCHINI SOUFFLÉ 199

CASSEROLES AND COMBINATIONS

ANDRE SOLTNER'S POTATO PIE 203
BAKED APPLES AND ONIONS 205
BAKED LIMA BEANS 206
BISCUITS AND GRAVY 207
BROWNED WHITE RICE CASSEROLE 209
CASSEROLE CARROTS 210
CASSOLETTE DE FRUITS DE MER (SEAFOOD CASSEROLE) 211

COOKED CHICKEN OR TURKEY LOAF	213
CORN RELISH	214
FISH SOUFFLÉ WITH MUSTARD SAUCE (AN ELEGANT AFTERMATH)	216
GORGONZOLA POLENTA	219
HAM AND MAC BAKE	220
HASH BROWN CASSEROLE	221
ITALIAN EASTER PIE (PIZZA RUSTICA)	223
KING RANCH CASSEROLE	225
MACARONI CROQUETTES	227
"NO CREAM" CREAM	229
ONION SHORTCAKE	230
RICHARD SAX'S COMFORTING CAFETERIA-STYLE MACARONI AND CHEESE	231
SPAGHETTI PIZZA PIE	233

MAIN DISHES (RED MEAT)

BOOKS' VEAL STEW	237
BRANDY BURGERS	239
BURGER BUNDLES	240
DOUBLE CUT PORK CHOPS WITH COUNTRY APPLESAUCE	241
HAM PATTIES	243
HENRY'S BEEF STROGANOFF	245
JEAN-LOUIS' LAMB STEW	248
MEAT LOAF	250
MEAT LOAF WITH MUSHROOM SAUCE	253
OSSO BUCO	255
REUBEN CROQUETTES	257
RIGATONI BOLOGNAISE	259
SALISBURY STEAK WITH MUSHROOM GRAVY	261
SHEPHERD'S PIE	263
SWEDISH MEATBALLS (KJOTTBOLLAR)	266
TEXAS CHILI	269

MAIN DISHES (POULTRY)

ANTHONY'S CHICKEN AL 273
AWESOME TURKEY LOAF 275
CAP'N CRUNCH CHICKEN WITH CREOLE
    MUSTARD SAUCE 277
CHICKEN ASIAGO PASTA 281
CHICKEN SAN REMO 283
CHICKEN SILANA 285
CHICKEN WELLINGTON 287
CHICKEN WITH FORTY CLOVES OF GARLIC 289
DRAGON PALACE MANGO CHICKEN 291
EASY, EASY CHICKEN 293
GROUND TURKEY STROGANOFF 294
HENRY'S COQ AU VIN 295
PALM CHICKEN 299
PETE'S CHICKEN PECAN 301
POTTED TURKEY LEGS 303
PRETZEL CHICKEN WITH BEURRE BLANC SAUCE 305
STUFFED CHICKEN BREASTS 309
TENDER POACHED CHICKEN BREASTS 311
TURKEY LOAVES WITH APRICOT GLAZE 312

MAIN DISHES (SEAFOOD)

ATLANTIC SALMON WITH SUN-DRIED TOMATO
    VINAIGRETTE 317
BAKED BEER BATTER SHRIMP 319
DOLPHIN ZINGARA 321
GRILLED LOBSTER CLUB SANDWICH 323
LA COQUILLE SHRIMP PASTA 325
MAHI MAHI MANGO MANGO 327
MONKFISH WITH PRUNES 329
OUT OF DENMARK SNAPPER EN PAPILLOTE 331
PAN-SEARED SCALLOPS IN MUSHROOM CREAM SAUCE 333

SALMON QUICHE 335
SEAFOOD CAKES 336
SEAFOOD NEWBURG 339
SHRIMP MOUSSE WITH SOLE 341
SNAPPER CALYPSO 343
STUFFED SOLE 345
THE WHALE'S RIB BAKED DOLPHIN 349
TUNA CATANIA 351

DESSERTS

APPLE POUND CAKE 355
AUNT JEN'S BLACKBERRY JAM CAKE 357
BANANA CREAM PIE 359
CHOCOLATE ALMOND BALLS 363
CREAM CHEESE CHOCOLATE CHIP POUND CAKE 365
EASY RICE PUDDING 366
FROZEN FRUIT YOGURTS 367
FROZEN KEY LIME-GINGER PIE 369
GREEN TOMATO FUDGE CAKE 372
GUINNESS FRUITCAKE 373
HOLY CROSS HOSPITAL OATMEAL RAISIN COOKIES 375
MARBLE CAKE (a.k.a. CONDO CAKE) 377
MOTHER-IN-LAW APPLE CAKE 379
OATMEAL LAYERED BROWNIES 381
PARSNIP TART 383
POTATO CHIP COOKIES 385
SAQUELLA CHOCOLATE ESPRESSO COOKIES 387
SHORTCUT GINGERSNAPS 389
SWEET POTATO CHEESECAKE 390
TOURTES DE BLETTES (SWISS CHARD AND APPLE PIE) 391
VEGETARIAN KEY WEST LIME CHEESECAKE 393

CULINARY TIPS AND TIDBITS 395

INDEXES

GENERAL INDEX 403
RECIPE INDEX 407

INTRODUCTION

After years of working as a food writer/author/editor, answering cooking and cooking-related questions, coping with customer's problems, and organizing and executing cooking classes and demonstrations, I decided to retire. Retirement lasted just long enough for Molly, my cat, and me to move from Florida to Louisiana where we are now comfortably settled in our new house, but where the innumerable requests for me to write a cookbook including my favorite recipes from those years of involvement have followed me.

You will have to thank my daughter Pam who not only encouraged the book project but who nicely nagged until I agreed to come out of my second retirement. Thanks also go to my granddaughter Jennifer Greene who was so very dedicated and helpful and willing to delve through the piles of organized and not-so-organized files of recipes predating WWII to the present to help make the difficult decisions about which of those thousands of "favorite" recipes to choose and use. And thanks to Jennifer whose artistic talent included the delightful design for the book's cover.

We hope you will enjoy reading and cooking as much as we enjoyed choosing, writing, and organizing. Thinking now of all the still-filed-away recipes, I wonder if a second (third, fourth or . . .) edition is lurking in the background. Stay tuned.

Suzanne S. Jones

APPETIZERS

American Café Homemade Ketchup

AMERICAN CAFÉ HOMEMADE KETCHUP

Here is a totally new way to view an otherwise ordinary condiment. One of the favorite ways to serve this gently simmered combination of piquant ingredients and seasonings known as ketchup is as an appetizer dip with a variety of chips: from Pringles to store-bought pita and tortillas. Of course, it will soon replace the Heinz jar in your refrigerator for using on your burgers or in your meatloaf or anywhere else this condiment is generally utilized.

Guaranteed to become a household favorite.

1 can (28 ounces) tomato puree (a good brand)
1/3 cup apple cider vinegar
2/3 cup sugar
1 whole clove
1 large bay leaf
1/2 teaspoon ground coriander
1/4 large cinnamon stick

3/4 teaspoon dry mustard
2 medium garlic cloves, minced
1/2 teaspoon salt, or to taste
1/4 teaspoon fresh-ground black pepper, or to taste
1/8 teaspoon cayenne pepper, or to taste

In a large heavy saucepot, combine all the ingredients well. Bring to a simmer over medium heat, stirring occasionally. When the mixture begins to simmer, adjust the heat to keep the simmer at a steady bubble; the French call it *en riant*. (A word of caution: make sure your saucepan is a deep one, or you may have tomato sauce spattering all over your stove. You may want to partially cover the pan, as we did.)

Continue simmering the mixture for 40 to 45 minutes, stirring occasionally or until it has reduced slightly and has thickened to a dipping consistency. Cool to room temperature, transfer to covered containers, and refrigerate. You may want to remove the cinnamon stick and bay leaf before serving. Serve with all manner of your favorite chips. Makes about 3 cups.

BAKED CHICKEN NUGGETS WITH HOT AND SWEET MUSTARD SAUCE

This is one of our favorite easy-and-delicious appetizers. Simply cut your fresh chicken breasts into 1-inch pieces; dip into a mixture of crumbs, herbs, and cheese; and bake to a golden brown. Try the dipping sauce as a tasty covering for a nice hunk of cream cheese for another easy appetizer!

Nuggets:

- 1 teaspoon salt
- 1 cup fine dry bread crumbs (plain or Italian seasoned for even more flavor)
- 1/2 teaspoon dried basil
- 1/2 teaspoon dried thyme
- 1/3 cup fresh-grated Parmesan cheese
- 4 large chicken breast halves (skinned, boned, and cut into 1-inch pieces)
- 1/2 cup (1 stick) butter, melted
- Hot and Sweet Mustard Sauce (recipe given)

Preheat the oven to 400 degrees.

In a medium bowl, combine the salt, bread crumbs, basil, thyme, and Parmesan cheese. Dip the chicken pieces in the melted butter, then in the crumb mixture, and place in a single layer, without touching, in a large ungreased baking dish. Bake in the center of the oven for about 10 minutes, or until nicely browned. Serve warm with the sauce. Makes about 10 servings.

Hot and Sweet Mustard Sauce:

- 1-1/4 cups apricot preserves
- 1 cup apple jelly
- 1/4 cup prepared horseradish
- 2 tablespoons dry mustard

In a large bowl, combine all the ingredients. Beat with an electric mixer at medium speed until well mixed. Makes about 2-1/2 cups.

BLUE CHEESE COOKIES

These are a delicious cocktail go-with or an accompaniment to soups as a first course. We have always considered these "cookies" a cousin to the ever-popular variations of cheese straws, which usually call for Cheddar cheese. If you enjoy blue cheese, this will become a favorite.

4 ounces (about 1 cup) crumbled blue cheese	1 cup all-purpose flour
	1/2 teaspoon seasoned salt
1/2 cup (1 stick) unsalted butter, cut into 8 pieces (at room temperature)	dash hot pepper sauce
	3/4 cup fine-chopped blanched almonds

Preheat the oven to 375 degrees. In a mixing bowl, cream the blue cheese and butter well. Mix in the flour, seasoned salt, and hot pepper sauce.

Shape the mixture into balls about an inch in diameter and roll each in the chopped almonds. Place on an ungreased baking sheet and flatten slightly with your fingertips.

Bake in the center of the oven for about 12 minutes, or until very lightly browned. These are best served slightly warm, but room temperature will do just fine.

Makes about 35 cookies.

CHEESE AND CHIVE SPREAD

This is served in a popular restaurant as a spread with their warm and/or toasted breads. However, we guarantee you will find it delicious on all manner of crackers, bagels, pitas, or whatever in addition to those breads. The slow simmering of the green onions (or scallions) and shallots in olive oil, which is often described as a "soft fry," gives the spread its wonderful caramelized flavor. Use a food processor to whip the cream cheese to a smooth and light texture before adding the warm onions. The cottage cheese and sour cream add to the final creaminess of the spread, and the slight tang from the sour cream is softly discernible.

5 medium scallions with fresh, crisp green stems
3 ounces shallots (each of our bulbs weighed an ounce)
1/4 cup olive oil
4 ounces cream cheese, at room temperature
1/2 cup sour cream
1/4 cup creamed cottage cheese
salt and white pepper to taste

Trim the bulb ends of the scallions and cut each scallion into 1-1/2-inch pieces, using about 4 inches of the green stems. In a food processor fitted with the metal blade, fine-chop the scallion pieces and the shallots. In a medium heavy skillet, heat the oil over medium heat. Stir in the chopped scallions and shallots and bring just to a light bubble. You want this mixture to look like a "soft fry." Adjust the heat to maintain the bubble and cook for 20 to 25 minutes, or until the mixture is lightly tanned. Be very careful not to let this scorch or burn. Remove from the heat.

In a food processor fitted with the metal blade, process the cream cheese until smooth. Add the warm onions and oil to the cream cheese, and process for a few seconds. Add the remaining ingredients and process until well blended. Adjust the seasoning. Transfer to a bowl, cover, and refrigerate for several hours.

Makes about 1-1/2 cups.

CHICKEN PATE WITH ALMONDS

To demonstrate how easily recipes could be done in the food processor, we developed this chicken pate recipe in our Cuisinart test kitchen many years ago. It is a delicious use for leftover chicken (or turkey). It is subtly flavored with a little dry sherry and toasted almonds.

1-1/2 cups cubed, cooked chicken (about 12 ounces)
1 small onion, peeled and cut into 8 pieces
1/4 cup butter, at room temperature
1 tablespoon dry sherry
5 tablespoons slivered, toasted almonds (divided*)

In a food processor fitted with the metal blade, add the chicken, onions, butter, sherry, and 4 tablespoons of the almonds. Process with on/off pulses until the mixture is almost minced. Do not process until smooth. You want a bit of texture. Transfer to a small bowl and refrigerate for at least 2 hours. Just before serving, sprinkle with the remaining tablespoon of almonds. Serve with your choice of crackers.

Makes about 1-2/3 cups.

*To toast the almonds, preheat the oven to 350 degrees. Place the almonds in a pie plate and bake for about 8 minutes, or until just beginning to turn a golden brown. Cool completely.

CORNED BEEF PATE

Thanks to a dear friend from Pennsylvania, here is a very different and delicious pate recipe. Instead of the more familiar seafood or chicken livers we are often accustomed to finding in a good pate recipe, here is an unusual combination of canned corned beef and liverwurst or braunschweiger that takes only minutes to prepare in a food processor or good blender and is a winner on crisp crackers or other crisp servers.

2 teaspoons instant minced onions
2/3 cup room temperature water
1 can (12 ounces) corned beef, broken up

8 ounces liverwurst or braunschweiger
1/2 cup mayonnaise
1 tablespoon vinegar (we like plain cider vinegar)
1/2 teaspoon dry mustard

Soften the onions in the water for 5 minutes. In a food processor fitted with the metal blade, process the corned beef, liverwurst or braunschweiger, mayonnaise, vinegar, dry mustard, and undrained onion mixture until thoroughly blended. (You can use a good blender, but divide the ingredients into two batches for best mixing.) Turn the mixture into a lightly oiled 3-1/2 cup mold or bowl, cover, and chill for at least 8 hours or overnight. Unmold onto a serving plate surrounded by crisp crackers or other crisp servers.

Makes about 3-1/2 cups.

CREAM CHEESE AND VEGETABLE SPREAD

This is a delicious change from seafood or meat spreads. A food processor or good blender will make preparation a breeze. We use it often to stuff celery or cherry tomatoes, but if you add a few more tablespoons of sour cream, the consistency will be just right as a dip for raw vegetables and/or crackers.

4 radishes, cut in half
4 scallions, white and an inch of green, cut into 1-inch pieces
2 inches of a medium cucumber, peeled, seeded, and cut into 4 pieces, patted dry
1 small celery rib, cut into 1-inch pieces
1/2 medium green pepper, seeded and cut into quarters

8 ounces cream cheese, cut into 8 pieces, at room temperature
2 tablespoons sour cream (more if you want this suitable as a dip)
1/2 teaspoon salt
1/4 teaspoon fresh-ground pepper

In a food processor fitted with the metal blade or a good blender, add the radishes, scallions, cucumber, celery, and green pepper. Process until the vegetables are coarsely chopped. Add the remaining ingredients and process until thoroughly mixed but still somewhat crunchy. Transfer to a bowl, cover, and refrigerate for several hours so the mixture firms up. Good for stuffing celery or cherry tomatoes or spread on crisp crackers. By adding the extra (1 or 2 tablespoons) sour cream, it will be of dipping consistency. Makes about 1-1/3 cups.

FAVORITE CHOPPED CHICKEN LIVERS

A reader once asked if we could help him duplicate the "nutty green kind of taste" in a chopped liver appetizer he and his family ate at a now out-of-business Italian restaurant in the Bronx, New York. We used our favorite chopped liver recipe from the first (volume 1) *Gourmet Cookbook*, published then by the Gourmet Distributing Corporation in New York in the fifties as the foundation. Adding chopped parsley, some brandy, and chopped pistachios gave us that "nutty green kind of taste" the reader remembered. (He wrote to let us know.) The original recipe called for rendered chicken fat. Since that is not readily available, we substituted butter or margarine, and no one has ever complained.

- 3 tablespoons butter or margarine
- 1/2 pound fresh chicken livers, trimmed
- 1 medium onion, finely chopped
- 1/2 slice stale white bread
- 1 large celery rib, finely diced
- 1 hard-cooked egg, chopped
- 2 tablespoons chopped fresh parsley
- 2 tablespoons brandy
- 1/4 cup chopped pistachios
- salt and fresh-ground pepper to taste
- additional butter or margarine, if necessary, softened

In a heavy skillet, melt the butter or margarine over medium heat. Sauté the livers and onions for about 3 minutes, or until the livers are no longer pink inside and the onions are soft but not brown. Let the mixture cool. You can finish the recipe by chopping the livers by hand, then adding the remaining ingredients, tasting for seasoning, or you can place the livers and onions in the work bowl of a food processor fitted with the metal blade. Pulse just a few times to chop the livers very coarsely. Add the remaining ingredients and pulse again just to combine. You want to retain some texture. If you think it necessary, add an additional teaspoon or more of butter or margarine to smooth out the mixture. Transfer to a serving crock or bowl and refrigerate for several hours to let the flavors marry.

Makes about 1-1/2 cup.

FROGGIES LA TARTE AU TOMATES ET FROMAGES CHEVRES
(Goat Cheese and Tomato Tart)

Froggies La Tarte au Tomates et Fromages
(Goat Cheese and Tomato Tart)

This is a wonderfully rich and flavorful appetizer. The contrast of the intense cheese flavor with the fresh tomatoes is a pleasurable tasting experience. You can choose the strength of the goat cheese for this recipe according to your taste—young goat cheeses are mild but become stronger as they mature. Though the crust becomes a bit soft, any leftover tart will keep well, refrigerated, for up to 5 days. It is best served warm, but no one complained when the last piece was served straight from the refrigerator. You can make and bake the pate brisee (pastry) several hours ahead.

Pate Brisee (for an 11-inch tart pan with removable bottom):

- 1/2 cup cold butter (no substitutions), cut into tablespoon-size pieces
- 1-1/2 cups all-purpose flour
- pinch salt
- 1 large egg yolk, lightly beaten
- 2 to 3 tablespoons ice water

In a mixing bowl, use a pastry blender to cut the butter into the flour and salt until the pieces are the size of small peas. Combine the egg yolk with 1 tablespoon of the water, and work into the flour mixture with a fork. Add additional water a tablespoon at a time, until all the dough is just moistened.

Use your clean fingers to work the dough until it forms a ball. Shape into a disk, wrap in plastic wrap, and refrigerate for about 30 minutes. This makes it easier to handle.

Roll the dough out on a lightly floured surface to a circle 2 inches larger than your tart pan. Fold the dough in half then in half again and lay it in the mold and unfold it. Press the dough lightly into the bottom and up the sides of the pan. Trim the dough to 1/2 inch and press the overhang inside against the edge of the pan.

Preheat the oven to 375 degrees. Line the tart shell with aluminum foil then pie weights or dry beans. Bake in the center of the oven for 8 to 9 minutes until the pastry is set. Remove the foil and prick the bottom of the pastry with a fork. Return to the oven for another 3 minutes. Cool on a wire rack while preparing the filling.

Filling:

- 12 ounces goat cheese at room temperature
- 3 large eggs
- 1-1/2 cups heavy cream
- 2 large garlic cloves, minced
- 1/4 teaspoon fresh-grated nutmeg
- salt and fresh-ground pepper, to taste
- 2 large or 3 medium fresh tomatoes, skinned, seeded, and cut into 1/4-inch dice, drained

Preheat the oven to 375 degrees.

In a large mixing bowl, beat the goat cheese on the medium speed of an electric mixer until smooth. Beat in the eggs one at a time. Add the cream slowly, beating constantly. Then on low speed, beat in the garlic, nutmeg, salt, and pepper. Spoon half the mixture into the baked tart shell. Sprinkle the diced tomatoes over the surface and spoon the remaining cheese mixture over all.

Bake in the center of the oven for 25 minutes, or until the tart is a light golden color and firm to the touch. Cool for up to 30 minutes before serving. Best warm, but can be served at room temperature. Remove the outer tart pan rim before serving.

Makes 12 appetizer servings.

HOLIDAY (OR OTHER) HAM BALLS

This was a popular recipe, thanks to the Bisquick people, many years ago. The original made around 7 dozen, so we cut it back, changed a couple of the ingredients, and served it with our tasty mustard-mayonnaise sauce. At holiday time or any other, this is an easy and tasty way to enjoy some leftover ham.

Ham Balls:

1-1/2 cups original Bisquick
1 cup fine-chopped cooked smoked ham
2 cups shredded Cheddar cheese (do not use fat-free)
1/4 cup fresh-grated Parmesan cheese

1-1/2 tablespoons chopped fresh parsley
1-1/2 teaspoons Dijon-style mustard
1/3 cup milk
Mustard-Mayonnaise Sauce (recipe given)

To make the ham balls, heat the oven to 350 degrees. Spray a large baking sheet with no-stick vegetable spray.

In a large mixing bowl, stir all the ingredients together thoroughly. With your (clean) hands, shape the mixture into balls about an inch in diameter. Place 2 inches apart on the baking sheet. Bake in the center of the oven for about 20 to 25 minutes or until nicely browned. Remove from the pan to serving trays or plates. Serve warm with the Mustard-Mayonnaise Sauce.

Makes about 40 ham balls.

Mustard-Mayonnaise Sauce:

1-1/2 cups fat-free mayonnaise
1/4 cup reduced-fat sour cream

1 tablespoon (or to taste) Dijon mustard

To make the sauce, in a medium-sized saucepan, stir all the ingredients together over medium-low heat just until heated through. Do not allow to boil.

Makes about 1-3/4 cups.

Hot Cheese and Crab Dip

HOT CHEESE AND CRAB DIP

We had a momentary problem when we first received this recipe from a popular restaurant. One of the ingredients called for was "shard Cheddar cheese." A phone call cleared up the mystery. What we thought might be a new (to us) category of Cheddar cheese turned out to be a typo that had changed "sharp" to "shard." Be sure you use fresh crabmeat, not canned, for the best results. The dip can be made several hours or even a day ahead and reheated just before serving. Fresh vegetables and/or an assortment of plain crackers make excellent "dippers."

- 1 tablespoon butter
- 1/4 cup minced onions
- 1/2 teaspoon cayenne pepper, or to taste
- 1 tablespoon dry mustard
- 1-1/2 teaspoons Old Bay Seasoning
- 1 cup heavy cream
- 8 ounces cream cheese at room temperature
- 1 cup shredded sharp Cheddar cheese
- 2 tablespoons fresh lemon juice
- 1-1/2 teaspoons Worcestershire sauce
- 8 ounces fresh crab claw meat
- 6 teaspoons chopped parsley, divided
- 3 tablespoons plain bread crumbs, divided
- 3 tablespoons grated Parmesan cheese, divided
- paprika for garnish

In a large heavy saucepan, melt the butter over medium heat. Sauté the onions for about 1-1/2 minutes, or until soft but not brown. Reduce the heat to low and add the cayenne pepper, dry mustard, Old Bay Seasoning, and heavy cream. Increase the heat to medium and use a whisk to mix the ingredients well. Add the cream cheese in large chunks, whisking to melt as it comes to a simmer. Slowly whisk in the Cheddar cheese. Remove from the heat and add the lemon juice and Worcestershire sauce. Stir to combine. Add the crabmeat and 3 teaspoons of the parsley. Stir well. Transfer the mixture to six 6-oz ovenproof ramekins. Can be made ahead to this point and refrigerated, covered, for up to 24 hours—adding the topping just before baking and serving or topping each serving now with 1-1/2 teaspoons each bread crumbs, Parmesan cheese, and the remaining parsley. Sprinkle each with a tad of paprika. Pop into a preheated 350-degree oven for about 5 minutes, or until well-heated through. (If refrigerated, remove from the refrigerator at least 30 minutes before baking. Add another minute or two to make sure the mixture is thoroughly heated through.)

Makes 6 servings.

JACQUES PEPIN'S SALMON TARTARE

One of the remarkable articles we worked on with Jacques Pepin for our Cuisinart *Pleasures of Cooking* magazine was a collection of his Alaskan salmon recipes. Among them was this recipe for Salmon Tartare. Remember, it is important you buy your salmon from a reliable fishmonger who can guarantee that it is super-fresh. Jacques liked to serve this on buttered black bread, but also suggested an alternative of hollowed-out cucumber slices. You will also enjoy it on your choice of sturdy crackers.

- 1 small onion, coarsely chopped
- 1-1/2 pounds boneless, skinless fresh salmon, cut into 1-inch pieces
- 2 medium scallions, trimmed and coarsely chopped
- 1 large garlic clove, peeled and crushed into a puree
- 2/3 cup fresh parsley leaves, finely chopped
- 1/3 cup fresh tarragon leaves, finely chopped
- 2 teaspoons fresh-grated lime zest
- 2 tablespoons fresh lime juice
- 4 tablespoons olive oil
- 1-1/2 teaspoons salt
- fresh-ground white pepper, to taste

Place the onions in a strainer and rinse under cold running water. Drain and press in paper towels to extract all excess water. This eliminates some of the strong taste and keeps the onion white.

In a food processor fitted with the metal blade, process the salmon just until coarsely chopped. Transfer to a large mixing bowl and combine well with the remaining ingredients, including the rinsed onions. Refrigerate for a couple of hours for the flavors to blend well.

Makes about 4-1/2 cups.

LOBSTER FRITTERS WITH LEMON SAUCE

We always thought this was a good way to stretch just 1 cup of chopped and cooked lobster into an unusual and delicious appetizer or even first course. And we like the fact that everything can be made several hours ahead. The fritters can be nicely reheated in a hot oven just before serving.

Fritters:

1/2 cup all-purpose flour	1 cup fine-chopped, cooked lobster meat
1 teaspoon baking powder	2 scallions, white and an inch of green, finely chopped
1/2 teaspoon ground coriander	1-1/2 tablespoons chopped fresh tarragon leaves
1/2 teaspoon salt	canola and olive oil for frying
1 large egg, lightly beaten	Lemon Sauce (recipe given)
1/4 cup milk	

To make the fritters, in a large mixing bowl whisk together the flour, baking powder, coriander, and salt. Transfer to a piece of wax paper. In the same bowl, mix the remaining ingredients, except the oils, together well. Add the dry ingredients and mix until the batter is thoroughly combined. Expect a thick and rather chunky mixture.

In a large skillet, pour enough of a combination of the oils to reach a depth of about 1/4 inch. Heat over medium heat until hot. Drop the batter by level tablespoons into the pan without crowding, and cook for about 50 to 60 seconds on each side or until golden brown. Transfer to paper towels to drain. Repeat with the remaining batter. Serve the fritters warm. (Can be made ahead: cooled, covered, and refrigerated. When ready to serve, reheat for about 10 minutes in a 400-degree oven.) Serve with the Lemon Sauce.

Makes 16 fritters.

Lemon Sauce:

1/2 cup real mayonnaise
2 tablespoons fine-chopped dill pickles
2 tablespoons fine-chopped scallions (white and 1 inch of green)

1 teaspoon fresh-grated lemon zest
2 teaspoons fresh lemon juice
1 tablespoon well-drained and chopped canned pimientos, optional but colorful

Combine all the ingredients in a small mixing bowl. Refrigerate until ready to use. Makes about 3/4 cup—about 2 heaping teaspoons for each fritter.

LOW-FAT (HOLIDAY) TERRINE

During our tenure at Cuisinarts Inc., we had many requests for low-fat pates or terrines. (The original definition of a *pate* was "a meat or fish dish enclosed in pastry." Now it is extended to mixtures baked in a mold or loaf pan and called *terrines*.) Thanks to the original owner—the late Carl Sontheimer who discovered a way to substitute cooked brown rice for some or most of the fat in those recipes—we not only developed the following delicious terrine, but other recipes as well. Flavorwise and texturewise, you and your guests will never guess it is not an original French Pate de Campagne recipe, though it contains less than 3 percent fat.

- 2 medium garlic cloves
- 1 pound boneless turkey thigh meat, cut into 1-inch pieces
- 2/3 cup water
- 3 tablespoons brandy
- 1-1/3 cups cooked brown rice
- 1/2 cup Egg Beaters or other liquid egg substitute*
- 1-1/2 teaspoons salt
- 1/2 teaspoon white pepper
- 1/8 teaspoon ground allspice
- 1/8 teaspoon ground cinnamon
- 2 tablespoons all-purpose flour
- pinch ground ginger
- 8 ounces turkey ham, cut into 1-inch pieces**

Place a cookie sheet on the middle rack of the oven and preheat the oven to 275 degrees. Lightly oil a 4-cup loaf pan.

In a food processor fitted with the metal blade, fine-chop the garlic. Add the turkey and process until smooth. With the motor running, slowly pour in the water and brandy. Remove the cover and add the remaining ingredients except the turkey ham; process until smooth, scraping down the sides of the bowl as necessary. Add the turkey ham and just pulse-chop it coarsely about 10 times.

Pack 1/3 of the mixture into the prepared pan, pressing down to fill the corners. Press in the remaining mixture 1/2 at a time, smoothing the top. Place on the baking sheet in the oven and bake about 1 hour and 30 minutes, or until the meat shrinks from the side of the pan and the internal temperature reaches 160 degrees.

Cool in the pan on a wire rack for 10 minutes, then invert onto the wire rack and cool to room temperature. Cover and refrigerate overnight.

To serve, cut into thin slices and garnish as desired. Serve with crusty French bread or plain crackers. You might put out some mustard and small sour pickles too.

Makes about 14 servings.

*You can use 2 large eggs, but that will increase the calorie count.
**Turkey ham can be found in the deli departments of most supermarkets or in the prepackaged cold meat sections.

MAX'S GRILLE SPINACH ARTICHOKE DIP

Max's Grille Spinach Artichoke Dip

The healthy dose of roasted garlic puree makes this dip special. It never ceases to amaze how that pungent and enticing flavor of fresh raw garlic changes when cooked, either braised or roasted. It refines an otherwise harsh taste into an almost delicate, mellow flavor with the consistency of soft butter. You might want to roast an extra bulb to enjoy on some crusty bread or crackers or to combine with the mashed potatoes you plan to serve another day. This dip can be made several hours ahead or even the night before. It can be finished in the microwave or a standard oven.

1/3 cup roasted garlic puree*
1/3 cup fresh-grated Parmesan cheese
2 boxes (10 ounces each) chopped frozen spinach, defrosted and squeezed dry
3 canned artichoke hearts, drained well and coarsely chopped
1 cup heavy cream
Salt and fresh-ground pepper, to taste
1-1/2 cups shredded Jack cheese

Combine all the ingredients except the Jack cheese in a mixing bowl. Make sure the squeezed spinach is well distributed (it tends to clump). This makes about 3 cups of dip. You can transfer the entire mixture to a 1-quart ceramic crock and sprinkle the top with the Jack cheese or use 6 individual ceramic 3/4-cup crocks and divide the mixture and the cheese among them.

The dip can be made ahead to this point. If you do not plan to use it within an hour, cover with saran and refrigerate until ready to finish. If using a microwave, cut a slit in the plastic wrap and zap on high for about 2 minutes. If finishing in the oven, preheat the oven to 375 degrees and bake for about 10 to 12 minutes, or until the cheese has melted and the dip is bubbling around the sides. Serve with tortilla chips. Some salsa and sour cream make delicious accompaniments.

Makes 6 servings.

*To roast the garlic, preheat the oven to 350 degrees. Loosen and remove the papery outside skin of the garlic heads. Cut off about 1/2 inch from the tip end of each head so most of the clove interiors are exposed. Place each head in the center of a large square of aluminum foil and drizzle about a teaspoon of oil over each. Sprinkle lightly with salt. Gather the corners of the foil over the heads and twist to seal. Place in a baking dish and roast in the center of the oven for an hour or until the garlic is very soft. Let packages cool, then remove from the foil and squeeze out the softened garlic into a bowl. Mash well with a fork or a wooden spoon. An average head will yield about 1/4 cup puree.

MELITZANOSALATA
(Greek Eggplant Dip)

Melitzanosalata
(Greek Eggplant Dip)

    Sam Kantzanelos, our friend and the owner of a popular Greek restaurant in Florida, generously shared his version of this delicious dip. We like to serve it with toasted pita bread, but it is equally delicious with a nice assortment of plain crackers. Make sure your eggplants are firm, shiny, and blemish-free. The yield will vary according to the weight/size of your eggplants and potato. Our yield was about 3-1/2 cups, which might seem like a generous amount until you begin tasting. We barely had enough to enjoy some leftovers.

2 large eggplants (about 1 pound each)
1 medium all-purpose potato (about 7 ounces), peeled, quartered, boiled, and roughly mashed
2 large garlic cloves, crushed
1 small onion, grated
2 tablespoons distilled white vinegar

2/3 cup olive oil
salt and fresh-ground pepper to taste
2 tablespoons chopped Italian parsley
1 tablespoon mayonnaise (optional)
20 Kalamata olives

Preheat the oven to 350 degrees. Puncture the eggplants with the sharp tip of a knife or a kitchen fork in several places. Place on a lightly oiled baking pan and bake for about an hour, or until very soft and the skin has turned dark. This will give the eggplant a slightly smoky flavor. Let the eggplants sit until cool enough to handle, but still warm. It is easier to peel them when still warm. Cut off the stem ends and peel off the skin. In a large mixing bowl, chop the eggplant into small pieces.* Continue chopping while slowly adding the potato, garlic, white vinegar, and olive oil. Taste for seasoning, then stir in the parsley. We did not add the mayonnaise since the texture seemed just right as it was.

Refrigerate the mixture for several hours or overnight so the flavors blend well. Stir well before serving. Serve on a plate garnished with the olives.

Makes about 3-1/2 cups.

*We used an old-fashioned potato masher to "chop" and combine the ingredients.

PISTACHIO BRIE WITH RASPBERRY SAUCE

This restaurant's appetizer serving of one 4-ounce wedge of Brie per person was a tad generous. We fudged a bit and cut an 8-ounce round of Brie into four 2-ounce wedges, which—when prepped, sautéed, baked, and garnished with the Raspberry Sauce—were declared the perfect size for a satisfactory before-dinner appetizer. You can make the Raspberry Sauce several hours ahead to make time for sieving, then reheat just before serving. You will declare these crisp, nutty-on-the-outside and soft, gooey-on-the-inside servings of Brie most decadent when pared deliciously with the slightly tart sauce drizzled over and/or around each.

Raspberry Sauce:

1 cup fresh or frozen raspberries

3 tablespoons sugar

In a small saucepan, bring the raspberries and sugar slowly to a simmer over medium-low heat, stirring frequently. Once they have begun to simmer and the sugar has completely melted, continue simmering for about 4 minutes. Let cool for about 15 minutes, stirring now and then. Pass the mixture through a fairly fine sieve to remove and discard the seeds. Can be held several hours at room temperature or refrigerated for up to 24 hours. Reheat slowly over low heat. Makes about 1/2 cup.

Pistachio Brie:

1 8-ounce round of Brie cheese, well chilled
1/2 cup all-purpose flour
1 large egg beaten with 2 teaspoons tepid water, for egg wash

2/3 cup fine-chopped (almost ground) pistachio nuts
vegetable oil for sautéing

With a sharp knife, cut the Brie into four equal wedges. Roll each in the flour then in the egg wash. Dredge each in the pistachio nuts and place on paper towels.

Preheat the oven to 350 degrees. In a heavy skillet, bring enough oil to measure about 1/2 inch in depth to a temperature of 350 degrees over medium heat. Sauté the coated cheese for about 1 minute a side or until nicely browned. Do not overcook, or you will have melted cheese before you want it.

SUZANNE S. JONES

Remove the cheese to a baking dish and place in the oven for about 3 minutes. This dries and crisps the coating perfectly. To serve, place each wedge of Brie on a warm serving dish and drizzle each (over the top and around the sides) with about 2 tablespoons of the warm Raspberry Sauce.

Makes 4 servings.

ROASTED SWEET POTATO DIP

This comes from a foodie friend who served it for a Thanksgiving party several years ago. It is easiest to roast the potatoes and other vegetables early in the day or even the day before you are planning to serve them so they will be completely cool when added to a food processor for the final whirl. We like to add a few toasted sesame seeds for crunch, flavor, and garnish. Serve with all kinds of vegetable dippers or bread sticks—preferably those thin, salty Italian *grissini*.

1-1/2 tablespoons sesame seeds
3 cups coarse-chopped sweet potatoes
2-1/2 cups coarse-chopped onions
1-1/2 cups coarse-chopped carrots
1-1/2 tablespoons olive oil
1/4 cup tahini (sesame seed paste)*
salt and white pepper, to taste

In a dry skillet over medium heat, toast the sesame seeds, stirring until they begin to take on color. This takes just a couple of minutes. You don't want them to be too brown. Set aside to cool.

Preheat the oven to 350 degrees. In a large bowl, combine the potatoes, onions, and carrots. Drizzle with the olive oil and toss gently to coat the vegetables. Transfer the mixture to a jelly roll pan and bake in the center of the oven, stirring once or twice, for about 45 minutes or until the potables are very tender. Cool to room temperature.

In a food processor fitted with the metal blade, process the potato mixture, tahini, and seasonings until smooth. Add half the toasted sesame seeds and pulse to combine. Transfer to a serving bowl. Just before serving, sprinkle the remaining toasted seeds on top. Best served at or near room temperature. Will keep for up to 3 days in the refrigerator. Serve with crudities or bread sticks.

Makes about 3 cups.

*Tahini is available in some supermarkets, gourmet shops, and Mideastern markets.

Seafood World Stuffed Mushrooms

SEAFOOD WORLD STUFFED MUSHROOMS

This positively delectable crabmeat stuffing makes enough to stuff 24 large (about 2-1/4 to 2-1/2 inches), fresh white mushrooms. Making the stuffing ahead of time to chill makes it easier to handle. You can also stuff the mushrooms ahead and bake them just before serving so they remain moist and warm and utterly delicious. In the event you don't wish to make the entire twenty-four, you will be delighted to know the stuffing makes superb crab cakes. Just shape the mixture into 3/4-inch patties, dust lightly with flour, and pan fry briefly. If you don't mind a culinary stutter, serve both the mushrooms and cakes at the same meal. No one will complain!

- 3 tablespoons unsalted butter, divided
- 1 small onion, finely chopped
- 2 large eggs, lightly beaten
- 1/3 cup heavy cream
- 2 tablespoons dry white wine
- 1 teaspoon dry mustard
- 1 pound fresh lump crabmeat, picked over to remove any shells
- 6 to 8 tablespoons Italian-seasoned dry bread crumbs
- 24 fresh white stuffing mushrooms (2-1/4 to 2-1/2 inches across), cleaned and any stems removed
- chopped fresh parsley for garnish

In a small skillet, melt 1 tablespoon of the butter over medium heat. Sauté the onions for about 2 minutes or until softened. Cool completely. In a nonreactive mixing bowl, whisk together the eggs, cream, wine, and mustard. Stir in the cooled onions and crabmeat. Add the bread crumbs a couple tablespoons at a time until the mixture is firm but not stiff. Cover and refrigerate for up to 8 hours or even overnight. This makes the mixture easier to handle.

When ready to prepare the mushrooms, preheat the oven to 350 degrees. Melt the remaining 2 tablespoons of butter and lightly brush the mushroom caps inside and out and place cap-side-down on a large baking sheet. Fill each mushroom cap with a heaping tablespoon of the crabmeat mixture, mounding the top. Brush the tops with any remaining melted butter. Bake in the center of the oven for 20 minutes, or until the mushrooms are soft and the crab mixture is very hot throughout. Transfer to serving platters or individual serving dishes and garnish with chopped parsley.

Makes 24 stuffed mushrooms.

SESAME CHEESE BREAD STICKS WITH SUN-DRIED TOMATO HUMMUS

This oh-so-flavorful hummus is the perfect partner for the crisp and flavorful bread sticks. The easy-to-execute dough should be put together several hours or, preferably, overnight. Chilling in the refrigerator gives it a chance to relax a bit, making it easier to roll out. The hummus is also best made ahead so the flavorful ingredients have a chance to become fully acquainted. You will be amused as we were when first reading through the recipe from a popular restaurant; it noted that we should "have a chef check the seasonings before serving." Since we do not have a resident chef, we checked them ourselves!

Sesame Cheese Bread Sticks:

- 1 package (1/4 ounce) dried yeast
- 2/3 cup warm (110-115 degrees) water
- 1 teaspoon sugar
- 5 tablespoons vegetable oil, divided
- 2 tablespoons chopped Italian parsley
- 2-1/4 cups all-purpose flour
- 3 teaspoons kosher salt, divided
- 3 teaspoons white sesame seeds
- 1 teaspoon black sesame seeds
- 1/4 cup fresh-grated Parmesan cheese

In a large bowl, stir together the yeast, water, and sugar. Let stand for 5 minutes or until the mixture bubbles. Stir in 2 tablespoons of the oil and parsley. Add 1 cup of the flour and 1-1/2 teaspoons of the salt and mix well. Slowly add enough of the remaining flour to make a smooth dough. Turn out onto a lightly floured surface and knead for 3 or 4 minutes. Shape into a ball and place in a lightly floured plastic storage bag. Press out the air and close with a twisty tie. Refrigerate for several hours or preferably overnight.

When ready to roll out, preheat the oven to 325 degrees and lightly oil a large baking sheet. Divide the dough in half. On a lightly floured surface, roll half the dough into a rectangle about 12 inches long and 10 inches wide. (The dough should be about 1/8 inch thick.) Brush the dough with half the remaining vegetable oil, half the remaining salt, and half each of the sesame seeds and Parmesan cheese. Press the toppings in lightly with the rolling pin. With a pizza cutter or sharp knife, cut the dough lengthwise into 10 strips and place an inch or so apart on the prepared baking sheet. Bake in the center of the oven for 25 to 30 minutes or until the strips are golden brown and crackerlike.* Transfer to wire racks to cool. Repeat with the remaining dough. (If stored airtight, these will stay fresh for several weeks.)

Makes 20 bread sticks.

*To make sure of fairly even browning, we rearranged the sticks on the baking sheet halfway through the baking, swapping the ones on the outside edges with the center ones.

Sun-Dried Tomato Hummus:

- 1 can (15 ounces) garbanzos (chickpeas), drained
- 3 tablespoons roasted garlic (we used the already roasted garlic in oil)
- 1/3 cup loose-packed Italian parsley leaves
- 3 tablespoons (about 6 smallish pieces) sun-dried tomatoes in oil, drained
- 1/2 teaspoon kosher salt
- 2 tablespoons sesame oil
- 2 tablespoons fresh lemon juice
- 2 to 3 tablespoons olive oil

In a food processor fitted with the metal blade, process all the ingredients except the olive oil until smooth. Drizzle the oil in slowly until the mixture is of dipping consistency. Transfer to a bowl, cover, and refrigerate until ready to use.

Makes about 1-3/4 cups.

SWISS ONION SQUARES

With the combination of bacon, onions, and Swiss cheese, these tasty appetizer squares are definitely reminiscent of our favorite quiche. We have always liked the fact that they are equally delicious served hot, warm, or at room temperature. (We even admit to enjoying some leftovers right from the refrigerator.)

1 cup crushed saltine crackers
4 tablespoons butter, melted
6 slices lean smoked bacon
1 cup coarse-chopped onions
2 cups shredded Swiss cheese
3/4 cup sour cream
2 eggs, lightly beaten
fresh-ground black pepper to taste
1/2 cup shredded Cheddar cheese

Preheat the oven to 375 degrees. Combine the cracker crumbs and melted butter and press onto the bottom of an 8-inch square baking pan. Set aside.

In a large skillet, cook the bacon until crisp. Drain, reserving 2 tablespoons of the drippings. Crumble the bacon and set aside. In the same skillet, sauté the onions in the drippings over medium heat for about 2 minutes or until soft.

In a mixing bowl combine the reserved bacon, onions, Swiss cheese, sour cream, eggs, and pepper. Pour the mixture over the prepared crust. Bake in the center of the oven for about 30 minutes or until almost set. Top with the Cheddar cheese and continue baking for another 2 to 3 minutes or until the cheese has melted. Let stand for about 15 minutes before cutting into squares.

Makes 12 servings.

TWO GEORGES CRAB DIP

This dense but creamy, flavorful, and splendidly spicy appetizer from a popular restaurant in Boynton Beach, Florida, needs to be made several hours or even a day ahead so the piquancy of the cayenne pepper, Tabasco sauce, and Old Bay seasoning have time to develop fully. You can reheat small servings conveniently in the microwave or in a double boiler for larger amounts to bring the dip to dipping consistency. You can also serve the dip closer to room temperature, but make sure to supply your guests with spreading knives since the mixture thickens upon cooling. By all means, do not use canned crabmeat, but go to your favorite fishmonger to get the best and freshest backfin crab (sometimes called backfin lump crab).

1 tablespoon butter
1/4 cup small-diced onions
1/4 teaspoon cayenne pepper, or to taste
7 to 8 drops Tabasco sauce, or to taste
1 tablespoon plus 1 teaspoon Old Bay seasoning, or to taste
1 pound cream cheese, at room temperature
8 ounces backfin crabmeat

In a medium skillet, melt the butter over medium heat. Sauté the onions for about 3 to 4 minutes or until soft and just beginning to take on color. Stir in the cayenne pepper, Tabasco sauce, and Old Bay seasoning. Add the cream cheese, mashing it down and around until everything is completely incorporated and well mixed. Add the crabmeat and mix gently but thoroughly.

Now, you have several choices. If you are going to serve the entire 3-cup amount in a large bowl for a large party immediately, place it in a 1-quart serving bowl and bake in a preheated 325-degree oven for about 20 minutes to heat thoroughly and to allow the flavors to develop. You can also transfer it to several smaller 1-cup or more or less bowls and heat it the same way. Or, we opted to let it cool, refrigerated it overnight, and reheated smaller amounts in the microwave. If reheating the entire refrigerated amount, you can transfer it to a double boiler to reheat comfortably and easily.

Makes about 3 cups.

SOUPS

Baked Potato Soup

BAKED POTATO SOUP

Just reading through this recipe, your mental taste buds are guaranteed to be in their anticipation mode. From the savory roux of butter, celery, onions, and flour right through the heavy cream, basil, baked potatoes, and chicken base—once the potatoes are baked (which can be done up to a day ahead), the recipe goes quickly. The soup can be served at once or cooled, covered, and refrigerated for up to three days. Just reheat slowly. The pale white but comforting appearance of this delicious soup is enhanced with colorful toppings of scallions, bacon bits, and fresh-shredded Cheddar cheese.

- 4 large or 5 medium Idaho baking potatoes*
- 6 tablespoons butter
- 3 medium ribs celery, chopped
- 1 small yellow onion, chopped
- 6 tablespoons all-purpose flour
- 1 quart heavy cream
- 1 quart half and half
- 1-1/2 teaspoons Better Than Bouillon chicken base
- 1 tablespoon salt or to taste
- 1/4 teaspoon white pepper or to taste
- 1/8 teaspoon hot pepper sauce (we used Tabasco) or to taste
- 2 tablespoons dry basil leaves, crushed
- chopped scallions for garnish
- crisp, crumbled bacon (can use the Hormel brand Real Bacon Bits) for garnish
- shredded Cheddar cheese, for garnish

Preheat the oven to 425 degrees. Scrub the potatoes and prick several places with a kitchen fork. Place directly on the oven rack in the center of the oven and bake for about 40 to 45 minutes or until easily pierced with a fork. Remove to a wire tack and cool completely. Peel and cut the potatoes into scant 1/2-inch dice. Set aside.

In a large pot, melt the butter over medium heat. Add the celery and onions and cook, stirring, for about 2 minutes or until translucent. Add the flour to make a roux and cook for 3 to 4 minutes, stirring frequently. Slowly add the heavy cream and half and half, stirring or whisking constantly to avoid any lumps. When the mixture is hot but not yet simmering, whisk in the chicken base. Keep whisking until the base is completely dissolved. Stir in the salt, pepper, hot pepper sauce, and basil leaves. Bring the mixture to a simmer and let simmer for about a minute. Add the diced potatoes, bring back to a simmer, and adjust the seasoning if necessary.

Serve immediately; or cool, cover, and refrigerate for up to 3 days. Reheat slowly over medium-low heat.

To serve, top each serving with about a teaspoon each of the scallions, bacon bits, and Cheddar cheese.

Makes about 14 cups.

*You can also use the microwave to bake the potatoes.

BUTTERNUT SQUASH SOUP WITH PEARS

Back in the '80s, we developed this delicious flavor combination—not to mention the enticing color—in our Cuisinart test kitchen for publication in the newsletter we called *The Cooking Edge*. Everyone who tasted our many tests voted the version below the best, although there was always a divided opinion on the optional cayenne pepper.

- 2 tablespoons unsalted butter
- 1 medium carrot, coarsely chopped
- 2 small celery ribs, coarsely chopped
- 1 large leek, trimmed, rinsed and coarsely chopped
- 1 medium butternut squash (about 1-1/4 pounds) peeled and cut into 1/2-inch cubes
- 2 large, ripe pears, peeled, seeded and coarsely chopped
- 4 cups chicken broth (we used 1-1/2 tablespoons Better Than Bouillon chicken base and 4 cups hot water)
- bouquet garni*
- 1/2 cup light cream or half and half
- 1/8 teaspoon fresh-grated nutmeg
- 1/8 teaspoon cayenne pepper (optional)
- salt and fresh-ground white pepper to taste

In a large saucepot, melt the butter over medium heat. Add the carrots, celery, and leek; and cook, stirring for about 10 minutes or until softened. Add the squash, pears, chicken broth, and bouquet garni. Bring to a boil, reduce the heat to low, and simmer, partially covered, for about 15 to 20 minutes or until the vegetables are tender.

Strain the soup through a colander placed over a large bowl. Discard the bouquet garni. Pour the liquid back into the saucepot. In a food processor fitted with the metal blade (or a good blender), process the solids until very smooth. Return to the pot. Stir in the cream and seasonings and cook over low heat, stirring, until heated through.

Makes about 10 cups.

*You can purchase ready-made bundles of bouquet garni at some gourmet shops. However, to make your own, tie together in a small square of cheesecloth one large bay leaf, a sprig of fresh thyme, some sprigs of fresh parsley, and celery leaves.

CABBAGE BORSCHT

We were asked a few years ago if we had a good recipe for a Jewish version of Cabbage Borscht. We had only to call our friend, the late Ray Rapoport—retired restaurateur and knowledgeable source for Jewish (and many other) recipes—and we soon had that recipe. Even if you have never been fond of borscht, you will change your mind when you taste this version, chock full of meaty, beefy flavor. Don't try to substitute canned beets for the real (fresh) thing, even though you don't relish the thought of peeling and cutting those fresh beets which tend to turn everything nice and red. The end result will not have that crimson color or the satisfying fresh beet flavor. You will need a nice big stockpot in which to make this great family-style recipe and several hours of your time. When the soup is ready, all you need are some nice serving bowls and a basket full of hearty brown bread.

- 2 pounds flanken beef short ribs, trimmed and cut between the bones
- 2 pounds meaty beef and marrow bones
- 2 quarts water
- 1-3/4 pounds fresh beets, peeled and cut into 1/4-inch julienne strips (about 2 cups)
- 3 cups shredded green cabbage (about 1 pound)
- 1-1/2 cups sliced onions
- 3/4 pound boiling potatoes, peeled and cut into 1/2-inch cubes (about 2 cups)
- 1 pound coarse-chopped fresh tomatoes (can use about 1-3/4 cups canned with juice)
- 2 tablespoons fresh lemon juice
- 1 tablespoon sugar
- salt and fresh-ground black pepper to taste

In a large stockpot, place the beef short ribs and marrow bones. Cover with the water. Bring to a simmer over medium-high heat and let simmer for about 2 minutes. Skim any foam (protein) from the surface.

Add the beets, cabbage, onions, potatoes, and tomatoes. Bring back to a simmer, reduce the heat to medium-low, cover, and cook for 2 hours. Add the lemon juice, sugar, and salt and pepper and cook an additional 15 minutes. Skim the surface, if necessary.

Carefully remove the meat and bones from the soup. If you prefer a smooth soup, you can puree the solids in a food processor fitted with the metal blade or in a good blender. You would have to do this in batches. Or, we preferred the larger chunks of vegetables. Remove all meat and marrow from the bones and return to the pot, discarding the bones. Serve hot.

Makes about 10 servings.

CHICKEN AND ESCAROLE SOUP

Many excellent chicken soups can be made with a good canned chicken stock or broth, but there are those that come by their excellence with the leisurely cooking of homemade chicken stock whose recipe you will find below. Make sure to give yourself plenty of time to cook the stock and allow it to cool before finishing the recipe. The ingredients are simple and few, but the end result with the bright green color and leafy taste and texture of the escarole added during the final moments of cooking make this soup special. Enjoy it as a savory first course or luncheon dish.

Chicken Stock:

- 2 fresh chickens (about 2-1/2 pounds each), quartered (add the gizzards, necks, and hearts if included for additional flavor)
- 12 cups water
- 2 large onions, quartered
- 3 large carrots, quartered
- 3 large celery ribs, cut into 1-inch pieces
- 8 black peppercorns
- 1 bay leaf

Put the quartered chicken (and innards if included) into a large stockpot. Add the remaining ingredients and bring to a boil over medium-high heat. Skim the foam that rises to the surface. Reduce the heat to medium-low (you want it to simmer gently), partially cover, and let cook for 2-1/2 hours.

Remove the pot to a wire rack, uncover and let the stock cool for up to an hour. Remove the chicken to a platter and refrigerate for about 30 minutes or until cool enough to handle. Remove the skin and bones from the meat and cut the meat into bite size pieces. Reserve.

Strain the stock, pressing down firmly on the vegetables and innards, if included. Discard the solids and skim off any fat from the liquid. You should have about 2 quarts of stock.

The Soup:

- 2 tablespoons butter
- 2 celery ribs, diced
- 2 medium onions, diced
- 2 large carrots, diced
- 2 quarts chicken stock, recipe given
- salt and fresh-ground black pepper
- cut-up reserved chicken
- 2 small or 1 large head(s) escarole (about 1-1/4 pounds total), trimmed and cut into 1/2-inch pieces

To finish the soup, melt the butter in a large pot over medium-low heat. Add the celery, onions and carrots and cook, stirring occasionally for about 8 minutes, or until soft but not brown. Add the stock and bring to a boil over medium heat. Taste for seasoning. Stir in the chicken, then the escarole, and simmer the mixture for about 4 minutes, or just until the escarole is tender. Check for seasoning again. Makes 8 servings.

CHICKEN "POZOLE"

You might have expected to see a recipe using hominy, since the original versions of pozole—a savory Mexican stew based on what the Aztecs called *mixtamal*, but what we now know as *hominy*—usually contained that ingredient. Here, the innovative chef of a popular restaurant substituted fresh roasted corn instead, which was definitely a culinary coup for anyone who happens to be ambiguous toward hominy. And for those unfamiliar with the ingredient epazote, it is a Latin American ingredient sometimes called goosefoot, Jerusalem oak pazote, Mexican tea, pigweed, or wormseed and is known to be a carminative—meaning that it reduces the gas usually associated with beans! Though hearty but not heavy, this is a deliciously spicy soup perfect as a first course or a light luncheon or supper dish.

For the Soup:

- 1 can (14.5 ounces) peeled whole tomatoes, drained
- 1 medium Spanish onion, peeled and quartered
- 4 large garlic cloves, peeled
- 1 tablespoon ground guajillo chili powder*
- 2 teaspoons ground epazote*
- 1/4 cup canola oil
- 2 quarts chicken stock
- 1 tablespoon chicken base (Better Than Bouillon brand)
- 1/3 cup chopped fresh cilantro
- salt and fresh-ground pepper to taste
- 2 tablespoons melted butter
- 4 ears fresh corn, husks and silk removed
- 1 pound cooked skinless, boneless chicken breasts (cut into 1/2-inch dice)

Suggested Garnishes:

chopped fresh oregano leaves, chopped fresh cilantro, diced onions, baked corn tortilla chips, thin-sliced radishes

To make the soup, in a good blender or a food processor fitted with the metal blade, process the tomatoes, onion, garlic, guajillo chili powder, and epazote. In a large saucepot, heat the oil over medium heat. Add the processed ingredients and bring to a simmer, stirring. Cook for about 2 minutes, then stir in the chicken stock and chicken base. Bring back to a simmer, lower the heat, cover, and continue to simmer for an hour, stirring occasionally. Add the chopped cilantro, taste for seasoning, and simmer just for a minute.

While the soup is simmering, preheat the oven to 475 degrees. Brush the ears of corn with the melted butter and wrap them in aluminum foil. Place the corn directly on the middle rack of the oven and "roast" for about 20 minutes. When cool enough to handle, slice off the kernels with a sharp knife. Reserve the kernels.

When the soup has finished cooking, stir in the corn and chicken and heat through. Garnish each serving with any or all of the above suggested garnishes.

Makes about 12 cups.

*Available in Latin American shops and some gourmet shops.

CHILLED APPLE VICHYSSOISE

This recipe was originally given to us to serve 110. We adjusted it to serve a more practical number. Once you taste this marvel of taste and textures, not only your whole concept of the meaning of vichyssoise (that familiar cold leek and potato soup) will undergo a dramatic change, but you may wish we had not adjusted it so far down. The Granny Smith apples have found a whole new venue in this creamy, rich, flavorful, and refreshing soup.

1-1/2 cups water
3/4 cup sugar
1-1/2 pounds Granny Smith apples, peeled, seeded and cut into large dice
2-1/2 tablespoons unsalted butter
1 ounce fresh gingerroot (about a 2-1/2 by 1-inch piece) peeled and chopped
1 cup plain ready-made applesauce (we used Mott's)
3/4 cup dry white wine
1/4 cup apple brandy (Calvados is good)
3/4 cup heavy cream
1-2/3 cups vanilla ice cream
2 teaspoons ground cinnamon (or to taste)
1-2/3 cups plain vanilla yogurt
fine-diced Granny Smith apples for garnish (about 1/4 cup per serving)

In a large saucepot, stir together the water and sugar over medium heat until the sugar dissolves and the mixture comes to a simmer. Add the large diced apples, reduce the heat, and cook for about 15 minutes at a low simmer or until the apples are very tender. Stir occasionally. Remove from the heat and reserve.

In another larger pot, melt the butter over medium heat and sauté the ginger for about 3 minutes to release the flavor. Don't let it burn. Stir in the applesauce, white wine, brandy, and heavy cream. Stir in the cooked apples and let everything cool to room temperature. In a food processor fitted with the metal blade, process the apple mixture with the ice cream (in batches if necessary) until very smooth. Pass everything through a fine sieve into a large bowl. Discard any solids remaining in the sieve. Whisk in the cinnamon and yogurt and refrigerate until well chilled—several hours or overnight. Cover when cool. Stir well before serving, and garnish each bowl with the diced apples. Makes about 9 cups.

COUNTRY-STYLE TOMATO SOUP

Country-Style Tomato Soup

Just glancing through the list of ingredients including tomato puree, tomato paste, and chopped canned plum tomatoes will convince you that this will be an outstanding tomato soup experience. You will thank the innovative chef who shared this soup recipe with its velvety texture and rich tomato flavor, and we guarantee you will never reach for what was once your favorite canned tomato soup again.

Soup:

- 2 tablespoons butter
- 1 tablespoon olive oil
- 2 small yellow onions, peeled and diced
- 2 medium garlic cloves, peeled and chopped
- 2 tablespoons all-purpose flour
- 3 cups tomato puree
- 2 tablespoons tomato paste
- 1 cup chicken stock (we used 1 heaping teaspoon Better Than Bouillon chicken base and 1 cup hot water)
- 2 cups half and half
- 3/4 cup chopped canned plum tomatoes
- 3 tablespoons chopped fresh basil
- salt and fresh-ground pepper to taste

Garnish:

8 toasted French baguette slices (about 3/4 inch thick by 3 inches in diameter)	3 tablespoons fresh-grated Parmesan cheese
1 tablespoon olive oil	2 tablespoons chopped fresh basil

To make the soup, in a large saucepot melt the butter with the olive oil over medium heat. When hot, add the onions and sauté for about 3 minutes or until translucent. Add the chopped garlic and sauté for about another 1-1/2 minutes. Add the flour and cook, stirring, for about 3 minutes. Slowly add the chicken stock (or base and hot water), tomato puree, and tomato paste. Bring to a simmer, reduce the heat if necessary, and cook at a slow simmer, stirring occasionally, for 10 minutes. Add the half and half, bring back to a simmer, and let cook for an additional 5 minutes, stirring occasionally.

Remove the soup from the heat and let cool for 15 to 20 minutes. In a good blender or a food processor fitted with the metal blade, puree the soup in batches, transferring each batch to a clean saucepot. When all has been pureed, return the saucepot to the stove and stir in the canned chopped plum tomatoes, fresh chopped basil, and salt and pepper to taste. Bring back to a simmer over medium heat and let cook for about 5 minutes more.

To serve, divide the soup among 8 warm serving bowls and garnish each with a toasted French baguette slice lightly brushed with a scant 1/2 teaspoon olive oil. Divide the Parmesan cheese and fresh-chopped basil over each bread slice.

Makes 8 servings.

CREAM OF BROCCOLI SOUP

Glancing through this recipe, you may wonder what makes this Cream of Broccoli Soup so special. It is yet another delicious example of how the freshest and simplest is often the best. That means making sure your head of broccoli shows no signs of distress such as yellowed patches on its flowerets and/or brownish and tired-looking leaves and stems. Here we chose a broccoli head weighing about 1-3/4 pounds. We cleaned and trimmed away all but 3/8 of an inch of the stems leaving about 8 firm-packed cups of small-cut flowerets. (Use those stems, trimmed and peeled, another day.) We guarantee even those who are not broccoli fans will enjoy the flavor and texture of this light but rich-tasting soup.

1/2 pound (2 sticks) unsalted butter, divided
1 small onion, peeled and cut into small pieces
5 medium garlic cloves, quartered
8 cups firm-packed fresh small-cut broccoli flowerets
1 large bay leaf
2 quarts (8 cups) hot water
4 heaping teaspoons Better Than Bouillon chicken base
1 cup whole milk
1/2 cup heavy cream
3 tablespoons all-purpose flour
salt and fresh-ground pepper to taste
extra virgin olive oil for garnish, optional
fresh-grated Parmesan cheese for garnish, optional

In a large saucepot, melt all but 3 tablespoons of the butter over medium heat. Sauté the onions and garlic for about 5 to 7 minutes or until soft, being careful not to let brown. Add the broccoli and bay leaf and toss well to coat. Stir in the water and chicken base, stirring to dissolve the base. Then stir in the milk. Bring the mixture to a boil, reduce the heat, and simmer, partially covered, for about 15 minutes or until the broccoli is very soft. Add the cream and let cook for another 5 minutes. Remove from the heat and let cool for 15 to 20 minutes, stirring occasionally.

With a large slotted ladle, spoon the solids (discarding the bay leaf) into the workbowl of a food processor fitted with the metal blade or a good blender (you may have to do this in batches) and process until pureed. Transfer the pureed mixture to a bowl until all has been processed. Stir the pureed mixture back into the liquid remaining in the saucepot. Place over medium heat and bring back to a slow simmer, stirring.

Meanwhile, make a roux with the remaining 3 tablespoons of butter and the flour. Melt the butter in a small saucepan over medium heat. Stir in the flour. Slowly stir the roux into the simmering soup and cook the soup, partially covered, for about 10 minutes, stirring occasionally.

To serve, if desired, drizzle about a teaspoon of the olive oil and Parmesan cheese over the top of each serving. Can be made several hours ahead and reheated slowly over low heat.

Makes about 11 cups.

CREAM OF GARLIC SOUP

Cream of Garlic Soup

The day we tested this soup was a day when anyone living on the third floor of our building was treated to an atmosphere of aromatic bliss. Even though the cooking time is relatively brief, the 1/4 cup of sautéed minced garlic was not to be ignored. The garlic—along with the green onions and chopped fresh parsley—is cooked just long enough to remove any sharp flavor edges, and combined with the other ingredients, the ensuing garlic flavor is smooth and soothing to the palate. Even with the addition of heavy cream, this soup is surprisingly light yet satisfying.

2 tablespoons unsalted butter or margarine
7 green onions (scallions), white part and 1-inch of green, chopped
2 tablespoons chopped fresh parsley
10 large garlic cloves, finely chopped
2 teaspoons chicken base (we used the Better Than Bouillon brand)
1/2 cup dry white wine
3 cups water
2 tablespoons all-purpose flour
1 cup heavy whipping cream
salt and fresh-ground white pepper, to taste

In a large heavy saucepan, melt the butter over medium heat. Sauté the onions and parsley for about 1 minute. Add the garlic and sauté for another 2 minutes, or until the onions and garlic are soft and fragrant. Stir in the chicken base and white wine and cook, stirring until the chicken base is completely melted. Stir in the water and bring the mixture to a boil. Whisk the flour with about 1/4 cup of the heavy cream. Stir the remaining cream into the soup and when that comes to a simmer, stir in the flour/cream mixture. Keep stirring for another 2 minutes or until the soup simmers again and has thickened slightly. Season to taste with salt and white pepper. Reduce the heat to medium-low and let the soup simmer slowly for another 2 minutes. Serve hot.

Makes about 4-1/3 cups.

CREAM OF MUSHROOM SOUP

Cream of Mushroom Soup

To mushroom lovers everywhere, this intensely flavored Cream of Mushroom Soup is destined to be a favorite. Every spoonful is chock-full of tender mushrooms that have been sautéed and simmered until every bit of flavor has been released. The aroma of the simmering mushrooms is a heady experience and a guarantee of an awesome taste treat. Chef Bill Willoughby, the generous chef who shared this recipe, told us that if you ever have any leftover soup it can be used as a sauce for turkey, chicken, or even meatloaf.

6 tablespoons unsalted butter or margarine
2 medium garlic cloves, minced
1 small onion, cut into small dice (less than 1/4 inch)
1-1/2 pounds white mushrooms, washed, stems trimmed and thinly sliced (about 12 cups)
1/2 cup dry sherry
2 cups heavy cream
1 can (14-1/2 ounces) low-sodium chicken broth
3 chicken bouillon cubes or 3 teaspoons chicken bouillon granules
1 quart whole milk
roux: 4 tablespoons unsalted butter or margarine and 1/3 cup all-purpose flour
salt and fresh-ground pepper
chopped parsley, for garnish

In a large sauté pan, melt the butter over medium-high heat. Add the garlic, onions, and mushrooms; and cook, stirring, until the mushrooms are tender—about 3 minutes. Stir in the sherry, reduce the heat, and simmer for 8 minutes.

Add the heavy cream and let reduce by 1/4 over medium heat. (This takes about 12 minutes.) Add the chicken broth and bouillon cubes or granules and simmer for an additional 15 minutes. Add the milk and bring just to a boil.

Meanwhile, in a small saucepan, make the roux. Melt the butter over medium heat. Stir in the flour and let bubble for 1 minute to "cook" the flour. Whisk the roux into the hot soup and keep whisking until the mixture thickens and is creamy—about 2 minutes. Season to taste with salt and pepper. Serve hot garnished with the chopped parsley.

Makes about 9 cups.

CUCUMBER AND DILL SOUP

Once we received and tested this delicious and thoroughly refreshing soup from a popular restaurant, it was high on our list of favorites whether the weather was warm or cold. Your taste buds will be pleased with the smooth richness of each mouthful but delighted to have the velvety smoothness interrupted with crunchy cubes of cucumber. Be sure to make the soup several hours or even the day before you plan to serve it. It is at its best when well chilled and all the flavorful ingredients have united.

- 1 cup chicken stock (we used a heaping teaspoon of Better than Bouillon chicken base and 1 cup hot water)
- 1/2 cup sugar
- 1/4 cup white vinegar (we used Heinz brand)
- 2-1/2 pounds (40 ounces) sour cream (not reduced fat or fat-free)
- 2 teaspoons prepared horseradish, or to taste
- 1 tablespoon fresh lemon juice
- dash or two of Worcestershire sauce
- salt and fresh-ground white pepper to taste
- 1/3 cup chopped fresh dill
- 2 large European cucumbers* (peeled, seeded, and diced)

In a large mixing bowl, whisk together all the ingredients except the cucumbers. Continue whisking until the mixture is very smooth. Stir in the cubed cucumbers and refrigerate for several hours or overnight. Stir before serving. This will keep for up to three days in the refrigerator.

Makes about 12 cups.

*Available in most supermarkets. They are the long cucumbers that have fewer and smaller seeds than the usual domestic varieties.

Horseradish Soup

HORSERADISH SOUP

We are apt to associate horseradish with roast beef or as part of the ubiquitous red cocktail sauce the late James Beard often referred to as the "red menace." Sometimes stirred into mustard, whipped cream, or sour cream, it can accompany all manner of fish, fowl, or other cooked meats. Here in this delightfully smooth and creamy soup, the usually pungent horseradish is cooked just long enough to diminish its sharp bite and leave a pleasant tickle on your taste buds.

1 tablespoon margarine or butter
10 thin-sliced scallions, white part and one inch of green
1 tablespoon chopped fresh parsley
3 tablespoons prepared horseradish
1 heaping tablespoon unsweetened applesauce
1/2 cup dry white wine
3 cups chicken broth (we used a tablespoons Better Than Bouillon chicken base and 3 cups water)
1 cup heavy cream
2-1/2 tablespoons all-purpose flour
fresh-ground white pepper to taste

In a large heavy saucepan, melt the margarine or butter over medium heat. Sauté the scallions and parsley for about 2 minutes or until the scallions are tender. Stir in the horseradish and applesauce and sauté for another minute. Stir in the wine and chicken broth and bring to a boil, stirring occasionally.

In a small bowl, whisk the flour into about 1/3 cup of the heavy cream. Add the remaining cream and whisk thoroughly. When the horseradish mixture comes to a boil, slowly stir in the heavy cream and flour. Keep stirring, just until it returns to a boil and the soup thickens. Check for seasoning, adding white pepper to taste. Serve hot.

Makes about 5-1/2 cups.

Nick's Minestrone Soup

NICK'S MINESTRONE SOUP

For the record and for a bit of history, there is actually no fixed recipe for Minestrone since it is usually made out of whatever vegetables are in season. Time was when it was also known in Italy as *cucina povera*—literally meaning "poor kitchen" as it was often made from leftovers. But times have changed, and Minestrone today varies widely depending upon traditional cooking times, available ingredients, and whether one wants a completely vegetarian dish or one with the addition of meat or poultry. Some also call for the addition of pasta. You will find the recipe below from a well-known restaurant an enjoyable way to eat your vegetables in a remarkably thick and flavorful way.

2 tablespoons olive oil
2 large carrots, peeled and diced
2 large celery ribs, diced
1 large onion, peeled and diced
2 medium shallots, peeled and diced
2 medium leeks, trimmed, well washed and roughly chopped
2 large garlic cloves, roughly chopped
2-1/2 cups firm-packed shredded cabbage
1-1/2 cups fresh or frozen green beans, cut into 1/2-inch pieces
1 can (15-1/2 ounces) chick peas, drained
1 can (7-3/4 ounces) chick peas, drained
6 cups water
1 can (14-1/2 ounces) diced tomatoes, undrained
1-1/4 cups canned, crushed tomatoes
1 heaping tablespoon chicken base (we use the Better Than Bouillon brand)
1 heaping tablespoon beef base (we use the Better Than Bouillon brand)
1 teaspoon crushed dry basil
1 teaspoon crushed dry oregano
8 sprigs fresh thyme
2 large bay leaves
salt and fresh-ground pepper to taste
fresh-grated Parmesan cheese, about 2 teaspoons for serving

In a large saucepot or stockpot, heat the oil over medium-high heat. Sauté the carrots, celery, onions, shallots, leeks, and garlic for about 1-1/2 minutes or until they are about 1/4 cooked. Stir in the cabbage and sauté for another 30 seconds. Add the remaining ingredients except the Parmesan cheese, stirring well to mix everything thoroughly and making sure the chicken and beef base have dissolved. Bring the mixture to a boil. Lower the heat, partially cover the pot, and let the soup simmer gently for about 35 to 40 minutes, or until it has thickened to your liking. Serve hot or at room temperature and pass the fresh-grated Parmesan cheese.

Makes about 14 cups.

PRIEST'S SOUP
(OR LENTIL SOUP OR ESAU'S POTAGE)

Lentils are one of the oldest known legumes, dating back to biblical times. It is said that the original Lentil soup was that "mess of potage" for which Esau exchanged his birthright, hence the name Esau's Potage. Then the name Priest's Soup evolved because the legend of Esau was told so often by some priests. Whatever you choose to call this soup, it is satisfyingly thick and flavorful. Many recipes call for chunk bacon or a ham bone to be cooked with the other ingredients. We eliminated those ingredients when we developed this version for my book *The Low-Cholesterol Food Processor Cookbook* (Doubleday, 1980) and used the imitation bacon bits made from soy protein for a tasty garnish instead.

- 1-1/2 cups dried lentils
- 2 medium cloves garlic, peeled and coarsely chopped
- 2 large onions, peeled and coarsely chopped
- 3 large carrots, peeled and coarsely chopped
- 3 ribs celery, coarsely chopped
- 1 large all-purpose potato, peeled and cut into 1-inch pieces
- 1/2 cup fresh Italian parsley leaves
- 6 cups chicken broth (we used 6 heaping teaspoons Better Than Bouillon chicken base and 6 cups warm water)
- Salt and fresh-ground pepper to taste
- 2 tablespoons dry sherry
- 3 tablespoons soy-based imitation bacon bits for garnish

Rinse and pick over the dried lentils. In a large saucepot, stir together all the ingredients except the sherry and bacon bits. Bring to a boil over medium-high heat, stirring. Lower the heat to medium-low, cover and simmer for 1-1/2 hours. Remove from the heat and let cool for 30 minutes.

In a food processor fitted with the metal blade, or a good blender, process the soup in batches until it is fairly smooth. Return to the pot and if it seems too thick, add more broth or water. Stir in the sherry and taste for seasoning. Serve sprinkled with some of the bacon bits.

Makes 8 servings.

Pumpkin Bisque

PUMPKIN BISQUE

This recipe for Pumpkin Bisque, kindly shared with us from a popular restaurant, is another example of culinary wizardry. It is a masterful blend and balance of readily accessible ingredients with no complicated steps in the execution. The resulting taste and texture make it a winner all around. Though we often associate pumpkin recipes with the holidays, you will find this soup is the perfect beginning for a meal at any time of the year. It keeps well for up to three days in the refrigerator and is just as smooth and flavorful as the day it was made.

- 4 cups chicken stock (we used 5 teaspoons chicken bouillon granules—1 extra to make it strong—and 4 cups water)
- 1/2 cup firm-packed light brown sugar
- 2 cans (15 ounces each) canned pumpkin puree (not for pumpkin pie)
- 1/4 cup undiluted frozen orange juice concentrate
- 1 teaspoon ground allspice
- 1 tablespoon ground cinnamon
- 2 cups heavy cream
- 3 tablespoons cornstarch
- 3/4 cup cool water
- salt and fresh-ground black pepper, to taste
- chopped fresh dill or dill sprigs, for garnish

In a 4-quart saucepan, bring the chicken stock just to the simmer over medium-high heat. Reduce the heat to medium. Stir in the brown sugar until dissolved. Whisk in the pumpkin, the orange juice concentrate, allspice and cinnamon until well mixed. Whisk in the cream.

Dissolve the cornstarch in the cool water and whisk into the pumpkin mixture. Keep whisking or stirring over medium heat until it has thickened slightly. Season to taste. Can be made several hours ahead and reheated slowly over medium-low heat, stirring. May also be covered and refrigerated for up to 3 days. Garnish each serving with chopped fresh dill or dill sprigs.

Makes about 12 cups.

PUREE CRECY
(A COLD CARRO/POTATO SOUP)

A la Crecy is the name given to various preparations, most notably soups. Some are composed exclusively of carrots, but all include an obligatory carrot garnish. Puree Crecy is another recipe we developed for my cookbook *The Low-Cholesterol Food Processor Cookbook* (Doubleday 1980, now out of print). It can be served either hot for cool-weather meals or chilled for warm summer dining. And you can disregard that obligatory garnish if you wish and toss in some chopped parsley just for a pleasing contrast in color. A tablespoon or two of sherry is also delicious. Whichever way you decide to serve this soup, you will enjoy the flavor and velvety texture.

2 tablespoons unsalted butter
1 large leek, white part only, washed and sliced
5 medium carrots, peeled and sliced
2 medium potatoes, peeled and diced

3 cups chicken bouillon (we use 3 heaping teaspoons Better Than Bouillon chicken base and three cups hot water)
salt to taste
pinch white pepper
1 cup evaporated skim milk
3 tablespoons fine-shredded or chopped raw carrots

In a large heavy saucepan, melt the butter over medium heat. Sauté the leek for 2 or 3 minutes, stirring constantly, or until it is limp but not brown. Add the sliced carrots, diced potatoes, and chicken bouillon. Bring to a boil, reduce heat to medium-low, and simmer partially covered for 20 to 25 minutes or until the vegetables are very tender. Remove the vegetables with a slotted spoon and in a food processor fitted with the metal blade (can also use a blender, but add some of the liquid to the vegetables as you puree) puree the vegetables in batches, if necessary, until smooth. Return the puree to the cooking liquid in the saucepan and stir in well. Add the salt and pepper to taste. If mixture seems too thick, add a bit of water. This is good served either warm or well chilled. Serve sprinkled with the shredded or chopped raw carrots. Try adding a tablespoon or two of sherry just before serving.

Makes 6 servings.

SALMON-TOMATO BISQUE

Salmon-Tomato Bisque

    We can thank the owner and chef of a popular restaurant in Boca Raton for this outstanding salmon-tomato bisque recipe. We were puzzled at first by one of the ingredients listed: salmon trimmings. Chef Tony explained that the restaurant saved what would be called the thinner tail sections of the fresh salmon fillets they serve and froze those trimmings until they had enough to make this delicious bisque. What an example of judicious planning! Check with your local fishmonger as we did, who will be happy to trim off those thin tail sections in the amount you need at a slightly reduced price. Just explain your need nicely. This bisque is rich in both flavor and texture. It does take a while to prepare, but the preparation is extraordinarily easy for an end result this is so exceptional. Do be sure to warm your cream and half and half as instructed. It is less likely to curdle when added to the tomato mixture.

- 2 cans (14.5 ounces each) peeled and diced tomatoes
- 1 can (15 ounces) crushed tomatoes
- 1-1/2 teaspoons dried basil leaves
- 1/2 teaspoon dried oregano
- 1-1/2 teaspoons granulated garlic (we like Lawry's coarse ground garlic with parsley)
- 1 tablespoon instant minced onions
- 1 teaspoon Lawry's Seasoned Salt
- Pinch fresh-ground black pepper
- 1 scant teaspoon chicken bouillon granules
- 2 small bay leaves
- 6 ounces fresh salmon*, skin removed and cut into small pieces
- 1 cup heavy cream, warmed
- 1/2 cup half and half, warmed
- 1/4 teaspoon sugar, if needed

Combine all the ingredients except the cream, half and half, and sugar in a large saucepot. Bring to a boil over medium-high heat, whisking often to break up the salmon. When the mixture comes to a boil, reduce the heat to low, partially cover, and let simmer, stirring occasionally for 1 hour.

Whisk in the warm cream and half and half and return just to a boil. Remove from the heat and taste for seasoning, adding the sugar if too acidic. Serve hot. Can be made ahead (even the day before), cooled, and refrigerated. Bring slowly to just below boiling before serving.

Makes about 7 cups.

*Ask your fishmonger for the "tails" of the salmon fillets he sells. He may give you a good price. Or watch for a nice sale on fresh salmon.

THE REAL GULASCHSUPPE

Someone once asked us if we had an authentic recipe for *gulaschsuppe* (a tasty variation on a thick stew) as prepared in the *gasthaeusers* (restaurants) in Southern Germany. (We think the Washington bunch could take a lesson in international cooperation from the friendly exchange that ensued.) We called one of our German friends, Rosemarie, who faxed her cousin Dorothee in Munich, Bavaria, with the request. Within days, we received a letter from Rosemarie complete with the recipe for *Gulaschsuppe*. Dorothee had faxed back, both in the original German and a translation. We then asked German neighbor Herta to check the translation, and the happy ending to this friendly cooperation is the delicious variation everyone enjoyed. We found that it was even more flavorful if made the day before you plan to serve it. The flavors just meld beautifully.

2 tablespoons pork lard* (can substitute vegetable oil, but some flavor is lost)
2 large onions, cut into 1/2-inch dice
1 tablespoon Hungarian paprika
1 large garlic clove, minced
1 pound well trimmed beef for stew, cut into small 1/2-inch cubes
1 pound potatoes, peeled and cut into small 1/2-inch cubes

2 large tomatoes, peeled and diced
1 large bell pepper, seeded and diced
3 medium carrots, scrubbed and thin-sliced
3 1/4-inch slices celery root (celeric), cut into 1/4-inch dice
1 tablespoon caraway seeds
salt to taste
3 cups water, about
1/2 cup sour cream, optional, but very nice

Melt the lard in a large heavy saucepot over medium-high heat. Sauté the onions until soft, but not brown, about 3 minutes. Add the paprika, garlic and beef and sauté until the beef is no longer red, about 3 minutes. Cover and let simmer over low heat until the meat juices have almost evaporated, about 15 minutes.

Add the remaining ingredients, cover with water, and bring to a boil. Cover, reduce the heat, and simmer gently until everything is very tender and "nearly disintegrated" (literal translation)—about 3 hours. Add the sour cream, if using, just before serving.

We like to serve this with rice to soak up some of the delectable juices. Makes 4 servings.

*In spite of its not-so-good reputation according to the Department of Agriculture in its book *Composition of Foods*, lard is better for use than butter. It has 1/3 the cholesterol and less than 2/3 the saturated fat content.

TOMATO BLEU CHEESE SOUP

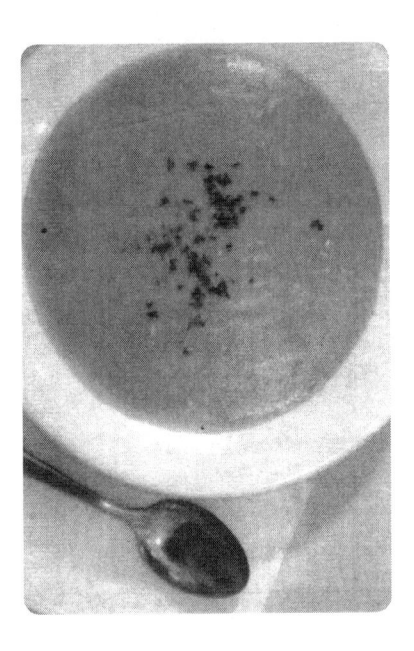

Tomato Bleu Cheese Soup

According to the restaurant owner who shared this unusual and outstanding recipe, when they first offered it on the menu none of their customers seemed interested in trying it. Then they began giving out free samples and it immediately became one of the favorites. You will find the same reaction—one spoonful and you will make immediate converts, even with those who are not bleu cheese enthusiasts. Do use a top quality of bleu cheese, not the crumbled variety. You will like the way the small amount of heavy cream along with the cheese added at the end temper and mellow the slight acidity of the tomato puree.

- 1/2 cup butter
- 1/2 cup all-purpose flour
- 2 quarts water
- 2 tablespoons chicken base (we use Better Than Bouillon chicken base)
- 3 cups tomato puree (do not use tomato sauce)
- fresh-ground white pepper to taste
- 1 cup heavy cream
- 6 ounces bleu cheese (bulk variety, not the precrumbled)

In a large heavy saucepot, melt the butter over medium heat. Stir in the flour and keep stirring constantly while the roux bubbles for about 2 minutes. Gradually whisk in the water. Whisk in the chicken base and tomato puree. Keep whisking or stirring until the mixture comes to a simmer. Reduce the heat, if necessary, and let simmer for about 5 minutes, stirring occasionally. Lastly, stir in the heavy cream and the bleu cheese which you have crumbled by hand. Keep stirring for about 5 minutes, or until it thickens slightly. Serve hot with your favorite saltines. This will keep well, refrigerated, for up to 3 days. Reheat slowly over low heat.

Makes about 13 cups.

VEGETARIAN PUMPKIN SOUP

The subtle flavor of the roasted cashews pureed with some of the vegetable stock adds a most pleasurable taste to this flavorful soup. The use of Bragg Liquid Aminos—that all-purpose seasoning made from soy protein and an excellent flavoring alternative to tamari or soy sauce but much lower in salt—also adds to the final flavor.

3/4 cup roasted cashew halves or pieces	sea salt and fresh-ground black pepper to taste
3-3/4 cups vegetable bouillon, divided*	3 cans (15 ounces each) pumpkin puree (not pumpkin pie mix)
3 tablespoons soy margarine	2-1/4 cups warm water
3/4 cup fine-diced onions	2-1/2 teaspoons Bragg Liquid Aminos
3/4 cup fine-diced carrots	
1/4 cup chopped fresh parsley	
1 teaspoon dried thyme leaves	

In a food processor fitted with the metal blade or a good blender, process the cashews with 3/4 cup of the vegetable bouillon until the mixture is as smooth as possible. Set aside.

In a large saucepot, melt the margarine over medium heat and sauté the onions and carrots for about 4 minutes, or until very tender but not brown. Add the parsley, thyme, salt, pepper and the pumpkin and stir well. Slowly add the remaining 3 cups of vegetable bouillon, the water, and the Bragg Liquid Aminos. Bring to a boil, stirring. Add the pureed cashews and bring back to a boil. If the soup seems too thick, you can add more bouillon or water. You can garnish this nicely with additional chopped parsley, some plain croutons, or some toasted pumpkin seeds. The soup keeps well, refrigerated for up to 3 days, and can be frozen. You can also turn this into a delicious "cream" soup by just a small addition of low-fat or evaporated milk—about a tablespoon per cup of the liquid.

Makes about 15 cups.

*You can use either vegetable bouillon cubes and water, canned vegetable bouillon, or the Better Than Bouillon vegetable base and water.

WATERCRESS SOUP

The piquant flavor and pleasing color from the watercress add to the enjoyment of this soup. We first decided to serve it as a holiday offering because of its green overtones, but it is now a year-round favorite. For best results, make sure your watercress is very fresh. This is a soup that is delicious served either warm or well chilled.

1 tablespoon butter
1 tablespoon vegetable oil
3 small leeks, white part only, thinly sliced
1 small onion, peeled and thinly sliced
3 small waxy potatoes, peeled and diced
4 cups chicken broth (we use 4 teaspoons of Better Than Bouillon chicken base and 4 cups water)
salt to taste
1 nice fresh bunch watercress (stems removed and discarded, coarsely chopped, divided)
1 cup milk
1 cup heavy cream
watercress leaves and/or 6 tablespoons sour cream for garnish

In a heavy saucepan, melt the butter with the vegetable oil over medium heat. Cook the leeks and onions, stirring occasionally, for about 3 minutes or until softened. Add the potatoes and cook, stirring for another 3 minutes. Stir in the chicken broth and salt and bring to a boil. Reduce the heat and simmer, partially covered, for about 15 minutes. Stir in 3/4 of the chopped watercress and milk, bring back to a simmer, and cook for about 5 minutes or until the watercress is wilted and the potatoes are very tender. Remove from the heat and let cool for 15 to 20 minutes, stirring occasionally.

In a food processor fitted with the metal blade or a good blender, puree the mixture in batches until smooth and velvety. Add the remaining chopped watercress to the last batch and process just until the soup is flecked with dark green.

Return the processed soup to the saucepan and stir in the heavy cream. Check for seasoning and reheat over medium-low heat. Serve warm or chilled; it is delicious either way. Garnish each serving with some watercress leaves and/or a tablespoon of sour cream.

Makes 6 servings.

SALADS

BARLEY AND SAUSAGE SALAD

Years ago, before barley was as well-known as it is today (thanks to all the emphasis given to the healthful advantages of eating more grains), the Cuisinart test kitchen experimented with several recipes using barley. We found the homey flavor and texture lent itself to many uses, one of which was this wonderful Barley and Sausage Salad. We recommend you serve this slightly warm or at room temperature for the best flavor. Do make the Red Pepper Vinaigrette first since you will need some of it in which to sauté the kielbasa sausage.

Red Pepper Vinaigrette:

2 medium garlic cloves
1/3 cup fresh basil leaves
2-1/2 tablespoons red wine vinegar
2 tablespoons Dijon mustard
1/3 cup olive oil

1/4 teaspoon dried rosemary leaves
1 whole canned pimento, drained well and chunked
salt and fresh-ground pepper to taste

In a food processor fitted with the metal blade, process the garlic until finely chopped. Add the remaining ingredients and process until smooth.
Makes about 3/4 cup.

Salad:

1/4 cup red pepper vinaigrette, recipe given
6 ounces kielbasa sausage, cut into 1/2-inch cubes
6 cups thin-sliced Savoy cabbage
3 tablespoons water

2 cups cooked barley (we used Quaker medium-pearled barley)
1 small red pepper, seeded and julienned
3 cups arugula torn into bite-size pieces
3 tablespoons toasted pine nuts*

In a large skillet, heat the vinaigrette over medium heat. Sauté the kielbasa for about 5 minutes or until lightly browned. Add the cabbage and water, cover, and cook for about 3 minutes or until the cabbage is tender. Stir in the barley.

In a large serving bowl, combine the red pepper strips and arugula. Add the contents of the skillet and toss well to combine. Drizzle with the remaining 1/2 cup vinaigrette and toss again. Sprinkle with the toasted pine nuts and serve.

Makes 6 servings.

*To toast the pine nuts, preheat the oven to 350 degrees. Spread the nuts in a pie plate and bake in the center of the oven for about 8 minutes or until lightly browned. Let cool.

CHICKEN PASTA SALAD

Chicken Pasta Salad

This Chicken Pasta Salad with its Balsamic Vinaigrette is truly an outstanding meal. A local caterer was kind enough to share the recipe after we had enjoyed it at a catered luncheon. There are several steps to the preparation, but most can and should be done ahead to allow all the ingredients to be at room or refrigerator temperature. Because the penne pasta will happily soak up the vinaigrette as it sits, you might want to save about 1/4 cup as we did to fold in just before serving. This is an eye-appealing dish with its colorful chopped sun-dried tomatoes, julienned strips of red peppers, and the bright green of the broccoli florets. The simple but flavorful Balsamic Vinaigrette will find its way into many other salads. It will not be as thick as a mayonnaise but the consistency of very lightly whipped cream. We have to admit, the yield always diminishes after the first taste for seasoning—we keep tasting just to be sure!

Salad:

- 1/2 cup firm-packed sun-dried tomato halves (not in oil), reconstituted
- 12 ounces penne pasta, cooked according to package directions
- 5-1/2 tablespoons olive oil, divided
- 4 large boneless, skinless chicken breast halves (about 5 ounces each)
- 2 large red peppers (seeded and cut into julienne strips about 1-1/2 by 1/4 inches)
- 1 large onion (peeled, halved, and cut into julienne strips about 1-1/2 by 1/4 inches)
- salt and fresh-ground pepper
- 2 large garlic cloves, peeled and chopped
- 5 cups broccoli florets (1 large head—save the stems for soup)
- 1/2 cup fresh-grated Parmesan cheese

Balsamic Vinaigrette:

- 1/2 cup Balsamic vinegar
- 2 heaping tablespoons Dijon mustard
- 2 tablespoons sugar
- 1 cup olive oil
- salt and fresh-ground pepper, to taste

To prepare the salad, place the tomatoes in a saucepan and add water to cover. Bring to a boil over medium-high heat. Reduce the heat and simmer for 4 to 5 minutes, just to soften. Drain well, cool, and coarsely chop. Set aside.

After the pasta has cooked according to package directions, drain well and toss with 1 tablespoon of the olive oil in a large mixing bowl. Set aside.

In a nonstick skillet, heat 2 tablespoons of the oil over medium-high heat. Sauté the chicken breasts for about 3 to 4 minutes a side, or just until no pink shows in the center. Let cool while roasting the vegetables.

Preheat the oven to 400 degrees. Toss the red peppers and onions in a bowl with 1 tablespoon of the olive oil. Season with salt and pepper. Place in a jelly roll pan and roast in the center of the oven for 5 minutes. Stir once, add the garlic, stir again, and continue roasting for another 10 minutes or until the vegetables begin to take on color. Transfer to paper towels to drain and cool.

Toss the broccoli florets with the remaining 1-1/2 tablespoons oil, season with salt and pepper, and roast in the same pan for about 5 minutes, or until heated through but still crisp.

Cut the cooled chicken breasts crosswise into about 1/2-inch strips. Add the chicken and all the cooked, cooled, and roasted ingredients and 3/4 of the Parmesan cheese to the pasta, and toss lightly to mix. Make the vinaigrette.

To make the vinaigrette, place the vinegar, mustard, and sugar in a bowl. Blend well on the medium speed of an electric mixer. With the mixer running full speed, slowly drizzle in the oil. It should emulsify nicely—not as a thick mayonnaise consistency but almost like a lightly whipped cream. Taste for seasoning.

Toss the pasta and chicken mixture with all but 1/4 cup of the dressing. The salad can be made several hours ahead to this point. Cover with plastic wrap and refrigerate until serving. Just before serving, drizzle the remaining dressing, if needed, over the salad. To serve, divide the salad among six serving dishes lined with greens and sprinkle with the remaining Parmesan cheese.

Makes 6 servings.

Chicken Salad with Grapes

CHICKEN SALAD WITH GRAPES

This delicious recipe for Chicken Salad with Grapes is thanks to the general manager of Charcuterie Too, the outstanding restaurant right in the middle of the main library in Fort Lauderdale, Florida. (Reading and eating: two favorite pastimes!) At first glance, you may wonder at the simplicity of the ingredient list and how this recipe could possibly be so special. We hasten to assure you that the short list, followed precisely, will give chicken salad a whole new image. *Precisely* means not to even think about substituting any other mustard for the imported Pommery (Moutarde de Meaux) mustard. This is the secret to an incredible and unusually flavorful chicken salad. Pommery Mustard may not be available in all supermarkets, so check your neighborhood gourmet food shops. FYI, this mustard has been served at the tables of the kings of France since 1632. This salad can also substitute for a delicious sandwich when piled on French baguettes, for example. As a salad, the restaurant serves it on assorted greens garnished with tomatoes, carrot curls, and sprouts.

2 pounds trimmed boneless, skinless, chicken breasts*
salt and fresh-ground black pepper
1-1/2 cups imported Pommery (Moutarde de Meaux) Mustard (NO substitutes)
1 cup good quality mayonnaise (not reduced fat)
1 cup sour cream (not reduced fat)
1 pound seedless red grapes, stemmed, washed and dried
1 cup sliced almonds, toasted**

Poach the chicken breasts, salted and peppered, in water to cover for about 6 minutes, uncovered, or until the center pink is just gone. Drain immediately and, when cool enough to handle, cut into 1/2-inch pieces.

Meanwhile, in a large mixing bowl, whisk together the mustard, mayonnaise, and sour cream until well blended and smooth. Fold in the chicken, then the grapes and almonds. Chill for a minimum of 4 hours to let the dressing mellow and mature. Can also be made one day ahead. Fold again before serving.

Makes 8 servings.

*You can use leftover cooked chicken and/or turkey, but by starting with uncooked chicken and poaching it briefly, you will be assured of moist and tender bites.
**To toast the almonds, spread them in a single layer on a baking sheet. Bake in a 350-degree oven for 6 to 8 minutes, stirring once until lightly browned and fragrant.

COLD LAMB SALAD

We have used leftover lamb in curries, shepherd's pies, and hash, but one of our favorites is a cold lamb salad that we developed for the then-popular Cuisinart newsletter in the late 1980s. Of course, we always use our food processor to slice and chop, but a sharp knife will do the job—it just takes a few more minutes of your time. From oven-baked to butterflied barbequed lamb, each lends itself to a flavorful salad. We did find that the barbequed lamb added a bit of additional flavor. Whatever leftover lamb you have, it is a salad to be enjoyed throughout the year.

3/4 pound cooked lamb (about 2-1/2 cups when trimmed and cubed)
4 medium mushrooms, trimmed, and thinly sliced
3 medium scallions, trimmed of all but 1/2-inch green and thinly sliced
1/2 bunch chives (about 1/4 ounce), finely chopped
1 tablespoon fresh parsley leaves, finely chopped

3 tablespoons olive oil
1 tablespoon tarragon vinegar (we've also used balsamic)
1/2 tablespoon Dijon mustard
1 teaspoon fresh lemon juice
1/2 teaspoon Worcestershire sauce
salt and fresh-ground pepper to taste
2 medium tomatoes, sliced about 1/4-inch thick
chopped parsley, for garnish

Trim the lamb of any fat and cut into 1/2-inch pieces. Transfer to a large mixing bowl. Add the mushrooms and scallions.

In another mixing bowl, whisk together the remaining ingredients except the tomatoes and parsley for garnish. Pour over the lamb and toss well to combine. Let sit, covered and refrigerated, for at least 1 hour so the flavors can meld. Toss again before serving.

To serve, arrange the tomato slices around the edge of a serving platter. Mound the lamb in the center and garnish with the chopped parsley.

Makes 4 servings.

COUSCOUS SALAD

Couscous Salad

If you are not a couscous fan or have not had occasion to enjoy what is sometimes referred to as "a fine pellet made from semolina flour," this recipe from the Big Bear Brewing Company restaurant will make a convert of you. The combination of readily available ingredients is outstanding. Teamed with an unusual yogurt-based dressing, this flavorful and light dish could become habit-forming. Unless you are a purist who owns a couscousiere, the instant product (such as the Near East Original Plain variety), is most satisfactory. We used our food processor to take the work out of processing all the ingredients and to make the dressing. The dressing should be started a day before you plan to use it since the yogurt needs to be drained for several hours and preferably overnight.

Couscous Dressing:

1 cup plain yogurt, drained
1/3 cup plus 1 tablespoon fresh lemon juice
1/4 cup water
1 large clove garlic, minced
1/4 cup cider vinegar

1/3 cup plus 1 tablespoon sugar
3/4 teaspoon kosher salt
3/4 teaspoon fresh-ground black pepper
1 cup extra virgin olive oil

To drain the yogurt, line a large strainer with dampened cheesecloth and place over a mixing bowl. Scrape the yogurt onto the cheesecloth and bring the sides of the cheesecloth over the yogurt. Place in the refrigerator and allow to drain for at least 6 to 8 hours or preferably overnight. The result will be about 1/2 cup of what is sometimes called yogo cheese.

In a food processor fitted with the metal blade, place the drained yogurt, lemon juice, water, garlic, vinegar, sugar, salt, and pepper. Process until well mixed. With the motor running, slowly add the olive oil through the feed tube. The dressing will emulsify into a texture resembling lightly whipped cream. Transfer to a covered container and refrigerate until ready to use. This will keep well for up to 3 days. Since it tends to separate a bit, whisk before using.

Makes about 2-1/4 cups.

Couscous Salad:

4 cups cooked couscous (we used a 10-oz box of Near East Original Plain couscous, cooked according to package directions. This will give you just a bit more than 4 cups but you will be happy with the extra amount and won't have to wonder what to do with the small amount remaining in the box.)	1/3 cup coarse-chopped peanuts 1/4 cup coarse-chopped scallions 3/4 cup coarse-chopped parsley 1/3 cup coarse-chopped carrots 1/4 cup chopped celery 1/2 cup coarse-chopped currants 1 cup julienned radishes 1 cup Couscous Dressing (recipe given)

Place the cooked couscous in a large mixing bowl and cool to room temperature. Fluff occasionally while cooling to ensure the grains stay separate and to hasten the cooling. Fold in the remaining ingredients. Serve at room temperature or chilled. This keeps well for up to three days. Since couscous—like other pasta and sometimes rice—seem to soak up moisture while sitting, you may want to toss the salad with a couple more tablespoons of the extra dressing after it has been refrigerated for a day or more.

Makes 6 generous servings.

EGG WHITE ONLY AND NO-EGG MAYONNAISE

Once the use of raw eggs was channeled to the "dangerous to eat" classification, we were besieged with questions on what one could substitute for those raw eggs in a variety of dishes (recipes). One category I myself researched was mayonnaise. While developing recipes for my now-out-of-print cookbook (*The Low-Cholesterol Food Processor Cookbook*, Doubleday 1980), I came up with several recipes for mayonnaise that didn't use raw fresh eggs. One was with the pasteurized and frozen Egg Beater Egg Whites and the other with the regular pasteurized Egg Beaters. Technically, these could be considered misnomers since Egg Beaters are a "real egg product." But, of course, we are talking "no fresh eggs" here!

Egg White Only Mayonnaise:

- equivalent of 2 frozen pasteurized Egg Beater Egg Whites, defrosted according to package directions
- 1 teaspoon prepared mustard (we like Dijon-style)
- 1 teaspoon cider vinegar
- 1 tablespoon fresh lemon juice
- dash salt
- dash cayenne pepper (optional but nice)
- 1 cup vegetable oil, divided
- 1 tablespoon evaporated skim milk

In a food processor fitted with the metal blade, combine the egg whites, mustard, vinegar, lemon juice, salt, cayenne, and 1 tablespoon of the oil. Pulse the machine 5 or 6 times to mix the ingredients well. Then, with the motor running, pour the remaining oil very slowly through the feed tube. When all the oil has been incorporated and the mixture has thickened, add the evaporated milk and pulse 2 or 3 times to incorporate it well.

Makes about 1-1/4 cups.

No-Egg Mayonnaise:

3 tablespoons frozen Fleischmann's Egg Beaters, defrosted according to package directions	fresh-ground black pepper to taste
pinch of sugar	1 teaspoon fresh lemon juice
pinch of salt	1 teaspoon cider vinegar
	1 teaspoon prepared mustard (we use Dijon-style)
	1 cup vegetable oil, divided

In a food processor fitted with the metal blade, combine the Egg Beaters, sugar, salt, pepper, lemon juice, vinegar, mustard, and 1 tablespoon of the oil. Pulse the machine 3 or 4 times to combine. With the motor running, pour the remaining oil slowly through the feed tube. This mayonnaise will thicken quickly, so turn the machine off as soon as all the oil has been added.

This keeps well, and because it is very thick, it is excellent for sandwiches or salads. Try mixing it with an equal amount of plain low-fat yogurt and some curry powder to taste and serve it over vegetables.

Makes about 1-1/4 cups.

FRESH CUCUMBER MOUSSE

Light in both texture and flavor with just a hint of tang from the horseradish called for, this is sure to become a favorite make-ahead salad. First published in our cookbook *The Low-Cholesterol Food Processor Cookbook* (Doubleday 1980, now out of print), we have served and shared this refreshing salad (recipe) always to rave reviews. If you wish, the added drop or two of green food coloring will give the mousse a more visual impact.

1 cup evaporated skim milk
2 cucumbers peeled and seeded
1 envelope (1 ounce) unflavored gelatin
1/3 cup boiling water
4 scallions, white part only, cut into 1/2-inch pieces
1/2 cup mayonnaise (reduced fat if desired)
1 tablespoon prepared horseradish, drained
salt and white pepper, to taste
1 to 2 drops green food coloring, optional
watercress for garnish
mayonnaise, to pass (optional)

Refrigerate the milk at least overnight so it is well-chilled.
Oil a 4-cup ring or other mold. Set aside.
Cut the cucumbers in chunks, and in a food processor fitted with the metal blade, puree the cucumbers. Place in a strainer to drain briefly. Set aside.
Empty the gelatin into the workbowl. Add the boiling water and scallions and process until the scallions are liquefied. Add the mayonnaise, horseradish, and seasonings to taste. Process on and off just to mix. Add the reserved cucumbers, and process on and off to mix. Pour in the chilled milk and green food coloring, if using, and let the machine run for about 15 seconds to mix well.
Pour the mixture into the prepared mold and refrigerate for at least 4 hours or until well-set. To serve, unmold onto a chilled serving plate and surround with watercress. If desired, pass additional mayonnaise.
Makes 6 servings.

Grilled Chicken Cobb Salad with
Key Lime Vinaigrette

GRILLED CHICKEN COBB SALAD WITH KEY LIME VINAIGRETTE

Originally named for the proprietor of the Brown Derby restaurant in Los Angeles in 1926 where it was first served, this popular salad, a variation on a California-style chef's salad, has survived through many modified versions over the years. Chef Chris Nealon's Grilled Chicken Cobb Salad with Key Lime Vinaigrette is one of the best versions we have yet to enjoy. We attribute this to his wonderfully tart but slightly sweet Key Lime Vinaigrette dressing that marries perfectly with the salad ingredients. You will want to file the recipe away to use in many other salad combinations where the tart/sweet flavor is appropriate. The vinaigrette can be made ahead and refrigerated until serving. Just be sure and give it a good whisk before using. Chef Chris says that if key limes are not available, substitute with bottled key lime juice or the fresh limes available in your supermarket. Only a highly educated palate will be able to notice any flavor difference.

Key Lime Vinaigrette:

- 2 tablespoons fresh key lime juice
- 2 tablespoons whole-grain Dijon mustard (we like Grey Poupon Country Dijon)
- 1 tablespoon red wine vinegar
- 1 tablespoon chopped Italian parsley
- 1 tablespoon light brown sugar
- pinch kosher salt
- fresh-ground black pepper, to taste
- 1/4 cup plus 2 tablespoons olive oil

Salad Ingredients:

4 cups chopped iceberg lettuce
1/4 cup coarse-chopped cooked bacon (about 5 strips)
1 large egg, hard-cooked, and coarsely chopped
1/4 cup crumbled blue cheese
1 small ripe tomato, cut into 3/4-inch dice
1 ripe Haas avocado (the one with bumpy blackish skin), peeled and diced
2 cooked boneless, skinless chicken breast halves, cut into 1/2-inch dice (the restaurant grills their chicken)

To make the vinaigrette, place all the ingredients except the olive oil in a nonreactive bowl and whisk to combine. Slowly whisk in the olive oil and continue whisking until a thick emulsion has formed. Can be made ahead and kept covered in the refrigerator for several hours. Whisk briskly again before using.

Makes about 1 cup.

To make the salad, in a large bowl, toss the chopped lettuce with about 3/4 cup of the vinaigrette. Divide the lettuce between two large shallow salad bowls. Divide the remaining ingredients and arrange attractively on top of the lettuce. Drizzle with the remaining vinaigrette.

Makes 2 servings.

HAM AND MACARONI SALAD

This is an easy salad for summer or any time using leftover ham—or even purchased-on-purpose ham. Many years ago in our BC (before Cuisinart) days, when we managed the Harrington's of Vermont store in Greenwich, Connecticut, one of the many recipes we developed and recommended as a delicious way to utilize any leftover Harrington ham was this Ham and Macaroni Salad. It makes a perfect light luncheon or supper dish.

2 cups cubed baked ham (about 8 ounces cut into 1/4-inch dice)
1/2 cup cubed sharp Cheddar cheese (1/4-inch cubes)
2 cups cooked elbow macaroni
1 cup chopped celery
1 small onion, chopped
1/2 cup diced dill pickle
1/2 cup real mayonnaise
2 teaspoons prepared mustard (we like the grainy kind here)

In a large mixing bowl combine the ham, cheese, macaroni, celery, onions and dill pickle. In a small bowl mix the mayonnaise and mustard well and add to the macaroni mixture. Stir well to combine. Cover and let chill in the refrigerator for several hours before serving. Stir again just before serving.

Makes 4 servings.

MANGO SALAD DRESSING

Thanks to a popular, local restaurant, this unusual and delicious salad dressing can be enjoyed as long as fresh mangoes are available. We have substituted frozen mangos when fresh were not available, and if defrosted and well drained and shredded, they are an okay substitute. The restaurant originally served the dressing on assorted greens. We discovered early on that it is also delectable on assorted fruits, seafood, and even poultry.

1 medium fresh mango, pitted and peeled
1-1/2 teaspoons honey
1/2 cup sour cream
1/2 cup mayonnaise
1 medium clove garlic, minced
2 tablespoons raspberry vinegar
1-1/2 teaspoons fine-chopped fresh dill
1 large, fresh basil leaf (finely chopped)
salt and fresh-ground pepper to taste

Use the coarse side of a 4-sided grater to grate the mango into a mixing bowl. Discard any stringy portions (or eat them). Add the remaining ingredients, stirring slowly until well mixed and smooth. Refrigerate several hours before using to allow the flavors to get well acquainted. This dressing keeps well for up to a week. Serve on a nice mix of fresh greens—or see suggestions above.

Makes about 1-1/3 cups.

MARTHA'S VINEYARD SALAD WITH RASPBERRY-MAPLE DRESSING

Martha's Vineyard Salad with Raspberry-Maple Dressing

When we first tasted what appeared to be just a nice, fresh green salad (Martha's Vineyard) adorned with some blue cheese and pine nuts, our taste buds went into overdrive. The adjectives that came to mind over the raspberry-maple dressing were "unique, delicious, flavorful, ambrosial, savory, palatable, toothsome, and delectable." The combination of the raspberry vinegar and pure maple syrup (make sure it is pure maple syrup and not any of the sweet imitations) is remarkable. The combination of the soft-textured and sweet-flavored Bibb and red-edged ruby lettuces is eminently satisfactory when tossed with that remarkable dressing. Just be sure to wash and thoroughly dry each leaf. Any moisture will dilute the flavorful dressing. The amounts here for the salad serves two—the dressing makes enough for eight servings.

Raspberry-Maple Dressing:

    1/2 cup raspberry vinegar*
    1/2 cup extra virgin olive oil
    1/2 cup vegetable oil
    1/2 cup pure maple syrup (do not substitute any of the maple-flavored varieties)
    2 tablespoons Dijon mustard
    2 tablespoons dried tarragon leaves (the original recipe indicated you could substitute 4 tablespoons chopped fresh, but the dry keeps better and longer in the refrigerated dressing)
    dash of salt (or to taste)

Salad Ingredients:

    2 cups washed and well-dried Bibb lettuce torn into bite-size pieces
    2 cups washed and well dried red leaf lettuce torn into bite-size pieces
    2 tablespoons crumbled blue cheese
    6 rings red onion, about 1/4 inch thick each
    4 teaspoons pine nuts, toasted** (can substitute coarse-chopped toasted walnuts or toasted slivered almonds—all good)

    To make the dressing, whisk together all the ingredients in a large mixing bowl. The dressing can and should be made several hours ahead or even the day before so the flavors can mingle well. Make sure to whisk briskly before using.

    To make the salad, just before serving, place the lettuce in a large bowl. Drizzle 1/4 cup of the dressing over and toss gently until all the leaves have a thin coating. Divide the lettuce between 2 chilled salad plates. Sprinkle each with half the blue cheese, place half the onion rings on each and sprinkle each with half the nuts. The remaining dressing will keep for several days refrigerated.

    Dressing makes 2 cups. Amount given for salads makes 2 servings.

*Raspberry vinegar is available in most supermarkets and gourmet shops.
**To toast the nuts, preheat the oven to 350 degrees. Spread nuts in a single layer in a pie plate or cake pan. Bake for 8 to 10 minutes or until lightly browned.

MOLDED POTATO AND HAM SALAD
(a.k.a. CAKE)

Sometimes called a salad and sometimes a cake, because you can "frost" the finished product with additional mayonnaise if desired, this makes an appetizing presentation every bit as good as it looks. We like the fact that the addition of some unflavored gelatin ensures that your salad will emerge from the mold in a nice, firm manner.

2-1/2 pounds small new potatoes (cooked, cooled, peeled, and sliced about 3/8 inch—you want about 6 cups sliced potatoes)
2 medium onions, minced
3 medium celery ribs, finely chopped
1/2 cup fine-chopped fresh parsley
1-1/2 teaspoons salt
1/4 teaspoon fresh-ground black pepper
16 thin slices cooked ham (they need to be approximately 7 by 4-1/2 inches)
2 envelopes (1/4 ounce each) unflavored gelatin
1/2 cup water
1-1/2 cups real mayonnaise
additional mayonnaise for "frosting" if desired
arugula for garnish
cherry tomatoes, for garnish

Line a 10 by 5 by 3-inch loaf pan completely with foil, letting it extend about 3 inches above each edge. Smooth the foil as much as possible and lightly spray it with vegetable no-stick spray. Set aside.

In a large bowl, combine the sliced potatoes, onions, celery, parsley, salt and pepper. With kitchen shears, coarsely snip 8 of the ham slices and add to the ingredients in the bowl. Toss well to mix.

In a small bowl, sprinkle the gelatin over the water. Place the bowl over hot water and stir to dissolve the gelatin completely. Whisk into the mayonnaise, then add to the potato mixture and mix well.

To assemble the mold, lay three overlapping ham slices along one 10-inch side of the prepared pan. They should be even with the edge of the pan, extend across the bottom and partially up the opposite long side. Repeat on the other long side of the pan. This will make a double thickness of ham on the bottom of the pan. Cover each end of the pan with the remaining ham slices, making sure all ham slices are even with the edge of the pan.

Pack the potato salad mixture gently but firmly into the ham lined pan. Cover the top with the overhanging foil and refrigerate overnight.

To serve, uncover the foil on top of the salad. Place a chilled platter on top and invert the salad onto the platter. Peel off the foil. (At this point, if you wish, you can "frost" the top and sides of the salad with additional mayonnaise and any suitable decorations.) Surround the salad with the arugula and cherry tomatoes.

Makes 12 servings.

ORIENTAL RICE SALAD

FYI, September is National Rice Month. Quite a few years ago, we came across this recipe to help celebrate one of our basic foods. We all agreed this Oriental Rice Salad recipe directing you to cook the rice in soy sauce-infused water was one we would make often. The original recipe called for shrimp, but we found that cooked, diced chicken was equally tasty. If you prefer, just substitute the small cooked salad shrimp for the chicken.

Salad:

- 2 cups water
- 3 tablespoons Kikkoman Lite Soy Sauce, divided (can use regular)
- 1 cup long-grain rice (we usually use the Mahatma brand)
- 2 cups cooked, diced chicken
- 1 medium carrot, peeled and shredded
- 1/2 cup frozen baby sweet peas, defrosted
- 1/2 cup fine-sliced scallions, white part and 1 inch of green
- 2 teaspoons minced fresh gingerroot

Dressing:

- 1/3 cup rice vinegar
- 2 tablespoons sugar
- 2 teaspoons toasted sesame seeds*
- 2 teaspoons water

To make the salad, combine the water and 2 tablespoons of the soy sauce in a large saucepan. Bring to a boil over medium-high heat. Stir in the rice, reduce the heat to medium-low, cover and simmer for 20 minutes or until the water has been absorbed. Remove from the heat and let cool in the pan. Fluff the rice occasionally to keep it from sticking together as it cools.

In a large bowl, combine the chicken, carrots, peas, scallions, and gingerroot. Fluff the rice again with a fork and fold into the chicken mixture. Refrigerate for 3 hours, or until completely chilled.

To make the dressing, in a small bowl, whisk together the remaining tablespoon of soy sauce, the vinegar, sugar, sesame seeds, and water until the sugar dissolves.

Pour over the chilled rice mixture and toss to coat all the ingredients well. Serve on salad greens of choice.

Makes 4 servings.

*To toast the sesame seeds, sprinkle them in a small dry skillet and cook over medium heat, stirring for about 3 to 4 minutes, or until they just begin to take on color. Let cool.

PATRICK'S CAESAR SALAD

Patrick's Caesar Salad

You will know why we chose to include yet another Caesar salad recipe when you take your first bite of Chef Patrick Brennan's exceptional dressing. The origin of Caesar salad has generally been attributed to the restaurateur Caesar Cardini, the Italian-born Mexican who lived in San Diego during the early 1900s. You will find other fascinating claims, but really, the only things that matter are the freshest ingredients (romaine lettuce particularly). The flair of having the salad tossed tableside is impressive, but Chef Patrick likes to do the vigorous tossing before it leaves his kitchen to make sure all the romaine and the crunchy garlic croutons are evenly coated. The consistency of the delicious dressing is like a light mayonnaise. The use of Egg Beaters in lieu of the original raw eggs was a (clever) very successful substitution.

3 tablespoons Fleischmann's Egg Beaters	2 tablespoons red wine vinegar
1 tablespoon Dijon or other strong mustard	1 teaspoon minced garlic
	3 anchovy fillets, coarsely chopped
1 cup plus 1 tablespoon vegetable oil	Garlic Croutons (recipe given)
1/8 teaspoon fresh-ground black pepper	1 cup fresh-grated Parmesan cheese
1/8 teaspoon salt	1 large head romaine lettuce, rinsed and dried thoroughly (important)
1 tablespoon fresh lemon juice	

Combine the Egg Beaters, mustard, and 1 tablespoon of the oil in a small mixing bowl. Beat the mixture on medium speed of an electric mixer for 1 minute. Change to high speed and add the remaining cup of oil very slowly. The resulting emulsion will be fairly thick. Add the lemon juice and vinegar on low speed, then add the garlic and anchovy fillets on medium speed. The dressing should be the consistency of a light mayonnaise.

Makes about 1-1/4 cups

To prepare the salad, in a large bowl, add the romaine lettuce (torn or sliced into bite-size pieces). Add about half the dressing and the croutons and toss vigorously (important) until the romaine is evenly coated, adding more dressing as necessary. Add 1/2 cup of the Parmesan cheese and toss thoroughly again. Divide the salad among 4 chilled plates, and pass the remaining Parmesan.

Makes 4 servings.

Garlic Croutons:

4 slices (about 1 ounce each) firm-textured white or wheat bread	2 medium garlic cloves, minced
	2 tablespoons vegetable oil

Preheat the oven to 350 degrees. Trim crusts from the bread. Combine the garlic and oil in a small bowl. Brush one side of each bread slice well with the garlic/oil mixture. Cut the bread into 1/2-inch cubes and toast in one layer on a baking sheet for about 12 minutes or until lightly browned. Cool completely before using.

ROASTED THREE-POTATO SALAD

One of our favorite potato salads using sweet potatoes, red-skinned potatoes, and Idaho or russet potatoes starts with roasting those potatoes sprinkled with a bit of olive oil, salt, and pepper. Roasting the potatoes gives the salad a delicious taste dimension ordinary potato salads sometimes lack. Do make this at least 2 to 3 hours before serving so the flavors have a chance to blend well. You can vary the dressing by substituting a commercial honey mustard, sweet vidalia onion, or even a good chunky blue cheese for the mayonnaise-sugar-vinegar combination suggested here. They are all savory substitutes for the other ingredients.

3 medium russet or Idaho potatoes, peeled and cut into 1-inch cubes
3 medium red-skinned potatoes, unpeeled and cut into 1-inch cubes
1 large sweet potato, peeled and cut into 1-inch cubes
3 tablespoons olive oil

salt and fresh-ground pepper to taste
1 cup small diced red onion
3/4 cup small diced celery
3/4 cup mayonnaise
2 tablespoons sugar
1 tablespoon white vinegar
1/4 cup chopped fresh parsley

Preheat the oven to 425 degrees. Place the potatoes in a single layer in a large shallow baking pan or roasting pan. Drizzle with the olive oil, salt, and pepper. Toss well to coat all the potatoes. Bake in the center of the oven for 35 to 40 minutes or until the potatoes are tender and golden, stirring a couple of times. Let the potatoes cool for about 15 minutes, then transfer to a large mixing bowl.

In another mixing bowl combine the remaining ingredients, adding more salt and pepper if desired. Pour this mixture over the potatoes and toss all together gently but thoroughly. Refrigerate for 2 to 3 hours before serving to allow the ingredients to marry, but remove from the refrigerator 30 minutes before serving for best flavor.

Makes 12 servings.

Shanghai Chicken Salad with Spicy
Honey Mustard Dressing

SHANGHAI CHICKEN SALAD WITH SPICY HONEY MUSTARD DRESSING

You will find that the dressing is the key to the gustatory appeal of this salad. It enhances each and every mouthful, from the combination of greens to the tender chicken strips to the crunchy fried wontons. The real bonus is any leftover dressing, which can be used for other salads or in stir fries. It keeps well, refrigerated, for up to a week. The popular restaurant who graciously shared this recipe used large quantities of assorted greens, cabbage and carrots in their original recipe. We recommend using one of the prewashed and premixed salad green combinations now readily available, such as the Dole brand "French" combination with some added napa cabbage.

Spicy Honey Mustard Dressing:

- 4 teaspoons Coleman's dry mustard
- 1/4 cup rice wine vinegar
- 1 piece peeled fresh ginger, about 1 by 1 inch, finely minced
- 1 large garlic clove, finely minced
- 1/4 cup egg substitute
- 1/4 cup clover honey
- 2 tablespoons light brown sugar
- 2-1/2 tablespoons hoisin sauce
- 1 tablespoon soy sauce
- 1/2 cup yellow mustard (we like French's Classic Yellow)
- 2 tablespoons sesame oil
- 1/4 teaspoon salt
- large pinch white pepper
- 10 drops Tabasco sauce
- 1/8 teaspoon, or to taste, cayenne pepper
- 1 cup olive oil

In a large mixing bowl, whisk together the dry mustard and vinegar until smooth. Stir in the minced ginger and garlic. Add the remaining ingredients in the order given. When all have been added, whisk energetically until the mixture is completely homogenized. Refrigerate, covered, for several hours before serving. The dressing keeps well for up to a week. Leftovers are delicious on other green salads or in stir fries.

Makes about 2-1/2 cups.

Salad:

8 wonton skins (3-1/2 by 2-1/2 inches) cut into 1/4 by 1-3/4 inch strips	4 cups prepackaged, prewashed salad greens (randomly cut into julienne pieces)
oil for frying	2 cups julienne-cut bok choy
2 large boneless, skinless chicken breast halves, each about 5 ounces	1/2 cup sliced scallions, white part and 1 inch of green
1 tablespoon unsalted butter	3/4 cup Spicy Honey Mustard Dressing (recipe given)

Separate the wonton strips so they will fry individually and not in clumps. Heat about 1-1/2 inches of oil in a deep 8- or 10-inch skillet to 365 degrees. Fry the wonton strips in a single layer, tossing with a slotted spoon so they fry evenly, for about 1 minute or until they are golden brown and crisp. Transfer to paper towels to cool and drain. Repeat until all are fried. Set aside. (Can be made a day ahead and kept in an airtight container.)

Pound the chicken breasts between pieces of plastic wrap to an even 1/4 inch. In a large skillet, preferably nonstick, heat the butter over medium-high heat. Sauté the chicken breasts for about 1-1/2 minutes a side, or until lightly browned and just cooked through. Do not overcook. Transfer to paper towels to drain and cool.

In a large mixing bowl, toss the sliced prepackaged greens and bok choy together. Cut the chicken breasts crosswise across the grain into 1/4 to 3/8 inches by about 1-inch long strips. Add to the greens with half the scallions and half the wonton skins. Drizzle the dressing over all and toss well again.

Divide the salad between two large serving plates and garnish with the remaining scallions and fried wonton skins.

Makes 2 generous luncheon or supper servings.

STRAWBERRY-PRETZEL SALAD

This almost dessert-like salad goes back many years to our Connecticut days. Our introduction to this unusual combination was thanks to a "cooking" neighbor, now long gone, whose many shared recipes remain in our files. Even though the recipe makes enough to serve twenty-four, it keeps well for several days in the refrigerator, and we have never had a problem with leftovers—they disappear rapidly.

Crust:

- 3 tablespoons sugar
- 1-1/2 sticks butter, softened
- 1-1/2 cups fine-chopped or crushed pretzels (we like the salty brand of Snyders)

Preheat the oven to 350 degrees. In a mixing bowl cream the sugar with the butter. Stir in the pretzels and mix well. Press onto the bottom of a 13 by 9-inch baking pan. Bake in the center of the oven for 10 minutes. Remove to a wire rack to cool completely.

Filling:

- 8 ounces cream cheese at room temperature
- 1 cup sugar
- 2 cups Cool Whip, defrosted
- 1 package (6 ounces) strawberry gelatin
- 2 cups boiling water
- 1/2 cup cold water
- 2 packages (10 ounces each) frozen strawberries, thawed

In a mixing bowl combine the cheese and sugar until smooth. Fold in the Cool Whip. Spread over the cooled pretzel crust. Refrigerate while making the next layer.

In a mixing bowl dissolve the gelatin in the boiling water. When dissolved, stir in the cold water and the strawberries. Chill until partially congealed, then spread over the cream cheese layer. Chill again for at least 4 hours, or until firm.

Makes 24 servings (or you can make them larger, of course).

TRISH'S HOT CHICKEN SALAD

Trish (Summers) of Winter Haven, Florida, made this delicious salad for us when she was visiting a while ago. She was reluctant to write down the recipe, claiming she was not a good cook, but anyone who has tasted any of her efforts would not agree. She cooks as she does everything—with considerable style and flair. We liked the fact that because she recommends cooking a whole chicken to get the best and moistest meat for the salad, you have a flavorful stock to use in other recipes. She uses Swiss cheese in the recipe, but you can substitute if you prefer. We like the fact that the salad can be made several hours ahead and refrigerated. Just remember to add an additional 10 to 15 minutes in the oven to make sure it is well heated through.

1 2-1/2 to 3-pound fryer—liver, gizzards, etc. removed (can freeze for later use)
leafy tops from 3 celery ribs
1 small onion, peeled and quartered
1 medium green pepper, seeded and cut into 8 pieces
2 large bay leaves
2-1/2 quarts water, about
2 cups thin-sliced celery
1 small can (4-1/2 ounces) chopped black olives
1/2 cup coarse-chopped roasted peanuts
1/2 teaspoon salt
2 tablespoons grated onion
1/4 cup fresh lemon juice
1 cup mayonnaise
1/2 cup grated cheese (Swiss suggested, but you choose)
1 cup crushed potato chips

Place the chicken, celery tops, quartered onion, bell pepper and bay leaves in a large pot. Add enough water to cover and bring to a boil over medium-high heat. Reduce the heat, cover and simmer until chicken is tender, about 1-1/2 hours. Let chicken cool in the broth overnight in the refrigerator.

The following day, remove and discard any surface fat from the broth. Remove the chicken, skin and bone it, and cut the flesh into bite-size pieces. You should have about 2 cups. Reserve, discarding the skin and bones.

Strain the broth, discarding the solids. Reserve for future soups or any recipe that calls for chicken broth or stock. You will note this is salt free.

Heat the oven to 400 degrees. In a large mixing bowl, combine the chicken with the remaining ingredients, except the cheese and potato chips. Pile the mixture lightly into a lightly greased 1-1/2-quart casserole. (We like to use a 10 by

7 by 2-inch ceramic casserole that makes it easy to cut the salad into nice squares.) Or you can use six 1-cup individual serving dishes. Sprinkle the top(s) with the cheese and potato chips.

The salad can be made ahead to this point and baked later. The individual dishes will take about 15 to 20 minutes to heat through if baked immediately, and the casserole about twice that long. If refrigerated and baked later, add an additional 10 to 15 minutes.

Makes 6 servings.

WALNUT AND WATERCRESS SALAD

On a trip out West some years ago, we enjoyed this salad at a popular restaurant. The owner very nicely shared a list of ingredients, including those for the special walnut oil vinaigrette. We like the pleasing bite of watercress tempered nicely with the other flavorful ingredients. You will find this delicious salad a perfect adjunct to any buffet table.

Walnut Oil Vinaigrette:

- 1/2 cup walnut oil
- 1 tablespoon red wine vinegar
- 1/2 teaspoon Dijon mustard
- coarse salt (we use Kosher) and fresh-ground black pepper to taste

In a small mixing bowl, whisk together all the ingredients. Cover and refrigerate until ready to use so the flavors have a chance to blend well. Whisk before using.
Makes about 1/2 cup.

Salad:

- 1 cup toasted walnut halves*
- 1 bunch watercress, tough stems removed
- 1 large apple peeled, cored, and diced (we like Fuji or Gala here)
- 1/4 cup diced Gruyere cheese
- 1/4 cup diced celery
- 2 teaspoons chopped scallions (white part only)
- 8 ripe pitted olives, optional but highly recommended

In a large bowl, combine all the ingredients. Drizzle with the vinaigrette. Toss gently but well.
Makes 4 servings.

*To toast the walnuts, preheat the oven to 350 degrees. Place the nuts in a pie plate. Bake in the center of the oven for 8 to 10 minutes or until fragrant and lightly browned. Let cool.

WILD RICE SALAD

Wild Rice Salad

This Wild Rice Salad has been called "outrageous" (among other adjectives) by most everyone who has had the pleasure of eating it. The original recipe—thanks to the regional (Florida) Whole Foods Market prepared foods coordinator who willingly shared it—called for their organic wild rice. We found that a good brand of your supermarket's wild rice will be just fine once it is cooked and combined with the pecans, sweetened dried cranberries, and other delicious ingredients. The raspberry vinaigrette makes this an ideal salad to take on picnics, on the boat, or just out on the terrace to accompany your grilled meats and fish with no mayonnaise to worry about. Of course, it is just as welcome any day of the year. Do make the salad a few hours ahead to allow the flavors to blend.

4 cups cooked and cooled wild rice
1/3 cup dried cranberries (we suggest the Ocean Spray brand Craisins—sweetened dried cranberries)
1 tablespoons fine-chopped fresh parsley
1/3 cup pecan halves
6 scallions, white and 1-inch green finely chopped
1/2 cup yellow tomato, cut into 1/4-inch cubes (can substitute sweet yellow pepper if a tomato is not available)
1-1/2 tablespoons balsamic vinegar
3 tablespoons Annie's Naturals brand raspberry vinaigrette*
salt and fresh-ground black pepper, to taste

In a large mixing bowl toss together the cooked and cooled wild rice, cranberries, parsley, pecans, scallions and tomato cubes. Whisk together the balsamic vinegar and raspberry vinaigrette. Pour over the rice mixture and toss well. Season to taste. Make the salad a few hours ahead to allow the flavors to blend. Toss again before serving. Keeps well, refrigerated, for up to 3 days.

Makes about 4-2/3 cups.

*Annie's Naturals brand raspberry vinaigrette is available in some natural food stores, some gourmet shops, and some supermarkets. You can substitute Old Cape Cod, Clinton House, or Maple Grove Farms—brands that are available in most supermarkets.

WHO'S ON FIRST FRESH TUNA SALAD

Who's On First Fresh Tuna Salad

The combination of ingredients is outstanding both in flavor and in visual presentation. You will thank executive chef Frank Allen from the Pete Rose Ballpark Café for his innovative Blackberry Vinaigrette, which contributes greatly to the total enjoyment of this salad. For ease of preparation (we are 100 percent for that), you can use the prepackaged salad blend of coleslaw, which contains both green and red cabbage but also some shredded carrots in lieu of coping with shredding the 6 cups of green and 2 cups of red originally called for. Your choice.

Blackberry Vinaigrette Dressing:

1/2 cup seedless blackberry preserves
2 tablespoons Dijon mustard
1-1/2 cups canola oil
3/4 cup red wine vinegar
1 teaspoon minced garlic
1/3 teaspoon dried oregano
1/3 teaspoon dried basil
4 scallions (white part only) finely chopped

Salad:

9 tablespoons unsalted butter, divided
6 cups shredded green cabbage*
2 cups shredded red cabbage*
1 tablespoon Lawry's Seasoning Salt
4 fresh tuna steaks (about 6 ounces each)
1 teaspoon blackened fish seasoning (we used Paul Prudhomme's Magic Seasoning Blend of Blackened Redfish Magic), or to taste
12 baguette slices, toasted
1-1/3 cups crumbled blue cheese
3/4 cup toasted slivered almonds**
4 teaspoons chopped fresh parsley

To make the vinaigrette, whisk together the blackberry preserves and mustard. Slowly add the oil, whisking constantly so the mixture emulsifies. Stir in the remaining ingredients, mix well and store, covered in the refrigerator until ready to use. This keeps well for a week to use on other salad combinations. Stir before using.
Makes about 3 cups.

To make the salad, melt 6 tablespoons of the butter in a large skillet over medium heat. Add the cabbage and sauté, sprinkling with the seasoning salt. Sauté for about 2 minutes, or until the cabbage just begins to wilt. You want to retain some crunch. Set aside while cooking the tuna.

To prepare the tuna, in a large heavy skillet, melt the remaining 3 tablespoons butter over medium-high heat until sizzling and just beginning to take on color. While the butter is melting, sprinkle both sides of the tuna steaks with the blackened fish seasoning. Cook the tuna steaks for about 2 minutes per side, or until a deep brown and just cooked through. (Be sure to turn your kitchen exhaust fan on, since you will get a bit of smoke from the seasoning and browned butter.)

To serve, divide the sautéed cabbage among each of four serving plates, spreading it over the bottom. Place a tuna steak on top of each. Place 3 slices of toasted baguettes around the edge of each plate. Drizzle about 1/4 cup (or to taste) of the blackberry vinaigrette over each. Sprinkle each serving with the blue cheese and almonds and sprinkle the tops and around the rim of the plates with the chopped parsley.
Makes 4 servings.

*For ease of preparation, use a 16-ounce bag (8 cups) of already-prepared Salad Blend Coleslaw, which will have less red cabbage and some shredded carrots but is eminently satisfactory.

**To toast the almonds, place in a single layer in a baking pan. Bake in the center of a 350-degree oven for about 8 minutes, or until lightly browned and fragrant.

BREADS

APPLE CREAM COFFEE CAKE

Back many years, living in a small private community in Connecticut, we frequently got together after church on a Sunday morning to share a delicious brunch, courtesy of the talented neighborhood cooks. This Apple Cream Coffee Cake was one of our favorites, called "quick and easy" by the neighbor who was willing to share. Don't wait to serve this delicious and eye-appealing coffee cake just for breakfast or brunch—it is equally delicious for afternoon tea or coffee or an anytime snack.

1/2 cup coarse-chopped walnuts
2 teaspoons ground cinnamon
1-1/2 cups sugar, divided
2 cups all-purpose flour
1 teaspoon baking soda
1/2 teaspoon salt
1 teaspoon baking powder
1 stick (1/2 cup) butter or stick margarine, softened
2 large eggs
1 teaspoon pure vanilla extract
1 cup sour cream
1 medium apple, peeled, cored, and thinly sliced (we like a Golden Delicious apple)
confectioners' sugar, for dusting

Preheat the oven to 375 degrees. Grease a 9-inch tube pan with a removable bottom.

In a small bowl, mix together the walnuts, cinnamon, and 1/2 cup of the sugar. Set aside.

In a large bowl, whisk together the flour, baking sodas, salt, and baking powder. Transfer to a large piece of wax paper. In the same bowl, beat the butter or margarine and remaining 1 cup sugar together until light and fluffy. Beat in the eggs 1 at a time, mixing well after each. Stir in the vanilla.

Add the dry ingredients alternately with the sour cream to the butter mixture, mixing well after each addition. Spread half the batter in the prepared pan and top with the apple slices. Sprinkle half the walnut mixture over the apples. Spread the remaining batter over all and top with the remaining walnut mixture.

Bake in the center of the oven for 40 minutes or until a skewer inserted in the center comes out clean. Let sit in the pan on a wire rack for 20 minutes, then remove from the pan onto a wire rack to cool completely. Dust with confectioners' sugar before serving.

Makes 12 servings.

BOURBON-PECAN BREAD

This delicious sweet bread—courtesy of our late Aunt Jen of West Virginia—could easily be included in the dessert section. We like to serve it with a fresh fruit salad for lunch, but we also serve it topped with vanilla ice cream, drizzled with some additional bourbon. Either way, it is impossible to resist. And you know the old saying: "I love cooking with wine (or any spirit). Sometimes I even put it in the food."

3 cups all-purpose flour
1 cup sugar
4 teaspoons baking powder
1-1/2 teaspoons salt
1/4 cup butter, cut into tablespoons
2 teaspoons grated orange zest
1-1/2 cups chopped pecans, divided
1 cup milk
1/2 cup plus 2 tablespoons bourbon, divided
1 large egg, lightly beaten

Preheat the oven to 350 degrees. Grease and flour a 9 by 5 by 3-inch loaf pan. Set aside.

In a large bowl, whisk together the flour, sugar, baking powder and salt. Cut in the butter with a pastry blender until the mixture is crumbly. Stir in the orange zest and 1-1/4 cups of the pecans.

Combine the milk, 1/2 cup bourbon, and the egg, stirring well and adding to the dry ingredients. Stir just until moistened. Transfer to the prepared pan, spreading evenly. Sprinkle the remaining 1/2 cup pecans over the top, pressing down lightly. Bake in the center of the oven for 50 to 60 minutes, or until a toothpick inserted in the center comes out clean. Cool in the pan on a wire rack for 10 minutes, then remove from the pan and cool completely. Drizzle the bread while still slightly warm with the remaining 2 tablespoons of bourbon.

Makes 12 servings.

BUTTERY CARAMEL QUICKS

Sticky Buns have always been a favorite breakfast or snack treat, but making them does take time. We recently were asked if there could possibly be a recipe for making Sticky Buns without having to go through the long process of using yeast. We were delighted to offer our baking powder version we call Buttery Caramel Quicks, which originated with a good friend in Connecticut. We guarantee you can make and eat these delicious cousins of the Sticky Buns in about an hour—if you hurry!

1/2 cup butter at room temperature
1/3 cup plus 1/2 cup firm-packed light brown sugar, divided
1 tablespoon warm water
2 cups all-purpose flour
1/4 cup granulated sugar
2-1/2 teaspoons baking powder
1 teaspoon salt
3/4 cup whole milk
1 teaspoon ground cinnamon
1/3 cup chopped pecans

Preheat the oven to 425 degrees. Melt the butter in a 9-inch square or 11 by 7-inch baking pan. Sprinkle the 1/3 cup brown sugar and the warm water over the melted butter. Set aside.

In a large mixing bowl, whisk together well the flour, granulated sugar, baking powder and salt. Stir in the milk until a soft dough forms. Turn the dough out onto a well-floured surface and coat the top with flour. Roll the dough out to a 12 by 10-inch rectangle, adding more flour as needed to prevent sticking.

In a small bowl, combine the remaining 1/2 cup brown sugar, cinnamon and nuts and sprinkle over the dough. Starting with the 12-inch side, roll up the dough jellyroll fashion, sealing the seam. With a sharp or serrated knife, cut the log into twelve 1-inch slices and place cut-side-down on the brown sugar mixture in the prepared pan.

Bake in the center of the oven for about 20 minutes or until golden brown. Turn out onto wire racks placed over wax paper to catch any drippings. After a few minutes, you can scoop up any drippings and drizzle them back over the buns.

Makes 12 buns.

CEREAL BRUNCH COFFEE CAKE

Having enjoyed Total Whole Grain Cereal packed with nutrition for years, we were pleased to find this recipe for Cereal Brunch Coffee Cake that included 2 cups of our favorite cereal. Of course, there are a few more calories involved with each serving, but the inclusion of orange juice, mashed bananas, and raisins in the "cake" and chopped nuts in the broiled topping—we like to consider all those as additional nutritional bonuses. However you want to consider this delicious offering, you will find it a tasty treat for breakfast, brunch or anytime with a good cup of coffee or tea.

Cake:

1-1/2 cups all-purpose flour
1 teaspoon baking soda
1 teaspoon ground cinnamon
1/2 teaspoon salt
2 cups Total Whole Grain Cereal flakes
1 cup orange juice
1/4 cup vegetable oil
1 large egg, lightly beaten
2 medium bananas, mashed (about 2/3 cup)
1/2 cup seedless raisins, optional but highly recommended
Streusel Topping (recipe given)

Preheat the oven to 350 degrees. Grease a 9-inch square baking pan. Set aside.

In a large bowl, whisk together the flour, soda, cinnamon, and salt. Transfer to a piece of wax paper. In the same bowl, mix the cereal and orange juice and let stand about 2 minutes or until softened. Stir in the oil, egg and bananas. Stir in the dry ingredients, then the raisins, if using. Spread in the prepared pan, and bake in the center of the oven for 40 to 45 minutes, or until the top springs back when touched. Sprinkle the streusel topping over the warm cake. Turn the oven to broil, and broil the cake with the top about 5 inches from the heat for about 1 minute, or just until bubbly. Watch carefully to avoid burning.

Makes 12 servings.

Streusel Topping:

- 1/2 cup firm-packed light brown sugar
- 1/2 cup chopped nuts (we like walnuts)
- 1/4 cup all-purpose flour
- 1/4 cup margarine or butter, at room temperature
- 1/2 teaspoon ground cinnamon

Mix all ingredients until crumbly. Makes about 1-1/2 cups

Chili Bread

CHILI BREAD

Should you happen to have about 3/4 cup of leftover beanless chili (see p. 269) we encourage you to try using it to make this delicious Chili Bread. We developed this recipe during the weeks the Cuisinart test kitchen worked on an article we published on chili. This is a wonderfully fragrant and flavorful bread. Try it for making toasted cheese sandwiches. We also like to add some crisp-cooked bacon with the cheese before cooking. You will need a food processor fitted with the metal blade or a good blender to fine-chop that chili with the flour to achieve the proper and satisfying results.

1 package (1/4 ounce) dry yeast
1 teaspoon sugar
1/3 cup warm water (110 to 115 degrees)
2-1/2 cups all-purpose flour
1/2 cup whole wheat flour
3/4 cup leftover chili (don't use the kind with beans!)
1/2 teaspoon salt
1/2 cup cold water*
1 large egg whisked with 1 tablespoon water for glaze

Dissolve the yeast and sugar in the warm water and set aside. In a food processor fitted with the metal blade, process the flours, chili and salt for about 45 seconds, or until the chili is evenly ground.

With the motor running, pour the yeast mixture through the feed tube followed by the cold water in a steady stream just as fast as the flour will absorb it. Process until the dough forms a ball and cleans the side of the bowl, then process for an additional 45 seconds more to knead the dough.

Carefully remove the dough and form it into a ball. Place it in an oiled bowl, turning so all sides are oiled. Cover with oiled plastic wrap and let rise in a warm place until doubled, about 1-1/2 hours.

Spray an 8-1/2 by 4-1/2 by 2-1/4-inch bread pan with no-stick vegetable spray. Punch down the dough and shape it into a loaf to fit snugly in the prepared pan. Cover again with oiled plastic wrap, place in a warm spot and let rise just to the top of the pan, about 45 minutes.

Meanwhile, preheat the oven to 375 degrees. Brush the top of the dough with the egg wash and bake in the lower third of the oven for 45 minutes, or until the loaf sounds hollow when tapped and is nicely browned. Remove from the pan and cool on a wire rack. When cool, be sure to store in the refrigerator.

Makes a 1-1/2 pound loaf, or about 20 slices 3/8-inch thick.

*Depending upon the chili you use, you may need a bit more or less water for the dough since some chilies are looser than others.

CHOCOLATE CHIP COFFEE CAKE

Chocolate chip cookies have been on top of just about everyone's favorite cookie from the first recipe that appeared many years ago. Now, thanks to an old friend from Connecticut, those chocolate chips have found their home in a super-delicious coffee cake, made to enjoy for breakfast, brunch, lunch, afternoon tea, or anytime between. The cream cheese in the batter seems to add a lightness to the texture, and you will enjoy the sugary, nutty topping with a dose of cinnamon. A warning: you may have to hide this delicious coffee cake so it won't disappear before you want to serve it. It is that good!

Cake:

2 cups all-purpose flour
1 teaspoon baking powder
1/2 teaspoon baking soda
1/4 teaspoon salt
4 tablespoons butter at room temperature
1 package (8 ounces) cream cheese at room temperature

1-1/4 cups sugar
2 large eggs
1 teaspoon pure vanilla extract
1/4 cup cold milk
1 cup semisweet chocolate chips
Pecan Topping, recipe given

Preheat the oven to 350 degrees. Grease well a 9 by 3-inch springform pan. Set aside.

In a large bowl, whisk together the flour, baking powder, baking soda, and salt. Transfer to a piece of wax paper. In the same bowl, cream together the butter, cream cheese, and sugar until light and fluffy. Add the eggs one at a time, beating well after each addition. Stir in the vanilla. Add the dry ingredients in two additions alternately with the milk, beginning and ending with the dry ingredients. Stir in the chocolate chips. The mixture will be quite thick. Transfer to the prepared pan and sprinkle with the Pecan Topping. Bake in the center of the oven for 50 to 55 minutes or until a toothpick inserted in the center comes out clean. Let cool for at least 15 to 20 minutes then remove the outside ring from the pan. Cool the cake completely before cutting and serving.

Makes 12 servings.

Pecan Topping:

    1/4 cup sugar   1/4 cup chopped pecans
    1 teaspoon ground cinnamon

In a small bowl, mix all the ingredients together.
Makes about 1/2 cup.

CHOCOLATE STICKY BUNS

The original recipe for these popular buns was developed by Margaret Rudkin, one of the founders of the well-known Pepperidge Farm Company. Thanks to her, this version of the ever-popular sticky buns became an even more popular treat for chocolate lovers. Chocolate Sticky Buns take time to make with their three separate parts, but one taste and you will agree it is worth the effort.

Dough:

- 1 package (1/4 ounce) dry yeast
- 1/3 cup warm water (110 to 115 degrees)
- 1/3 cup sugar
- 1 teaspoon salt
- 1/2 cup (1 stick) butter, cut into 8 pieces
- 3/4 cup milk
- 3-1/2 cups all-purpose flour, divided
- 1 large egg
- 2 tablespoons melted butter

Topping:

- 1/2 cup (1 stick) butter
- 1 cup light brown sugar, packed
- 1/4 cup light corn syrup
- 3 tablespoons baking cocoa
- 1 cup whole pecans

Filling:

- 1 cup sugar
- 3 tablespoons baking cocoa
- 2 teaspoons ground cinnamon

To make the dough, in a 1-cup measure, dissolve the yeast in the warm water. In a mixing bowl, combine the sugar, salt and butter. In a saucepan, heat the milk to the bubbling stage over medium heat and pour over the sugar mixture. Stir until the butter melts. Cool to lukewarm.

Add 1-1/2 cups of the flour to the milk mixture and blend with an electric mixer at medium speed for 2 minutes. Add the egg and yeast mixture and continue beating for about 30 seconds. With a spoon add the remaining 2 cups of flour and beat as well as you can. The dough will be stiff. Cover the bowl with oiled plastic wrap and let rise in a warm place for about 50 minute or until doubled.

To make the topping, in a saucepan melt the butter and add the brown sugar, corn syrup and cocoa. Bring to a boil over medium heat, stirring, and cook for 1 minute. Divide the syrup between two 9-inch round cake pans. Arrange half the pecans over the bottom of each pan. Set aside.

To make the filling, combine all the ingredients together and set aside.

When the dough has risen, stir down and turn out onto a well-floured board. Cover and let rest for 5 minutes. Divide the dough in half and roll out each piece into a rectangle about 14 by 9-inches. Brush each lightly with half the melted butter. Sprinkle each rectangle with half the filling. Roll up as for a jelly roll from the short side to make a roll about 9 inches long. Cut each into 9 equal pieces and place cut-side-down in the prepared pans. Cover and let rise until doubled, about 1 hour.

Preheat the oven to 350 degrees and bake for about 35 minutes or until nicely browned and firm. Turn out of the pans immediately onto platters so the "topping" is on the top. Best served warm.

Makes 18 sticky buns.

DRIED CRANBERRY/NUT MUFFINS

Dried Cranberry/Nut Muffins

Talented pastry chef Annie Kelley graciously agreed to share her recipe for these Dried Cranberry/Nut Muffins served at a popular restaurant in Boca Raton, Florida. She described the recipe as "very basic" and that other small berries such as cherries or blueberries could be substituted. Once you try them, you will understand their popularity. They are rich, moist, and flavorful—thanks to the inclusion of yogurt, orange zest and juice, cranberries, and nuts. We found it impossible to eat just one and also found they were delicious served warm, at room temperature, or even chilled.

3 cups all-purpose flour
1-1/2 teaspoons baking soda
1/2 teaspoon salt
1 cup (2 sticks) unsalted butter, at room temperature
1-1/2 cups sugar
6 large eggs

zest from one large orange
1 cup plain yogurt
1/2 cup fresh orange juice
1/3 cup coarse-chopped pecans or walnuts
1/2 cup freeze-dried cranberries (or cherries or blueberries)

Preheat the oven to 350 degrees. Line 24 muffin cups (2-1/2 inches) with paper liners, or spray with no-stick vegetable spray.

In a large mixing bowl, whisk together the flour, baking soda and salt. Transfer to a piece of wax paper. In the same mixing bowl cream the butter and sugar on the medium speed of an electric mixer until light and fluffy. Add the eggs one at a time, beating well after each addition. Stir in the zest. Stir in the dry ingredients alternately with the yogurt and orange juice. Do not over blend. Fold in the fruit and nuts.

Fill the prepared muffin cups 3/4 full and bake in the center of the oven for about 15 minutes or until a toothpick inserted in the center comes out clean. Remove the muffins immediately from the muffin cups to wire racks to cool. Serve warm, at room temperature, chilled—you will enjoy every bite at any temperature.

Makes 24 muffins.

EASY ONION CASSEROLE BREAD

The original recipe for Easy Onion Casserole Bread was one of the winners in a Pillsbury Bake-Off in the '70s. The first time we tried it, nothing happened. It remained a soft, heavy mass. We realized that we had frozen the yeast cells by following the recipe's directions of dumping the cold sour cream and cold egg into the dissolving yeast. So in addition to adding some sugar to the yeast to give it food to feast on, we warmed the sour cream in the microwave and let the egg rest in warm water for about 10 minutes before using. This is a very tasty, oniony bread that we prefer to bake in a loaf pan as opposed to the original casserole dish. We shape our hamburgers to fit the bread slices before broiling, and toasted cheese sandwiches are heavenly. Just warmed or toasted, the slices are a perfect accompaniment to soups and salads.

1 box (16 ounces) Pillsbury Hot Roll Mix
3/4 cup warm water (110 to 115 degrees)
1 teaspoon sugar
1/2 cup sour cream, warmed to room temperature (can use microwave oven)
1 large egg, warmed to room temperature (place in warm water for 10 minutes)
1 can (2.8 ounces) French-fried onions, crumbled (use a rolling pin and crush on a large sheet of wax paper)

Dissolve the yeast from the Hot Roll Mix in the warm water with the sugar in a one-cup measure. Let sit until it begins to foam, about 4 minutes.

Pour the yeast mixture into a warm mixing bowl and whisk in the sour cream and egg. Add the dry package ingredients in 3 batches, using a whisk or large spoon to beat well after the first 2 additions. Stir in the onions with the final addition of dry ingredients. Turn out onto a floured surface and knead for about 5 minutes, adding more flour as necessary to keep it from sticking. Shape into a ball and place in an oiled bowl, turning so all sides are oiled. Cover with plastic wrap and let rise in a warm place until doubled—about 50 minutes.

Punch the dough down and shape into a loaf to fit into a 9 by 5 by 3-inch loaf pan sprayed with no-stick vegetable spray. Cover again with plastic wrap and let rise again until almost double, about 30 minutes.

Preheat the oven to 375 degrees. Bake the bread in the center of the oven until nicely browned, pulling away from the sides of the pan and sounding hollow when tapped, about 35 minutes. Turn the bread onto a wire rack to cool, preferably on its side to prevent the loaf from losing any volume.

Makes about 18 slices.

ENGLISH MUFFIN BREAD

A few years ago we had a request for an English Muffin Bread recipe such as the one found in a local area supermarket. Since the supermarket did not share their recipes, we went to work with the list of ingredients from the supermarket's bread, and the ingredients from some English Muffins we had developed. The addition of Malted Barley, farina, and baking soda proved to be the answer. You will find this bread delightfully crusty, with a marvelous texture (holes included), and it toasts like a dream.

3-1/2 cups all-purpose flour
1/4 cup dry skim milk
1 teaspoon sugar
1/4 teaspoon salt
1/4 teaspoon baking soda
2 tablespoons Farina*
1 envelope (1/4 ounce) dry yeast

1 tablespoon barley malt**
1 cup warm water (110 to 115 degrees)
2 tablespoons vegetable oil
2 large eggs, lightly beaten
corn meal

In a food processor fitted with the metal blade, process the flour, dry milk, sugar, salt, baking soda and farina for about 6 seconds or until well mixed. Leave in the workbowl. By hand, whisk the same ingredients together in a large bowl. Set aside.

In a 2-cup measure dissolve the yeast with the barley malt in the warm water. Let sit for about 5 minutes or until a foam forms on top. Stir in the oil and the egg.

In the food processor fitted with the metal blade and the motor running, pour the liquid through the feed tube as fast as the flour mixture will absorb it. Continue processing for about 30 seconds to knead the dough. The dough will be soft and slightly sticky. Flour you hands and remove to a floured surface. Knead lightly for a few seconds to incorporate any needed flour to make the dough soft but no longer sticky.

By hand, pour the liquid mixture into the flour mixture in the bowl and mix well with a wooden spoon. Knead on a floured surface until soft, about 7 minutes.

Place the dough in a floured 1-gallon plastic storage bag. Squeeze out all the air and close the very top with a twisty tie. Let rise until doubled a bout 1 to 1-1/2 hours. Oil an 8-1/2 by 4-1/5 by 2-1/2-inch loaf pan and sprinkle lightly with cornmeal.

Punch down the dough and shape it into a loaf to fit the prepared pan. Cover with oiled plastic wrap and let rise until doubled, about 1 hour. While the dough is rising, preheat the oven to 350 degrees. Bake the bread in the center of the oven until nicely browned and sounds hollow when tapped—about 35 to 40 minutes. Remove from the pan to a wire rack. Turn on its side until completely cool.

Makes 1 loaf, about sixteen 1/2-inch slices.

*Plain Farina can be found in the breakfast cereal isles of most supermarkets beside (usually) the Cream of Wheat, which is enriched Farina. We used 2 tablespoons of the Quick Cream of Wheat we already had on our shelf.

**We were introduced to barley malt long ago by Kie Craye, a retired baker from Pepperidge Farm who came with his "formulas" (recipes to us) to Cuisinarts to teach us how to make homemade crackers in the food processor. One of the major ingredients was the Barley Malt, which most bakers use in their products to ensure tenderness, available in health food stores.

HERBED OATMEAL PAN BREAD

We can thank the Pillsbury people who published the original Herbed Oatmeal Pan Bread recipe years ago. It has since appeared in other publications with a few adjustments (or changes). Once tried you can understand why it keeps reappearing, as most good recipes do. Even though it is a yeast dough, the preparation is not difficult. Just press all the dough into a large baking pan and cut diagonal lines in opposite directions to shape the "rolls." The fragrant topping that includes garlic, basil, oregano, and Parmesan cheese is guaranteed to tease your taste buds as the bread bakes. If you need an excuse to eat more than one, just explain that these "rolls" are a tasty way to get your oats!

Bread:

- 1-1/2 cups boiling water
- 1 cup oatmeal, quick or regular is fine
- 2 packages (1/4-ounce each) dry yeast
- 1/2 cup warm water (110 to 115 degrees)
- 1/4 cup sugar
- 3 tablespoons butter, softened
- 2 teaspoons salt
- 1 large egg, lightly beaten
- 4 to 4-1/2 cups all-purpose flour

Topping:

- 6 tablespoons melted butter, divided
- 2 tablespoons grated Parmesan cheese
- 1 teaspoon dried basil
- 1/2 teaspoon dried oregano
- 1/4 teaspoon garlic powder

In a small bowl, combine boiling water and oats. Cool to about 115 degrees. In a large bowl, dissolve the yeast in the warm water. Add the sugar, butter, salt, eggs, oat mixture and 2 cups of flour. Beat until smooth. Add enough remaining flour to form a soft dough. Turn onto a floured surface and knead for about 6 minutes or until smooth and elastic. Shape dough into a ball and cover with a large bowl. Let rest for 30 minutes. Grease a 13 by 9-inch baking pan. Punch the dough down and press evenly into the greased pan. Using a sharp knife, cut diagonal lines about 1-1/2 inches apart completely through the dough. Repeat in the opposite direction, making a diamond pattern. Cover and let rise for about 45 minutes, or until doubled.

Preheat the oven to 375 degrees. Redefine the cuts by poking along the cut lines with the knife tip. Don't pull the knife through or you will deflate the dough. Brush the top with 4 tablespoons of the butter. Bake the rolls for 15 minutes.

While the rolls are baking combine the Parmesan cheese, basil, oregano, and garlic powder. Brush the rolls with the remaining 2 tablespoons of butter and sprinkle with the cheese mixture. Bake for an additional 10 to 12 minutes, or until golden brown. Best served warm.

Makes 16 rolls.

HERO BREAD

Hero Bread

Like the Stuffing Bread before it (see p. 165), this is another simply super bread recipe developed during Cuisinart days. It became an all-time favorite at trade show demonstrations and cooking classes. We called it Hero Bread, and as the name denotes (you may recognize it as a Submarine, Hoagie, or Grinder), the flavors of the filling of these sandwiches are reflected in the bread itself, hence intensifying the appeal. In addition to the standard loaf, we found it a wonderful dough for a pizza crust, hamburger buns, English muffins and melba toast, and of course, the long loaf for a hero sandwich. Although this is a food processor recipe, you can use your blender to process the various ingredients and put it together by hand.

1 package (1/4 ounce) dry yeast
1 teaspoon sugar
1/4 cup warm water (105-115 degrees)
4 medium ice cubes
1 small onion, peeled and halved
1 small ripe tomato, peeled and seeded
2 teaspoons vegetable oil
3 1-inch pieces Parmesan cheese
1 medium garlic clove, peeled
2 ounces pepperoni, peeled, if necessary, and cut into 1-inch pieces
3 cups all-purpose flour
1/2 teaspoon salt
1 teaspoon dried oregano
1 large egg, lightly beaten with 1/2 teaspoon salt, for glaze

Stir the yeast and sugar into the warm water. In a food processor fitted with the medium shredding disc, process the ice cubes. Reserve.

With the metal blade, process the onion and tomato until pureed. In a small skillet, cook the mixture in the oil over medium heat, stirring, until the mixture comes to a boil. Transfer to a 1-cup liquid measure and immediately stir in enough shredded ice to bring the mixture to the 3/4-cup measure. Set aside.

Process the cheese, garlic, and pepperoni with the metal blade until finely chopped. Add the flour, salt, and oregano; and with the motor running, pour the yeast mixture then the tomato mixture through the feed tube as fast as the flour will absorb it. After the dough cleans the side of the work bowl, process for 45 seconds.

Shape the dough into a ball and place it in a lightly floured 1-gallon plastic storage bag. Squeeze out the air and close the bag at the top with a wire twist. Let rise in a warm place until doubled, about 1-1/2 hours. Remove the wire twist and punch down the dough in the bag. Oil an 8-1/2 by 4-1/2 by 2-1/2-inch loaf pan. Shape the dough into a loaf to fit in the pan. Cover with oiled plastic wrap and let rise again until doubled, about 1 hour.

Preheat the oven to 375 degrees. Brush the top of the dough with the egg glaze and bake in the center of the oven for about 30 to 35 minutes, or until the loaf is nicely browned and sounds hollow when tapped. Makes 1 loaf—about 2 pounds, 16 slices.

HOLLY'S MYSTERY MUFFINS

When someone asks if we have a good recipe for an easy high-fiber muffin, we like to share Holly's Mystery Muffins recipe. We have no idea who Holly is or was since the recipe was passed on to us from a friend in Connecticut who got it from another friend in Vermont, and neither of them knew Holly. Made entirely with whole wheat flour as well as old-fashioned oatmeal, these muffins are slightly dense and very moist. The mashed bananas, walnuts, and raisins add to the delicious flavor and pleasing texture. If you are fortunate enough to have any leftovers, they do freeze well for up to 6 months.

1 cup whole wheat flour
2 teaspoons baking powder
1/4 teaspoon baking soda
1/2 teaspoon ground cinnamon
1/4 teaspoon salt
1 cup old-fashioned oatmeal (we used quick-cooking)
1 large egg
1/2 cup honey
1/3 cup vegetable oil (we used safflower)
2/3 cup mashed ripe bananas (about 1-1/2 medium)
3/4 cup toasted walnuts, chopped*
1/2 cup golden raisins

Preheat the oven to 350 degrees. Line twelve 1/2-cup muffin pans with paper liners.

In a large mixing bowl, whisk together the flour, baking powder, baking soda, cinnamon and salt. Stir in the oatmeal. Transfer to a piece of wax paper.

In the same bowl, whisk (or use an electric mixer on medium speed) together the egg, honey, and vegetable oil until well mixed. Stir in the dry ingredients, walnuts, and raisins. Do not overmix.

Divide the mixture among the prepared muffin pans, filling each about 3/4 full. Bake in the center of the oven for about 20 to 24 minutes, or until a toothpick inserted in the center comes out clean. Remove immediately from the pan to wire racks. Best if served warm, but they do reheat well.

Makes 12 muffins.

*To toast the walnuts, spread them out on a baking sheet and bake for about 8 minutes in a preheated 350 degree oven, or until fragrant and lightly brown. Cool completely before chopping.

Honey Graham Crackers

HONEY GRAHAM CRACKERS

This recipe for Honey Graham Crackers was developed in the Cuisinart Test Kitchen many years ago after we had a number of requests from readers who asked if it was possible to make their own graham crackers. We had a great deal of culinary fun during their development with in-house (or kitchen) bashes making lots of S'mores with all the samples. For all intents and purposes (and recipes) Graham flour and whole wheat flour are interchangeable. Graham flour was named after a Sylvester Graham, a Presbyterian minister in the nineteenth century who denounced white bread (and other foods) as pernicious and extolled whole grain flour, soon to become known as Graham flour. Since whole wheat or Graham flour contain more fiber than other flours, we like to use it in combination with all-purpose or bread flour to give the finished product more baking strength.

2 cups all-purpose flour
1/3 cup whole wheat flour
1/2 cup tightly packed dark brown sugar
3/4 teaspoon baking soda
1/2 teaspoon salt
1/2 stick (4 tablespoons) unsalted butter, cut into 4 pieces
1/3 cup honey
1 teaspoon pure vanilla extract
5 tablespoons water

In a food processor fitted with the metal blade, combine the flours, brown sugar, soda, salt, and butter. Process for about 10 seconds. Add the remaining ingredients and process until the mixture forms a mass, about 20 seconds. Remove the dough, press it into a ball, and divide it in half. Cover one half with plastic wrap.

Preheat the oven to 325 degrees.

Roll out the uncovered dough on a buttered rimless 14 by 17-inch baking sheet. Lightly flour the surface of the dough and roll until it is very thin and covers the baking sheet. Use the sharp side of a knife to cut the dough into 3-inch squares, then use the dull side of the knife to divide the squares in half. Prick evenly with a fork. Bake for 12 to 15 minutes, or until evenly browned and firm to the touch. Repeat with the remaining dough on a second baking sheet.

Follow the scored lines to cut the crackers apart while warm; they will crisp as they cool. Gently lift them from the baking sheet with a spatula. Separate the crackers and store in airtight containers.

Makes about 40 crackers.

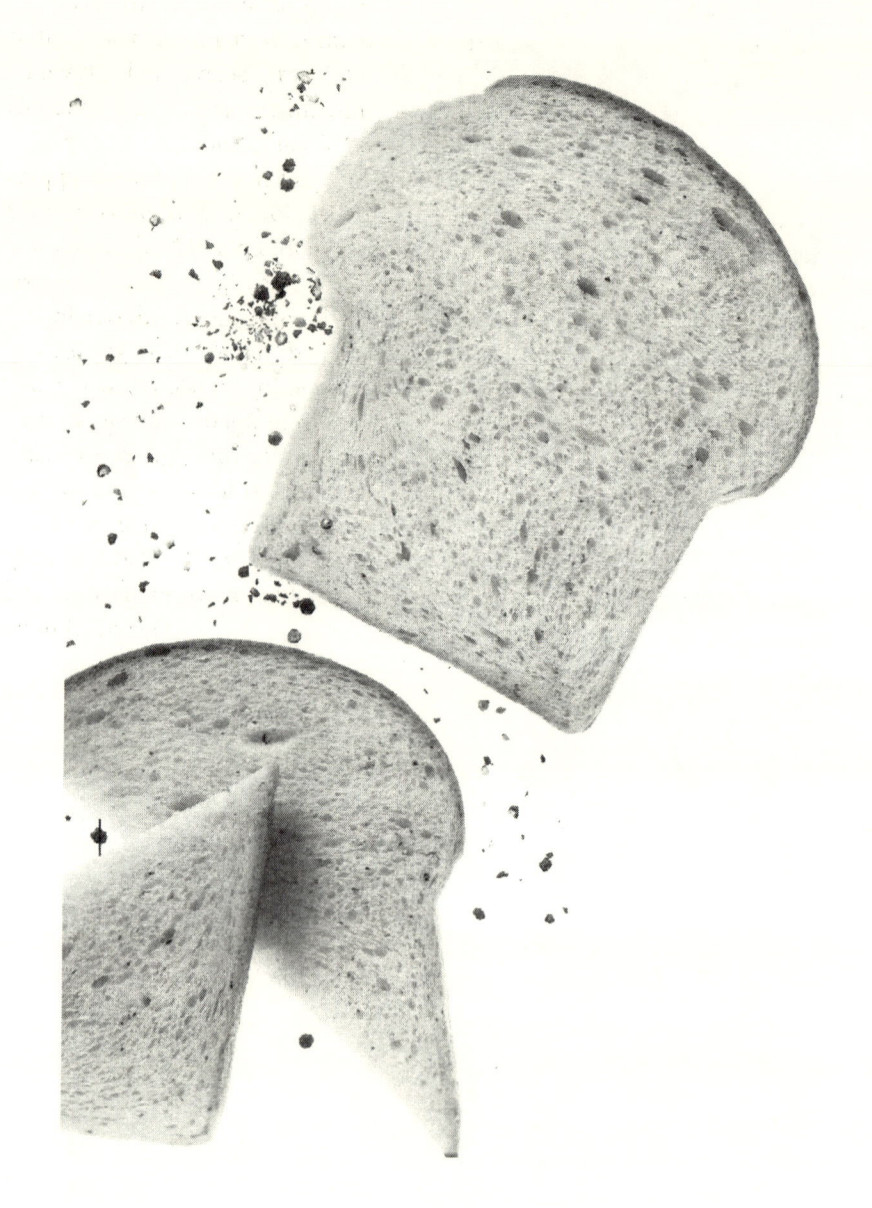

Mayburn's Pepper Cheese Bread

MAYBURN'S PEPPER CHEESE BREAD

We had a recipe request for a bread recipe with black pepper and Cheddar cheese as two of the main ingredients. Thanks to Mayburn Koss, the former PR Director and Editorial Consultant for Cuisinarts at that time, we quickly published the recipe for her Pepper Cheese Bread for everyone to enjoy. Though a food processor recipe, by hand will accomplish the job though taking much longer. This savory bread makes delicious sandwiches filled with ham, chicken, or turkey—or simply toasted to accompany a bowl of soup or a salad.

- 3 ounces extra-sharp Cheddar cheese (about 3/4 cup shredded)
- 1 package (1/4 ounce) dry yeast
- 1 tablespoon sugar
- 1/3 cup warm water (110 to 115 degrees)
- 3 cups all-purpose flour
- 1/4 stick (2 tablespoons) unsalted butter
- 1-1/4 teaspoons coarsely ground Java black pepper
- 1 teaspoon salt
- 1/4 teaspoon hot pepper sauce
- 2/3 cup plus 2 teaspoons cold water

Process the cheese with the medium shredding disc of a food processor. Set aside.

Stir the yeast and sugar into the warm water in a 2-cup measure. Let stand until foamy—about 5 minutes.

Process the flour, butter, black pepper, salt and hot pepper sauce in the food processor fitted with the metal blade for 20 seconds, scraping down the bowl once. Add the cold water to the yeast mixture and, with the motor running, pour the liquid through the feed tube in a steady stream as fast as the flour absorbs it. After the dough cleans the side of the bowl, add the shredded cheese and process for 1 minute more to knead the dough.

Remove the dough from the bowl, shape into a smooth ball and place in a lightly floured 1-gallon plastic storage bag. Squeeze out the air and close with a wire twist, allowing room for the dough to rise.

Let rise until doubled, about 1 hour. Shape into a loaf and place in a greased 8 by 4-inch loaf pan. Cover with oiled plastic wrap and let rise until the center of the loaf is about 1-1/2 inches above the rim of the pan, about 1 hour.

Preheat the oven to 375 degrees. Bake the loaf in the center of the oven for 30 to 35 minutes or until the loaf is well browned and sounds hollow when tapped.

Makes 1 loaf of about 16 slices.

ORANGE JUICE MUFFINS WITH HONEY SPREAD

If you are looking for a quick and delicious addition to breakfast or any meal or even in between, these Orange Juice Muffins with their easy Honey Spread are the answer. This recipe was shared by a good friend who will cook or bake anything if the word "easy" is in the title, the execution bears it out and the end result is satisfying. Although "easy" was not in the title, she knew with Bisquick as the first ingredient, these muffins were bound to clinch her criteria.

- 2 cups Original Bisquick
- 4 tablespoons sugar, divided
- 1 large egg
- 1 teaspoon grated orange zest
- 2/3 cup orange juice
- 1/4 teaspoon ground cinnamon
- 1/8 teaspoon ground nutmeg
- Honey Spread (recipe given)

Preheat the oven to 400 degrees. Grease the bottoms only of 12 medium muffin cups. In a large bowl, mix together the Bisquick, 2 tablespoons of the sugar, the egg, orange zest and orange juice. Beat vigorously for 30 seconds. Fill the muffin cups about 2/3 full. Mix the remaining 2 tablespoons sugar, the cinnamon and nutmeg and sprinkle the top of each muffin with about 1/2 teaspoon. Bake in the center of the oven for 15 minutes or until firm and beginning to brown. Serve warm with Honey Spread—also good reheated.

Makes 12 muffins.

Honey Spread:

- 1/2 cup butter, at room temperature
- 1/3 cup honey

Beat the butter and honey together until well mixed and smooth. Keep refrigerated. It will become firm but not hard.

Makes about 3/4 cup plus a tablespoon.

RISEN BISCUITS

Risen Biscuits

Someone asked if we had a recipe we could share called Angel Cloud Biscuits, which had been misplaced. The description fit what we know as Risen Biscuits, but often called Angel Cloud Biscuits, Kentucky Riz Biscuits, Alabama Biscuits, or Quaker Bonnet Biscuits. This is just another instance where a good recipe can travel the country over the years and appear in similar form under different names in different regions. As some astute cook once remarked, a good recipe never dies, it just keeps resurfacing under a different name.

This recipe for Risen Biscuits was given to us along with other handwritten recipes years ago by Ms. Belle Perry of Mount Hope, West Virginia. The name Quaker Bonnet Biscuits is even more fitting than the other known names since the top tier often is slightly askew, reminding one of a Quaker bonnet.

1 package (1/4 ounce) dry yeast
1/4 cup warm water (110-115 degrees)
1 tablespoon sugar
2-1/2 cups all-purpose flour
1/2 teaspoon salt
1/2 teaspoon baking soda
1/3 cup (about 5-1/3 tablespoons) unsalted butter*
3/4 cup room temperature buttermilk
1/2 cup unsalted butter, melted (for dipping)

Dissolve the yeast in the warm water with the sugar in a 2-cup measure. Let stand for 5 minutes or until foamy.

In a large mixing bowl, whisk together the flour, salt, and baking soda. Cut in the shortening with a pastry blender until the consistency of coarse meal. Stir the buttermilk into the yeast mixture. Combine this with the dry ingredient, mixing quickly. Turn out onto a floured board and knead 20 to 30 times. Roll out to 1/4-inch thickness and cut out biscuits with a 2-inch cutter. Dip each biscuit in melted butter and place half of them about 1-1/2 inches apart on a greased cookie sheet. Top each biscuit with a second biscuit dipped in butter. If necessary, you can reknead and reroll leftover dough. Cover the biscuits with oiled plastic wrap and let rise for about 1 hour, or until not quite doubled.

Meanwhile preheat the oven to 375 degrees. Bake the biscuits in the center of the oven for 12 to 14 minutes, or until nicely browned. Remove to wire racks to cool slightly. Best served warm.

Makes about two dozen biscuits.

*The original recipe called for lard, but we liked the flavor when made with butter.

RIVERSIDE HOTEL BROWN BREAD

Riverside Hotel Brown Bread

One Easter Sunday, several years ago, we had dinner at the Riverside Hotel in Fort Lauderdale, Florida. We were served the most delicious brown bread to accompany our meal. Upon request, the kitchen manager, Mr. Reed, brought out Ivanie, the gracious and talented woman who had been baking this bread (at that time) for over thirteen years. Both agreed to share this not-too-sweet but remarkably moist and fruity bread recipe with pleasant overtones of molasses. The sliced apples in corn syrup called for in the original recipe were not available to the home cook, so we substituted with Del Monte reconstituted dried apples with great success. This bread is superb for breakfast, lunch, teatime, dinner, or anytime.

2-1/2 cups all-purpose flour
1 teaspoon baking powder
1 teaspoon baking soda
1 teaspoon fresh-grated nutmeg
1 teaspoon ground cinnamon
2 large eggs
1/4 cup firm-packed light brown sugar
1/2 cup granulated sugar
1/2 cup plus 2 tablespoons vegetable oil

1 teaspoon pure vanilla extract
1 cup dark molasses
1/3 cup mashed bananas
1 cup fresh or frozen cranberries
1/3 cup raisins
1/3 cup coarse-chopped walnuts
1/3 cup coarse-chopped Del Monte reconstituted dried apples*

Preheat the oven to 350 degrees. Prepare two 8-1/2 by 4-1/2 by 2-1/2-inch bread pans with no-stick cooking spray.

In a large mixing bowl, whisk the flour, baking powder, soda, nutmeg, and cinnamon together. Transfer to a piece of wax paper.

In the same bowl, beat the eggs until light and lemon color. Beat in the sugar, oil, vanilla, and molasses. Add the dry ingredients, and beat for 1 minute on medium speed. Stir in the bananas, cranberries, raisins, walnuts, and apples.

Divide the mixture between the prepared pans. Bake in the center of the oven for 50 to 60 minutes, or until a toothpick inserted in the center comes out clean. Cool for 10 minutes in the pans, then transfer to wire racks to cool completely.

Makes 2 loaves, about 10 slices each.

*Del Monte sliced dried apples (8-ounce packages) are available in most supermarkets. Cook the entire package according to directions. The yield is about 4-1/2 cups. After using what is needed in the recipe, try sprinkling 1/4 cup confectioners' sugar and 1/8 teaspoon ground cinnamon on the apples remaining, tossing to mix. Serve as a side dish or use to make your favorite apple tart.

STOUFFER'S COFFEE CAKE

We had been asked from some transplanted New Yorkers if it would be possible to get or recreate the delicious coffee cake served in the Stouffer's cafeteria years ago. Thanks to a culinary friend—Rita Rossi who, for years, managed the kitchen at Carson Pirie Scott in Chicago—who shared many of her recipes, which included the New York recipe for Stouffer's Coffee Cake, we can all enjoy it. She said it originally was written to accommodate a large sheet pan serving about seventy-five people, but she successfully broke the recipe down. The result is the cinnamony, nutty, delicious coffee cake below, serving a comfortable twelve.

Cake:

- 1-1/2 cups all-purpose flour
- 3 teaspoons baking powder
- 1/2 teaspoon salt
- 3/4 cups sugar
- 1/4 cup cold unsalted butter, cut into 4 tablespoons
- 1/4 cup cold solid shortening (we used Crisco)
- 1 large egg, well beaten
- 1/2 cup milk
- 1-1/2 teaspoons pure vanilla extract

Filling:

- 1/2 cup sugar
- 2 tablespoons all-purpose flour
- 2 teaspoons ground cinnamon
- 2 tablespoons melted and cooled butter
- 3/4 cup coarse-chopped pecans or walnuts

Preheat the oven to 375 degrees. Grease an 8-inch square baking pan. Set aside.

To make the Cake: Sift together into a large mixing bowl, the flour, baking powder, salt and sugar. Cut in the butter and shortening with a pastry blender until the consistency of corn meal. Mix the egg with the milk and vanilla and pour over the flour mixture. Stir just enough to blend well, but do not overmix.

To make the filling: Stir all the ingredients together until well mixed.

To assemble the coffee cake, spread a scant half of the cake batter in the prepared baking pan. Sprinkle half the filling mixture evenly over the top. Drop the rest of the batter by the spoonful over the filling. Use a knife to spread it as evenly as possible to all sides and corners. (This may seem difficult, but persevere!) Sprinkle with the remaining filling.

Bake in the center of the oven for 25 to 30 minutes, or until nicely browned and a toothpick inserted in the center comes out clean

Best served warm or at room temperature with, of course, lots of butter.

Makes 12 servings.

STUFFING BREAD

We have had numerous requests for a recipe we developed several years ago called Stuffing Bread. It had in it many of the ingredients fond in a good basic stuffing for poultry or pork, such as onions, celery seeds, sage, black pepper and corn meal. This bead sliced is the ideal vehicle for leftover turkey or chicken sandwiches. Dried and cubed and sautéed in butter, it makes a quick and flavorful stuffing. When baking, the aroma emanating from the oven is downright irresistible. It also makes great grilled cheese sandwiches. Toasted, it is equally good with breakfast eggs, chicken soup, or most any salad. The original recipe was developed for the food processor, but you will also find a by-hand version below.

Food Processor Version:

- 1 package dry yeast (1/4 ounce)
- 1 teaspoon sugar
- 1/4 cup warm water (110 to 115 degrees)
- 1 small onion (2 ounces) peeled and quartered
- 2-1/2 to 2/3/4 cups all-purpose flour
- 1/2 cup yellow cornmeal
- 3 tablespoons unsalted butter, at room temperature
- 1-1/2 teaspoons salt
- 1 teaspoon celery seed
- 2 teaspoons dried sage
- 1 teaspoon crushed dried rosemary
- 1/4 teaspoon coarse-ground black pepper
- 1 large egg
- 1/2 cup ice water

Dissolve the yeast and sugar in the warm water and let stand until foamy, about 10 minutes.

In a food processor fitted with the metal blade, coarse-chop the onion. Add 2-1/2 cups flour, cornmeal, butter and seasonings and process for 30 seconds. Add the yeast mixture and the egg. Then with the machine running, pour the ice water through the feed tube in a steady stream as fast as the flour absorbs it. When the dough forms a ball, check its consistency, it should be slightly sticky. If too wet, process in the remaining flour a tablespoon at a time. Process the dough for about 45 seconds.

With floured hands, remove the dough and shape into a smooth ball. Put it in a lightly floured 1-gallon plastic storage bag and seal with a wire twist. Let rise until doubled, about 1-1/2 hours.

Remove the twist and punch down the dough in the bag. Shape into a loaf and put into a greased 8 by 4 by 2-1/2 inch loaf pan. Cover with oiled plastic wrap and let rise until doubled, about 45 minutes. Preheat the oven to 375 degrees. Bake the loaf in the center of the oven for about 35 minutes, or until nicely browned and sounds hollow when tapped. Remove loaf from the pan and cool on its side on a wire rack

Makes one 1-1/2 pound loaf: about 16 slices.

By-Hand Version:

Dissolve yeast as above in a 2-cup measure, but use 3/4 cups of warm water. Fine-chop the onion. Melt and cool the butter.

In a large mixing bowl, whisk together all the dry ingredients, using 2-1/2 cups flour. Transfer to a large piece of wax paper. In the same bowl, whisk the onion, butter, and egg together. Stir in the yeast mixture then half the dry ingredients. Add the remaining dry ingredients and stir well. The mixture will be sticky. Turn out onto a well-floured surface and knead in enough of the remaining flour (or more) to arrive at a soft, but not sticky, dough. Knead for about 8 minutes. Follow the directions above for finishing the loaf.

SWEET TOMATOES TANGY LEMON MUFFINS

The majority of restaurant chains are not willing to share their recipes. We were fortunate, however, when we contacted one of the Account Executives for Sweet Tomatoes at the Corporate Offices in California who graciously agreed to share their Tangy Lemon Muffin recipe. The "tang" in these delicious muffins comes from not only fresh lemon zest and juice, but also frozen lemonade concentrate, instant lemon pudding mix, and lemon-flavored extract. How much more lemony can you get? In spite of the thick batter, thanks to the addition of the lemon pudding mix, these muffins bake into deliciously lemony and light treasures. Eating just one can be a problem. They make a wonderful treat for breakfast, lunch, supper, or anytime in between.

Dry Mix:

- 3 cups all-purpose flour
- 1/2 cup whole wheat flour
- 1 tablespoon baking powder
- 1/2 teaspoon salt

Wet Mix:

- 1/3 cup plus 2 tablespoons buttermilk
- 1/3 cup frozen lemonade concentrate
- 1/3 cup canola oil
- 1/3 cup fresh lemon juice
- 1 teaspoon fine-diced lemon zest
- 2-3/4 teaspoons pure lemon extract
- 3/4 cup sugar
- 1/4 cup water
- 1 large egg
- 1/3 cup instant lemon pudding mix
- 2 tablespoons confectioners' sugar, for sprinkling

Preheat the oven to 350 degrees. Spray 18 standard muffin pans with no-stick vegetable spray or line with paper liners. Set aside.

In a large mixing bowl, whisk together the Dry Mix ingredients until thoroughly combined. In another large bowl, combine all the Wet Mix ingredients. Beat well to make sure the sugar is dissolved. Combine the wet and dry ingredients and mix just until well combined. Do not overmix. (You will note that the small amount of instant pudding mix will thicken the batter quickly, so be ready to fill the muffin tins right away.) Fill the prepared muffin tins about 3/4 full and sprinkle the tops with confectioners' sugar. Bake in the center of the oven for 15 to 20 minutes or until a toothpick inserted in the center comes out clean. Remove immediately from the pans to wire racks to cool. These are delicious served slightly warm or at room temperature.

Makes 18 muffins.

WHOLE WHEAT BISCOTTI

We became addicted to biscotti years and years ago once we tasted these Whole Wheat Biscotti made by a delightful Italian couple who—during our time at Northwestern University in Evanston, Illinois—taught our class in Italian and favored us frequently with some of their treasured recipes. You can use either pecans or walnuts and almost any dried fruits. We do prefer the Sun-Maid Fruit Bits, which gives you a variety of fruits in the biscotti. These are as delicious to eat out of hand as they are to dunk in your coffee or milk.

2 cups whole wheat flour
1-1/2 teaspoons baking powder
1/4 teaspoon baking soda
1/2 teaspoon salt
1-1/2 teaspoons ground cinnamon
1/4 teaspoon ground cloves
1/4 teaspoon ground allspice
1 stick (1/2 cup) unsalted butter at room temperature

1 cup sugar
2 large eggs
1-1/2 teaspoons pure vanilla extract
1/4 cup toasted pecans or walnuts, coarsely chopped*
1/4 cup Sun-Maid brand Fruit Bits, coarsely chopped

Preheat the oven o 350 degrees. Lightly spray a large baking sheet with no-stick vegetable spray.

In a large mixing bowl, whisk together the flour, baking powder, soda, salt, cinnamon, cloves and allspice. Transfer to a piece of wax paper. In the same bowl, cream the butter and sugar until light. Add the eggs one at a time, mixing well. Stir in the vanilla. Add the dry ingredients in three batches, mixing well after each addition. Stir in the chopped nuts and the chopped Fruit Bits.

The mixture will be firm but slightly sticky, so if need be lightly flour your hands. Shape the dough into three loaves, each about 1/2 inch high, 2 inches across and about 10-1/2 inches long. Place 2 inches apart on the prepared baking sheet. Bake in the center of the oven for about 25 minutes, or until lightly brown and firm to the touch. Cool the pan on a wire rack for about 15 to 20 minutes, or until the logs are cool enough to handle. Slice each loaf diagonally at about a 45-degree angle about 1/2-inch thick. Lay the slices on their cut side and bake

again for about 10 minutes or until they are slightly dry. Remove to wire racks to cool completely. Delicious to eat out of hand or to dunk in your coffee or milk.
  Makes about 48 biscotti.

*To toast the nuts, preheat the oven to 350 degrees. Spread the nuts in one layer on a baking sheet. Bake in the center of the oven for about 10 minutes or until fragrant and beginning to take on color.

VEGETABLES

Bahamian Peas and Rice

BAHAMIAN PEAS AND RICE

Hugh Ganter (Papa Hughie), the owner of the popular Seafood World Restaurant, sat down with us and dictated his recipe for Bahamian Peas and Rice at the same time that we were able to sample this flavorful side dish. You will find it is equally at home with poultry and pork as well as seafood. Pigeon peas are closely related to cow peas or field peas and are often the choice paired with rice in Hispanic and Caribbean cooking. Make sure you do not use instant rice here!

- 2 tablespoons peanut oil
- 1 small onion, cut into 1/4-inch dice
- 2 celery ribs, cut into 1/4-inch dice
- 1/2 medium green pepper, cut into 1/4-inch dice
- 1 can (15.5 ounces) pigeon peas, drained (we used the Goya brand)
- 1 tablespoon Kitchen Bouquet
- 2 heaping teaspoons instant chicken bouillon granules
- 1/4 teaspoon black pepper
- 1/2 teaspoon dried thyme leaves, crushed
- 1/4 cup tomato paste
- 2 tablespoons Worcestershire sauce (can also use teriyaki sauce)
- pinch cayenne or to taste
- 3 cups water
- 1-1/4 cups long grain white rice

In a large saucepot, heat the oil over medium-high heat. Stir in the onions, celery and green pepper and cook, stirring for about 5 minutes, or until the vegetables are soft but not brown.

Stir in the remaining ingredients except the rice and bring to a boil, stirring. Stir in the rice and bring back to a boil. Reduce the heat to medium-low, cover and simmer for 20 minutes, or until all the liquid has been absorbed. Stir the mixture a couple of times during the cooking, to keep it from sticking to the bottom of the pan. Serve warm.

This keeps well for two to three days, refrigerated. Reheat in the microwave or over very low heat. Add additional water if the mixture seems too dry.

Makes 8 servings.

Beer Batter Fried Asparagus

BEER BATTER FRIED ASPARAGUS

This simple recipe is from the man whose extraordinary knowledge of food and cookery has had so much influence on Americans and their cooking—the late James Beard. We had the immense pleasure of working with him and so appreciated his willingness to share his knowledge. He loved fresh asparagus, and Beer Batter Fried Asparagus was one of many recipes he did share with us. He talked about the large asparagus bed he once had and the satisfaction of cutting his own asparagus every day or two.

1-1/4 cups all-purpose flour
1 can (12 fluid ounces) beer at room temperature
1 teaspoon salt
1 teaspoon paprika

2 pounds fresh asparagus, trimmed*, washed, and well dried
vegetable oil for frying

Process 1 cup of the flour, the beer, salt, and paprika with the metal blade of a food processor, pulsing 2 to 4 times or just until mixed. Transfer to a 2-quart mixing bowl. The batter can be used immediately or covered and refrigerated for up to 24 hours. Stir before using.

Dust the asparagus lightly with the remaining flour. Heat about 2 inches of oil in a medium sauté pan or skillet to 360 degrees.

Dip the asparagus spears into the batter and lower carefully into the hot oil. Do not fry too many at a time or the temperature of the oil will drop. Cook, turning with a slotted spoon, until golden brown—about 2 minutes. Remove and drain on paper towels. Keep warm in a 250-degree oven until all the asparagus is cooked. Serve immediately.

Makes 6 servings.

*To be sure of tender asparagus, you may want to peel the spears. Remove the tough outer skin using a swivel-bladed peeler: moving the blade toward you, peel each spear from the root end to a point 2 or 3 inches from the tip.

BROCCOLI CUSTARD BAKE

This is another tempting way to introduce broccoli to anyone who claims not to like it or refuse to eat it. The original recipe for Broccoli Custard Bake was copied from an old magazine in our dentist's office many years ago. We like to make it with fresh broccoli florets, but frozen and defrosted can be substituted. It makes a delicious and filling side dish for just about any grilled, broiled or baked meat or fish.

2 cups fresh broccoli florets (or one 10-ounce package frozen, defrosted and drained)
1 cup chopped fresh mushrooms
1 cup shredded Swiss or Gruyere cheese

6 large eggs
1/2 cup milk
1/2 cup ranch dressing (we used Wish Bone brand)
3 tablespoons all-purpose flour

Preheat the oven to 350 degrees. Lightly oil a 1-1/2-quart casserole dish.

In a large mixing bowl, toss together the broccoli florets, mushrooms, and Swiss or Gruyere cheese. Transfer to the oiled casserole.

In the same bowl, thoroughly whisk the eggs, then whisk in the milk, dressing and flour until well mixed. Carefully pour the mixture over the broccoli mixture, making sure all is covered. Bake in the center of the oven for about 40 minutes or until puffy and set. Let sit for about 5 minutes before serving.

Makes 6 servings.

CAULIFLOWER AU GRATIN

From a small family restaurant (now unfortunately gone) comes this comforting, flavorful, and satisfying way to serve a sometimes otherwise uninteresting vegetable. There are no special or exotic ingredients required, and the preparation before baking can be done ahead. You can use either fresh or frozen cauliflower flowerets. Just be sure to follow the package instructions for cooking, but cut the time in half. You only want the cauliflower to be half done. It will finish cooking in the oven surrounded by a blanket of creamy, lightly nutmeg- and cheese-flavored sauce.

1 pound cauliflower flowerets, fresh or frozen (about 4-1/2 cups)
5 tablespoons butter or margarine
5 tablespoons all-purpose flour
2-1/2 cups warm milk
1 heaping teaspoon chicken base (or chicken bouillon granules)
1/4 teaspoon fresh-grated nutmeg
pinch white pepper, or to taste
4 tablespoons Parmesan cheese, divided
1 large egg, lightly beaten

Cook the cauliflower until just half done. If using frozen, check the package directions. If using fresh, it should take about 2 minutes. Immediately drain well. Let cool about 15 minutes, then spread in a baking dish or pan. Set aside.

In a large saucepan, melt the butter over medium heat. Stir in the flour and let bubble for a minute or two, stirring. Slowly add the warm milk, stirring constantly so no lumps form. When thickened, stir in the chicken base, nutmeg, pepper, and 3 tablespoons of the Parmesan cheese.

Slowly pour about 1/2 cup of the hot sauce over the beaten egg, stirring or whisking briskly to prevent the egg from curdling. Then whisk the egg mixture into the remaining sauce.

Pour the sauce over the cauliflower. Use a spatula or spoon to separate the flowerets to allow the sauce to cover all of it nicely. Sprinkle with the remaining Parmesan cheese. (Can be made ahead to this point.) Preheat the oven to 375 degrees. Bake the prepared cauliflower in the center of the oven for 30 minutes, or until the top is nicely browned.

Makes 4 servings.

Curtis' Broccoli Soufflé

CURTIS' BROCCOLI SOUFFLE

We had no problem getting the recipe for this Broccoli Soufflé from Chef Curtis Harralson who oversees the comfort and feeding of about one thousand people a day at one of the better-known retirement communities in South Florida. Unfortunately, the dining room there is not a public facility, but you can enjoy this special soufflé at home now with its high proportion of egg whites that ensures a wonderfully light texture, even when the soufflé begins to sigh and sink while it sits. We have found that even some people who vow they do not like broccoli will willingly take a second helping! Instead of the standard straight-sided soufflé dish, Chef Curtis makes the soufflé in large rectangular serving containers that fit into the slots on the steam table. To simulate this, we have baked our soufflé in an 11 by 7 by 1-3/4-inch baking dish.

1 package (10 ounces) frozen chopped broccoli
5 tablespoons unsalted butter
6 tablespoons (1/4 cup plus 2 tablespoons) all-purpose flour
1-1/4 cups milk
1/2 cup grated sharp Cheddar cheese
6 large eggs, separated
1/2 teaspoon salt
1/2 teaspoon garlic salt
1/8 teaspoon fresh-ground black pepper
1/4 teaspoon cream of tartar

Cook the broccoli according to package directions. Drain well, then place on a triple thickness of paper towels to drain further. (You want the broccoli to be as moisture-free as possible.)

Preheat the oven to 350 degrees. Lightly grease the bottom only of an 11 by 7 by 1-3/4-inch baking dish. Set aside.

Melt the butter in a medium saucepan over medium heat. Stir in the flour and let it bubble for 1 minute. Gradually stir or whisk in the milk and continue stirring until the mixture thickens. (It will be quite thick.) Remove from the heat and stir in the cheese until it has melted.

In a large mixing bowl, beat the egg yolks on the medium speed of an electric mixer until light. Start whisking or stirring in the warm cheese sauce, a small amount at a time. When all the sauce has been added, stir in the drained broccoli, the salt, garlic salt, and pepper. Set aside to cool.

While that mixture is cooling, in another mixing bowl with clean beaters on your mixer, start beating the egg whites with the cream of tartar on medium speed. When the whites are foamy, turn the beater to high and continue beating until stiff, but do not let dry peaks form. Stir about 1/3 of the whites into the egg yolk mixture to loosen it. Then gently fold in the remaining whites. Do not overmix.

Transfer the mixture to the prepared baking dish smoothing the top, and bake in the center of the oven for 35 to 40 minutes, or until firm throughout. Serve at once.

Makes 8 servings.

HENRY'S SWEET POTATO GRATIN

Henry's Sweet Potato Gratin

This Sweet Potato Gratin dish—with its layers of thin-sliced sweet potatoes "shingled" (Henry's restaurant owner Burt Rapoport's word for layering) and sandwiched between fresh-grated Parmesan cheese and topped with a reduction of heavy cream, pure maple syrup, and fresh thyme—may well remind you of your grandmother's sweet potato pie. The recipe calls for very thin-sliced sweet potatoes (about 1/16 of an inch thick). A food processor with a thin (2mm) disc is a real time saver here. Otherwise use your sharpest knife and a steady slicing hand. After our first taste as a guest of Rapoport's on Thanksgiving some years ago, we declared this dish to be the definitive way to serve sweet potatoes. And remember, sweet potatoes are high in nutrition—ranked even ahead of spinach and broccoli because of their high levels of fiber, complex carbohydrates, protein, vitamins A and C, iron, and calcium. WOW!

- 2 pounds sweet potatoes (about 4 medium weighing 8 ounces each)
- 2 tablespoons unsalted butter
- 1 medium white onion, cut into 1/4-inch dice
- 2 cups heavy cream
- 1/2 cup pure maple syrup
- 2 teaspoons chopped fresh thyme leaves
- 1/2 teaspoon salt
- 1/2 teaspoon fresh-ground black pepper
- 1 cup fresh-grated Parmesan cheese

Peel and slice the sweet potatoes into 1/16-inch slices. (Use your food processor's 2-mm slicing disc for quick slicing.) Bring a large pot of water to a boil over high heat. Add the potatoes, separating the slices if necessary, and bring back to a boil. Reduce the heat to medium, and simmer the potatoes uncovered for 2 minutes, or until they are barely cooked (al dente). Drain well and set aside.

In a large heavy saucepan, melt the butter over medium-high heat. Add the onions and cook, stirring for about 5 minutes, or until lightly caramelized. Remove from the heat.

In a 4-cup measuring cup, mix together the cream, maple syrup, thyme, salt and pepper. Off heat, add this mixture to the caramelized onions. Return the pan to medium heat, bring to a boil and reduce the mixture by half. (Measure the depth on the handle of a wooden spoon and mark with a pencil. Remeasure occasionally until the mixture reaches the halfway mark.)

Preheat the oven to 350 degrees. Spray a 1-1/2-quart gratin dish with no-stick cooking spray. Arrange slices of sweet potatoes (as Rapaport says, "shingle" them) in a single layer. Our dish took 3 rows just slightly overlapping. Sprinkle the top with 1 tablespoon of the Parmesan cheese. Repeat with two more layers, but after the third layer, spoon half the reduced cream mixture and 1/4 cup Parmesan over that third layer. Repeat the process with three more layers with the remaining reduced cream mixture and remaining 1/4 cup Parmesan over the top. You now have 6 layers in all. (You may have a few slices and/or pieces of sweet potatoes left over. No problem, they are a wonderful snack.)

Cover the top with heavy duty aluminum foil and bake in the center of the oven for 30 to 35 minutes, or until the mixture is bubbling nicely and the cheese has melted.

Makes 6 servings.

HIMMEL UND ERDE (HEAVEN AND EARTH)

This simple but savory side dish comes from a good friend of German descent. As we enjoyed it one evening, she explained that Himmel und Erde was an expandable recipe, and the seasonings depended upon the cook's whim and palate. Variations of this dish can be found in other countries including Scotland and Scandinavia as well as some parts of our country. You can use either turnips or rutabagas. Though some may think they are the same, botanically they are quite different. Small white turnips have a more delicate taste and a higher water content than the stronger-flavored yellow-orange rutabaga, which are sometimes called yellow turnips or Canadian turnips and sometimes Swede turnips.

2 pounds rutabaga or turnips, trimmed, peeled and cut into 1-inch pieces
2 pounds baking potatoes, peeled and cut into 1-inch pieces
1-1/2 pounds apples such as Granny Smith or Pippin (peeled, cored, and cut into 1-inch pieces)

1 cup light cream
1/2 cup plus 2 tablespoons unsalted butter, cut into tablespoon-size pieces
salt and fresh-ground pepper, to taste

Cook the rutabaga (or turnips) and potatoes together in water to cover until tender, about 25 minutes. Drain well. Cook the apples separately in about 1/2 cup water until tender, about 20 minutes. Drain.

With an electric mixer on low, mash the vegetables and apples together, adding the cream and butter until the desired consistency. Season to taste. Return to a saucepan and keep warm until serving.

Makes 8 servings.

LIGHT CORN FRITTERS

The original recipe for these Light Corn Fritters was from the well-known French chef Roger Verge. The fritters are made from a "pate a choux" base (the mixture used to make cream puffs) and are more delicate than those made from many of the standard corn fritter recipes. For anyone hesitant about making "pate a choux," be assured it is simple, and you will be pleased with the fritters. These are not deep fried, but sautéed in a little oil and butter in a skillet.

3 tablespoons water
1 tablespoon unsalted butter
1/8 teaspoon salt
1/8 teaspoon sugar
1/4 cup all-purpose flour
1 large egg
pinch fresh-grated nutmeg
pinch fresh-grated black pepper

1 package (10 ounces) frozen corn, defrosted and well drained (about 2 cups) or 2 cups canned niblet corn, drained, or 2 cups leftover corn niblets
2 tablespoons unsalted butter, for frying
2 tablespoons vegetable oil, for frying

In a 1-quart heavy saucepan, bring the water, butter, salt, and sugar to a boil. Remove from the heat and add the flour all at once. Beat vigorously with a wooden spoon to blend thoroughly. Then beat over low heat for 1 to 2 minutes until the mixture leaves the sides of the pan and the spoon, forms a mass, and begins to film the bottom of the pan. Remove from the heat and let sit for 1 minute. Make a well in the center of the paste with your spoon and immediately break the egg into the center. Beat it into the paste for several seconds until it has been well absorbed. Then beat for several moments more to be sure all is well blended. Stir in the nutmeg and pepper. Add the corn and stir well to combine.

In a heavy 10-inch skillet (preferably nonstick) heat 1 tablespoon of the butter and oil for frying over moderate heat. Drop the corn fritter batter by heaping tablespoons into the pan, flattening each fritter slightly with the back of the spoon. Do not overcrowd the pan. Cook for 2 to 3 minutes, or until the undersides are golden brown. Turn, flatten slightly again and brown the other side. Drain on paper towels and keep warm in a covered dish while you fry the rest, adding more butter and oil to the pan if necessary.

Makes about 12 fritters.

MASHED POTATO PUFFS FOR TWO

We discovered an easy and tasty way to dress up those instant mashed potatoes with this Mashed Potato Puffs For Two. We like the fact that we can whip it together ahead and bake it at the last minute. The Pillsbury Idaho Mashed Potatoes have been our first choice, but you can easily substitute. Just make sure to get the plain ones.

2 servings instant mashed potatoes (Pillsbury Idaho preferred), made according to package directions
2 additional tablespoons milk
2 tablespoons fresh-grated Parmesan cheese, divided
1/4 teaspoon dried rosemary leaves, crushed in a mortar with pestle
1 large egg
salt and fresh-ground black pepper to taste

Preheat the oven to 375 degrees. Lightly butter an oval baking dish about 7 by 5 by 2 inches. Set aside.

Cool down the prepared mashed potatoes by stirring in the additional milk, 1 tablespoon of the Parmesan cheese and crushed rosemary leaves. When the potatoes have come to room temperature, beat in the egg well with a wire whisk. Season to taste. Transfer to the prepared baking dish and sprinkle with the remaining Parmesan cheese. Bake in the center of the oven for 20 to 25 minutes or until puffed and lightly browned.

Makes 2 servings.

NUTTY BAKED CABBAGE

The addition of chopped, salted peanuts to what one could call an ordinary cheese sauced cabbage dish gives this Nutty Baked Cabbage its out of the ordinary texture and flavor. Of course make sure none of your guests is allergic to peanuts. We have substituted salted and chopped cashews when peanuts might be a problem. The sharp Cheddar cheese and a bit of fresh-grated nutmeg give another delicious dimension to this baked cabbage.

1 medium head green cabbage, about 1-1/2 pounds	1 cup milk
salt and fresh-ground black pepper	1/4 teaspoon fresh-grated nutmeg
3 tablespoons unsalted butter	1 cup chopped salted peanuts (can substitute salted cashews)
3 tablespoons all-purpose flour	1 cup grated sharp Cheddar cheese

Discard any damaged outer leaves from the cabbage and cut the rest into quarters. Cut away the center core and cut each quarter into fine shreds.

In a large heavy saucepan, heat about 1/2 inch of water over medium-high heat. Stir in a teaspoon of salt. Add the cabbage, a good handful at a time, seasoning with some pepper. When all the cabbage has been added, reduce the heat to low, cover the pan and let the cabbage steam for about 10 minutes. Do not overcook. You want it to still have a bit of crispness. Drain well.

In a small saucepan, melt the butter over medium heat. Stir in the flour and let it bubble for a minute or two. Slowly add the milk and cook, stirring, until it comes just to a simmer and thickens. Stir in the nutmeg and season with salt.

Preheat the oven to 400 degrees. Butter a 1-1/2 quart casserole dish. Arrange about a third of the cabbage over the bottom. Cover with 1/3 of the sauce, a third of the nuts and a third of the cheese. Repeat the layers ending with the cheese, of course. Bake in the center of the oven for 15 to 20 minutes, or until the cheese is golden brown. Serve at once.

Makes 6 servings.

ORANGE GLAZED CARROTS

We developed this recipe years ago in our Cuisinart test kitchen to include in one of our publications. By using the metal blade of your food processor to finely chop the orange zest and sugar together, it gives the sauce its eminently smooth and intense orange flavor. The recipe can easily be doubled or even tripled for a large crowd.

1 pound fresh young carrots, peeled and cut into 1/4-inch slices (we like these cut on the diagonal)
2 strips orange zest, about 1/2 by 2 inches
2 tablespoons sugar
2 tablespoons butter
2/3 cup orange juice
1-1/2 teaspoons cornstarch

Preheat the oven to 375 degrees. Lightly butter an 8 by 8-inch baking dish.

In a saucepan, cook the carrots in water to cover for about 10 minutes, or until tender. Drain well and arrange in the prepared baking dish. Save the saucepan.

Fine-chop the zest and sugar together in a food processor fitted with the metal blade (or a good blender). Add the mixture along with the butter to the saucepan and bring to a boil over medium heat, stirring constantly. Let simmer for 1 minute. Combine the juice and cornstarch and stir into the mixture in the saucepan. Bring back to a boil and stir briskly until thick. Pour over the carrots and bake in the center of the oven for about 20 minutes, or until hot and bubbly. Makes 4 servings.

Ratatouille

RATATOUILLE

Chef/owner Jon Howe of the Brooks Restaurant once again shared another of his excellent recipes, that robust Mediterranean vegetable dish known as Ratatouille. Abounding in a mélange of tomatoes, eggplant, zucchini, onions, bell peppers and a variety of herbs and spices, it can be served hot or cold and keeps well for a week, refrigerated. The flavor seems to improve with age, whether it is served cold or reheated. We applaud Chef Jon's use of canned crushed tomatoes rather than fresh, since the availability at any one time of year of really flavorful tomatoes is unfortunately questionable. This ensures consistent results any time of the year. There are many ways to serve the Ratatouille—as a side dish, a topping for pasta, or as an appetizer topped with sour cream. One we haven't tried is one the legendary chef Fernand Point at his Restaurant de la Pyramid in France served: Ratatouille topped with a cold soft-poached egg, garnished with ketchup!

1/4 cup extra virgin olive oil
2 large onions (1 pound total, peeled, cut into 1-inch pieces
3 medium zucchini (1 pound total), ends trimmed, cut into 1-inch cubes
1 large red pepper (8 ounces), seeded, cut into 1-inch pieces
1 large yellow pepper (8 ounces), seeded, cut into 1-inch pieces
1 large eggplant (1 pound total), ends trimmed, unpeeled, cut into 1-inch cubes

1/2 teaspoon sugar
1 to 2 teaspoons salt
1 teaspoon fresh-ground black pepper
leaves from 1 large sprig fresh thyme (about 2 teaspoons worth)
2 cups crushed canned tomatoes
2-1/2 tablespoons tomato paste
5 large, fresh basil leaves, rolled and cut crosswise into narrow julienne strips

Heat the olive oil in a large sauté pan over medium heat. Add the onions and sauté until transparent, about 5 minutes. Add the remaining ingredients except the tomatoes, tomato paste and basil. Stir well. Lower the heat, cover and cook until all the vegetables have softened but are not mushy, about 20 minutes, stirring occasionally.

Add the tomatoes, tomato paste and basil, stir well and let simmer, uncovered, until the liquid has reduced a bit, about 8 minutes. Adjust the seasoning.

Makes about 6 cups.

ROASTED GARLIC BREAD PUDDING

This awesome Roasted Garlic Bread Pudding is the brainchild of a talented chef we knew several years ago. He told us it was a savory version of the bread pudding hailing from his hometown of New Orleans. He recommended using crusty, stale French bread for the best results. The aromatic roasted garlic and fresh fennel blend wonderfully with the other dried and fresh herbs and spices. We recommend roasting a whole bulb of garlic here. It is easiest to do and will last for several weeks in the refrigerator. You will find it is a wonderful addition to mashed potatoes, among other things.

4 tablespoons unsalted butter
1-1/2 cups coarse-chopped onions
1/4 cup coarse-chopped celery
1/4 cup coarse-chopped fresh fennel
1/4 cup coarse-chopped shallots (about 2 large)
6 large cloves garlic (about 1/4 ounce each), roasted and pureed*
1 large whole egg
1 large egg yolk
1 cup heavy cream
1/2 teaspoon ground cumin
1/2 teaspoon ground coriander
1/2 teaspoon dried thyme leaves
1 tablespoon plus 1 teaspoon light brown sugar
2 teaspoons chopped fresh sage leaves
1 teaspoon fresh thyme leaves
Salt and fresh-ground pepper to taste
4 cups crusty stale French bread cubes (about 1/2 inch in size)

Preheat the oven to 350 degrees. Lightly oil an 8 by 8 by 2-inch square baking dish. Set aside.

In a large heavy skillet, melt the butter over medium heat. Sauté the onions, celery, fennel, and shallots about 10 minutes, or until soft. Remove from the heat. Stir in the garlic and let the mixture cool for about 10 minutes.

In a large mixing bowl, whisk together the large egg and egg yolk until frothy. Whisk in the milk, cumin, coriander, thyme and brown sugar until the sugar is dissolved. Stir in the fresh sage and thyme and the vegetable mixture. Season with salt and pepper to taste. Fold in the bread cubes, making certain they are all nicely drenched with the aromatic egg mixture.

Transfer to the prepared baking dish, spreading evenly. Bake in the center of the oven for about 30 minutes, or until nicely brown on top and crisp around the edges.

Makes 4 side dish servings.

*To roast the garlic (we recommend doing the whole bulb—it is easiest, will last for several weeks, and is a wonderful addition to mashed potatoes, among other things), heat the oven to 350 degrees. Peel the paperlike skin from around the bulb of garlic, leaving just enough to hold the cloves together. Cut about 1/2 inch off the top to expose the cloves. Place cut side up on a piece of aluminum foil, drizzle with 2 teaspoons oil and sprinkle with salt and pepper. Wrap securely in foil and place on a pie plate. Bake 45 to 50 minutes or until the garlic is toothpick tender. Cool, then squeeze the soft flesh of the cloves out of their papery skins.

SAUTEED BRUSSELS SPROUTS WITH NUTS

This miniature variety of the cabbage family, which is supposed to have originated in the early thirteenth century near Brussels (of course), has some bad rap attributed to it. Some of it is due to the fact that these small sprouts "ripen" quickly during storage and are often over the hill when purchased. And of course, overcooking any member of the cabbage family will create unpleasant aromas and tastes. We have learned to enjoy this vegetable in the recipe for Sautéed Brussels Sprouts with Nuts. Steamed briefly, split in half, and tossed in some butter, salt, pepper, and fresh lemon juice with any kind of toasted nuts (or even crumbled, crisp bacon), you will change your mind and enjoy these sometimes maligned "mini-cabbages."

- 1/3 cup coarsely chopped toasted nuts (we like pecans or cashews)
- 1-1/2 pounds fresh brussels sprouts, trimmed
- 4 tablespoons butter
- 1 tablespoon olive oil
- 1 small yellow onion, peeled and chopped
- 2 medium garlic cloves, chopped
- 2 teaspoons fresh lemon juice
- salt and fresh-ground black pepper

To toast the nuts, preheat the oven to 350 degrees. Spread the nuts in a baking dish and bake for 8 to 10 minutes or until they begin to take on color. Set aside.

Cook the brussels sprouts in boiling water to cover for about 4 to 5 minutes, or until just tender. Drain and set aside. When cool enough to handle, cut the sprouts in half lengthwise. Set aside.

In a large skillet, heat the butter and oil over medium-high heat. Sauté the onions for about 3 minutes, or until golden. Add the garlic and brussels sprouts and sauté for about 5 minutes, or until the sprouts begin to brown in spots. Drizzle with the lemon juice, add the nuts, and season to taste. Toss again before serving.

Makes 6 servings.

Spinach Rosemary Cakes

SPINACH ROSEMARY CAKES

The recipe for these delicious Spinach Rosemary Cakes is again thanks to the regional (Florida) Whole Foods Market Prepared Foods Coordinator who willingly shared it. These "cakes" can be served as a side vegetable or as a main dish; they are that substantial. Just reading through the ingredient list of minced garlic, fresh rosemary and oregano, feta cheese, and a touch of fresh-grated nutmeg, your mental taste buds are already on alert. For easier handling and shaping, we found it best to put the mixture together several hours ahead, covered and refrigerated.

8 ounces Idaho potato (1 very large), peeled and shredded
1-1/2 boxes (10 ounces each) frozen chopped spinach, defrosted
3/4 tablespoon extra virgin olive oil
2 tablespoons minced garlic
1 sprig fresh rosemary (strip leaves from stem), minced
1 sprig fresh oregano (strip leaves from stem), minced
2/3 cup fresh bread crumbs
1/4 cup feta cheese, crumbled
1/2 teaspoon fresh-ground black pepper
1/4 teaspoon fresh-grated nutmeg
1/2 teaspoon kosher salt
2 tablespoons olive oil, for cooking

Steam the shredded potato for 2 minutes, or just long enough to soften. When cool enough to handle, press out any excess water. Place in a large mixing bowl. Press out excess water from the spinach and add to the potatoes.

In a small skillet, heat the oil over medium heat. Sauté the garlic for about 2 minutes, or until just beginning to brown. Do not let it burn. Allow to cool, then add to the potato/spinach mixture. Add the remaining ingredients, except the oil for cooking, and mix well. (We found our clean hands got the best results.) Refrigerate for at least 3 hours to make shaping easier. Divide the mixture into 6 cakes, about 3 inches across and 3/4 inch thick.

Preheat the oven to 375 degrees. Use a large skillet, preferably nonstick, with an oven-proof handle. If the handle is not oven-proof, wrap it with a double layer of aluminum foil to protect it. Heat the 2 tablespoons oil over medium heat. When hot, sear the cakes for about 1 to 2 minutes a side or until nicely browned. Finish cooking in the center of the oven for about 10 minutes. Serve hot.

Makes 6 cakes.

Sweet Potato Mash

SWEET POTATO MASH

This Sweet Potato Mash was a specialty of the Boca Raton Restaurant, Brassiere Mon Ami. It is the wonderful flavor of pure maple syrup with just enough spices, including the white pepper to put a tiny tang on the taste buds, which makes these sweet potatoes so special. We guarantee that once you have made this recipe, you won't want to serve sweet potatoes any other way. The recipe can be increased or decreased to suit the number of diners. Seasonings can be adjusted to your personal taste with no harm done—except watch the white pepper.

1-1/2 pounds sweet potatoes, peeled and cut into 1-1/2-inch chunks, cooked
3 tablespoons unsalted butter
pinch ground white pepper (or to taste)
kosher salt, to taste
1/8 teaspoon ground nutmeg
1/8 teaspoon ground cinnamon
1-1/2 tablespoons pure maple syrup
1 tablespoon light brown sugar

The sweet potatoes can either be simmered in water to cover for 12 to 15 minutes and drained well, or cooked in a steamer for about 20 minutes. Either way, you want them to be very tender.

Place the hot, cooked potatoes in a large mixing bowl and add the remaining ingredients. Mash thoroughly with a good potato masher. You can use a food processor fitted with the metal blade or an electric mixer, but we like the way the potato masher leaves behind just enough small savory chunks to create a pleasing texture. Serve hot.

Makes 4 servings.

Zucchini Soufflé

ZUCCHINI SOUFFLÉ

Once you taste this Zucchini Soufflé, you will understand why it was one of the most popular dishes offered on a local restaurant's buffet table. It makes your mother's admonition to eat your vegetables easier to do. Slightly on the sweet side thanks to the amount of confectioners' sugar called for (this can be reduced if desired), it could almost be offered as a dessert along with the myriad of other "vegetables as sweets" recipes: Carrot Cookies, Chocolate Beet Cakes, Parsnip Tarts (see p. 383), Pumpkin Drop Cookies, Pinto Bean Pie, just to name a few. This soufflé is easy to make. There is no separation of eggs, and once the zucchini is fully cooked, it is just a matter of whipping everything together.

4 medium zucchini (about 1-1/2 pounds total) ends trimmed and coarsely chopped into about 1/2-inch pieces
2 large eggs
2 cups heavy cream
1 cup confectioners' sugar
1/2 cup corn starch
salt and fresh-ground white pepper, to taste

In a large saucepan, cover the zucchini with water. Bring to a boil over medium-high heat. Reduce the heat to medium-low, cover, and cook for about 10 minutes, or until the zucchini is very soft. Drain well and let cool for 15 minutes.

Preheat the oven to 350 degrees. Lightly butter a 10 by 7 by 2-inch baking dish (1-1/2 quarts).

Transfer the cooled zucchini to a large (deep) mixing bowl. Add the remaining ingredients and beat for 2 minutes with an electric mixer on medium speed. (I indicated a deep bowl since the mixture tends to spatter a bit—on the kitchen counter, walls, and front of cook—due to the zucchini skins.) Pour the mixture into the prepared baking dish and bake in the center of the oven for 35 to 40 minutes or until firm to the touch.

The restaurant does not suggest any topping, but we dusted the top with some confectioners' sugar and a pinch of ground nutmeg just before serving.

Makes 8 servings.

CASSEROLES AND COMBINATIONS

ANDRE SOLTNER'S POTATO PIE

Chef Andre Soltner of the French Culinary Institute and chef-owner of New York's fabled Lutece restaurant for thirty-four years shared this delicious recipe for potato pie with us when he did an article for our Cuisinart magazine some years ago. He informed us that, as children, he and his brother and sister often had it for dinner, accompanied by a green salad. Soltner used his own pastry recipe, but we found the Pillsbury ready-made crusts to be an easy substitute. You will find this a wonderfully filling dish, perfect for dinner. Be sure to add that green salad.

1 box Pillsbury Ready-Made pie crusts
6 ounces smoked slab bacon
1-3/4 pounds all-purpose potatoes, peeled and very thinly (important) sliced
1 teaspoon salt
1/2 teaspoon fresh-ground black pepper
1/2 cup loosely-packed fresh parsley, coarsely chopped
4 hard-cooked eggs, shells removed and sliced evenly with an egg slicer
1/2 cup heavy cream
1 large raw egg, lightly beaten

On a lightly floured surface, roll out one portion of the pie crust into a circle about 12 inches in diameter and about 1/16-inch thick. Press the dough lightly into the bottom and against the sides of a 10-inch tart pan with a removable bottom, leaving about a 1/2 inch overhang. Refrigerate while preparing the filling.

Preheat the oven to 400 degrees.

Cut the bacon into 1-inch slices. Stack the slices and cut into 1/4-inch strips. (FYI, these are called "lardoons" in French.) Fry the lardoons in a medium skillet over high heat for about 4 minutes, or until they are lightly browned. Transfer to paper towels with a slotted spoon.

Rinse the thin-sliced potatoes under cold running water. Drain and dry with paper towels. Transfer them to a 2-quart mixing bowl and sprinkle with the salt and pepper. Toss to mix well.

Arrange about 2/3 of the potatoes on the bottom of the prepared tart shell. Arrange the bacon, parsley, hard-cooked egg slices, and the remaining potato slices on top; and pour the cream over all.

Turn the overhang of dough from the lower crust over the edge of the filling and wet with a pastry brush dipped in water. Roll the remaining pastry portion into a 12-inch circle about 1/16 of an inch thick. Transfer to the top of the pie. Trim the sides to make it fit and press so it adheres to the lower crust. Brush the surface with the beaten egg and decorate by gently pulling a fork across the top in a pinwheel fashion. Cut a 3/4-inch hole in the center of the top crust.

Bake in the center of the oven for 20 minutes. Reduce the heat to 350 degrees and bake for 1 hour more. Reduce the heat to 300 degrees and bake for a final 10 minutes. Let cool on a wire rack for at least 20 minutes before serving.

Makes 6 hearty servings.

BAKED APPLES AND ONIONS

This delicious recipe for Baked Apples and Onions came from a book we have mentioned now and then, *Treasured Recipes from Early New England Kitchens* by the late Marjorie Page Blanchard and published by Harrington's in Vermont in the early '70s. You might recall we worked with Marjorie on her book while managing the Connecticut retail outlet for Harrington's, and we always made copies of the recipe for customers who purchased our famous hams and asked for suggestions for a side dish. Don't wait to make this only for your ham dinner; it is equally at home with other meats, poultry, and even seafood.

- 8 tart apples such as Granny Smith, cored and sliced into rings about 1/4-inch thick
- 8 large sweet onions, peeled and sliced into 1/4-inch-thick rings
- 2 tablespoons unsalted butter
- salt and fresh-ground pepper to taste
- 2 tablespoons sugar
- 1/4 cup hot water

Topping: 1/2 cup cracker crumbs (try Whole Wheat Ritz) tossed with 2 tablespoons melted butter

Preheat the oven to 350 degrees. Butter a deep 2-quart covered baking dish. Arrange half the apple slices in the bottom and cover with half the onions. Dot with half the butter and sprinkle with half the sugar. Repeat the layers. Pour the hot water over all and sprinkle with the buttered crumbs. Cover and bake for 1 to 1-1/4 hours, or until very tender. Remove the cover the last 15 minutes to let the top brown. Makes 6 servings.

BAKED LIMA BEANS

A kind of second cousin to Boston baked beans, Baked Lima Beans is a delicious casserole you will want to serve along with your hamburgers, hot dogs, grilled chicken, fish, or whatever all year long. A food friend who owns a cooking school in Pennsylvania introduced us to this version using the large dried lima beans, and it quickly became a favorite. It includes a cup of sour cream in the baking mixture, which gives the final dish a nice flavor.

1 pound dried lima beans (the large ones are best here)
3 strips lean bacon, diced
1 small onion, chopped
1/3 cup butter, melted
3/4 cup packed light brown sugar
1 tablespoon dry mustard
1/4 cup ketchup
1 cup sour cream
1 tablespoon molasses (we like Grandma's "robust flavor")

Rinse the beans and cover with water by 1-inch in a large bowl. Let sit overnight. Drain well. Put the beans in a large saucepan, cover with water, bring to a boil over medium-high heat and simmer for about 40 minutes or until tender. Drain and rinse under cold water.

In a small skillet, cook the bacon over medium heat for about 3 to 4 minutes, or until crisp. Transfer the bacon to paper towels to drain. Leave about a tablespoon of bacon fat in the skillet and sauté the onions for about 2 minutes, or until softened. Transfer to a large bowl and cool completely.

Preheat the oven to 350 degrees. Add the remaining ingredients, except the beans, to the onions and mix well. Stir in the beans. Transfer to a 2-quart baking dish and bake for about an hour, or until bubbly and thick.

Makes 6 servings.

BISCUITS AND GRAVY

When asked some years ago for a biscuits and gravy recipe, it brought back memories of summers spent on the Powell's farm in Winnebago, Illinois. I accumulated a wealth of knowledge from the age of four on, including how to milk a cow, how to pluck a freshly killed chicken, how to collect the daily production of eggs without being pecked, and to steer clear of mother pigs, among other things. But I enjoyed most of all learning to cook on a wood-burning stove. Jean Powell's biscuits and gravy were one of the favorites. She made her own sausage and made her delicious gravy in an old cast iron pot in which she had just fried the chicken. The brown bits scraped up from the bottom added yet more flavor, but you will agree that the recipe given here following Jean's basic rules is tasty and comforting as it is.

1 tablespoon vegetable oil
1 medium onion, finely chopped
1 garlic clove, finely chopped
8 ounces spicy bulk sausage (we used Jimmy Dean's hot sausage)
1/2 teaspoon dried sage
1/2 teaspoon dried thyme

1/3 cup plus 1 tablespoon all-purpose flour
3 cups milk
salt and fresh-ground black pepper, to taste
1 tablespoon chopped parsley, optional, but adds color
1 can (7-1/2 ounces) Pillsbury Refrigerated Biscuits*

Heat the oil in a large skillet over medium heat. Sauté the onions and garlic until soft but not brown, about 3 minutes. Add the sausage, breaking it up with a spoon, and cook, stirring occasionally, until the sausage is lightly browned, about 5 minutes. There should be about 3 tablespoons of fat in the skillet. If more than 3 tablespoons, drain off excess. If less, add enough vegetable oil to make 3 tablespoons.

Stir in the flour, sage, and thyme. Add the milk and cook, stirring until thickened. Season to taste. Just before serving, stir in the parsley.

Meanwhile, bake the biscuits according to the package directions. Since there are ten biscuits in the tube, you will have four left over to heat and serve for breakfast!

To serve, split 6 biscuits and place on individual serving plates. Divide the gravy over them.

Makes 6 servings.

*Substitute your own biscuit recipe, if you wish. However, the Pillsbury biscuits are excellent and so convenient.

BROWNED WHITE RICE CASSEROLE

This Browned White Rice Casserole is one we always like to make for a dinner party. It is so incredibly delicious we have found that some guests take more than one helping. That means, of course, that even though the recipe specifies 10 servings, count on 8 at the very most. We also like the fact that the rice can be browned several hours before you add the remaining ingredients and finish it in the oven. You can use the time to address your attention to other dinner preparations.

1/2 cup unsalted butter
2 cups uncooked white rice
  (not instant)
2 teaspoons salt
1/4 teaspoon fresh-ground
  black pepper

2 cans (14-1/2 ounces each)
  beef broth
2 cups water
1/2 cup chopped, blanched
  almonds

In a large skillet, melt the butter over medium-low heat. Add the rice and cook, stirring often, for about 5 to 7 minutes, or until the rice is golden brown. Place in a 2-quart casserole and sprinkle with the salt and pepper. This can be prepared to this point several hours ahead.

When ready to bake, preheat the oven to 300 degrees. Add the beef broth, water and chopped nuts to the browned rice and mix gently but well. Bake in the center of the oven for 1 hour and 15 minutes. Do not stir. All the liquid should have evaporated, and the rice will be moist and savory.

Makes 10 servings.

CASSEROLE CARROTS

This Casserole Carrots recipe will remind you of that ever-popular green bean casserole with its French-fried onion topping. Here, the cooked carrots are mixed into a flavorful cream sauce (not canned soup). The dry mustard gives it a nice tang and the Parmesan cheese additional flavor. This is definitely a tasty way to get your vitamin A.

2 pounds carrots
2 tablespoons unsalted butter
2 tablespoons all-purpose flour
3/4 teaspoon dry mustard
Salt and fresh-ground white pepper to taste
1/4 teaspoon paprika
2 cups whole milk
1/4 cup fresh-grated Parmesan cheese
3/4 cup canned French-fried onions

Peel the carrots and cut on the diagonal into 1/4-inch pieces. Place in a large pot, cover with water, and bring to a boil over medium-high heat. Reduce the heat, cover, and simmer about 10 minutes, or until just tender. Drain well. Set aside.

In the same pot, melt the butter over medium heat. Stir in the flour, dry mustard, salt, pepper and paprika. Let bubble for a minute. Gradually add the milk, using a whisk to prevent lumps. Continue cooking and whisking until the mixture thickens and begins to bubble. Stir in the cheese then carefully fold in the cooked carrots.

Preheat the oven to 350 degrees. Lightly grease a 1-1/2-quart casserole. Transfer carrot mixture to the casserole, cover and bake in the center of the oven for about 20 minutes, or until bubbling. Uncover and sprinkle with the French-fried onions. Continue baking, uncovered, for about 5 minutes.

Makes 8 servings.

CASSOLETTE DE FRUITS DE MER (SEAFOOD CASSEROLE)

(Seafood Casserole)
Cassolette De Fruits De Mer

You will find that the flavors of this Seafood Casserole (or cassolette) are remarkable. Even though the reduced sauce is intense, the distinct flavor of the individual seafoods (scallops, shrimp and crabmeat) comes through. The recipe can be made several hours ahead and refrigerated, covered, until ready to heat through. We found this to be a wonderfully rich and filling entrée that needed only a green salad and some crusty French bread to serve what can only be described as a "meal made in heaven." That is an overused cliché, but no other description seems as appropriate for this unusual dish.

4 tablespoons butter, divided
2 tablespoons all-purpose flour
1/4 cup virgin olive oil
8 ounces sea scallops, rinsed, dried and small mussel on the side removed (you may want to cut them in half if they are large)
8 ounces cleaned and deveined medium shrimp
8 ounces crabmeat
1 teaspoon tomato paste
1-1/4 cups Cabernet wine
1 cup heavy cream
2 tablespoons fresh lemon juice
salt and cayenne pepper to taste
3/4 cup shredded Swiss cheese

Mix 2 tablespoons of the butter and the flour together (a beurre manie). Reserve.

Melt the remaining butter with the oil in a large skillet over medium-high heat. Sauté the scallops, shrimp, and crabmeat for 2 minutes. Remove with a slotted spoon to paper towels.

Stir the tomato paste and wine into the skillet, and reduce the mixture by half. This will take about 12 minutes. Halfway through the reduction, return the seafood to the skillet and continue cooking over moderate heat until the reduction is complete, stirring occasionally.

When the reduction is complete, pour in the cream, lemon juice, salt and cayenne pepper. Stir in the beurre manie, 2 teaspoons at a time, letting it cook, stirring, for a minute after each addition. Keep adding the beurre manie until the sauce is lightly thickened. Taste for seasonings.

Preheat the oven to 350 degrees. Pour the seafood mixture into a lightly buttered 1-1/2 to 2-quart casserole dish. Sprinkle the top with the cheese and bake in the center of the oven until heated through and the cheese has melted, about 15 minutes. Serve immediately.

If you have made the dish ahead, remove from the refrigerator 30 minutes before baking, then bake until heated through: about 20 minutes.

Makes 6 servings.

COOKED CHICKEN OR TURKEY LOAF

Here is yet another savory way to utilize that leftover chicken or turkey—in a Cooked Chicken or Turkey Loaf. The recipe that has been our guide over the years is from an early 1940s edition of one of those cookbook bibles: *The Joy of Cooking* (Bobbs-Merrill). There have been numerous jokes about leftovers, but one of our favorites was written by Calvin Trillin—the remarkably diverse journalist, humorist, food writer, poet, memoirist, and novelist. To quote: "The most remarkable thing about my mother is that for thirty years she served the family nothing but leftovers. We had a team of anthropologists looking for the original meal, but it was never found."

1 tablespoon butter
1-1/2 tablespoons fine-chopped onions
1 tablespoon fine-diced green or red bell peppers
2 tablespoons fine-diced celery
2-1/2 cups fine-diced cooked turkey or chicken
salt and fresh-ground black pepper, to taste
1/8 teaspoon rubbed sage, optional
1 cup cracker crumbs (we like crushed Ritz brand crackers for their buttery flavor)
3/4 cup leftover turkey or chicken gravy*
3/4 cup milk
2 large eggs, beaten
water

Preheat the oven to 350 degrees. Spray an 8 by 4 by 2-1/2-inch loaf pan well with no-stick cooking spray.

In a medium skillet, melt the butter over medium heat. Sauté the onions, peppers, and celery about 2 minutes or until softened and fragrant. Let cool.

In a large mixing bowl, combine all ingredients (except water) well and pack into the prepared loaf pan. Place loaf pan in a larger pan on the middle oven shelf. Pour hot water into the larger pan so that it comes about halfway up the loaf pan. Bake about 45 minutes, or until firm and lightly browned. Remove from the water bath and unmold the loaf onto a serving platter.

Makes about 6 servings.

*If you don't have leftover gravy, use a packaged mix or thicken 3/4 cup canned chicken broth with 1-1/2 tablespoons all-purpose flour. This is nice served with additional leftover or prepared gravy with some chopped parsley or chives stirred in.

CORN RELISH

Corn Relish is just one of the many wonderful so-called sweets-and-sours that can be traced back to descendants of eighteenth-century German settlers. We make this in pint jars, and it does make wonderful gifts for your noncooking friends. We like the two-piece vacuum caps (lids and screw bands). You can choose large or small jars, whichever are most useful for you. This recipe came from our friends in Pennsylvania and is absolutely delicious. If you can't get fresh corn, frozen corn works well. We give you some canning tips at the end of the recipe.

2 medium onions, peeled, and finely chopped	8 cups fresh or defrosted frozen corn kernels
2 medium red peppers, cored, seeded, and finely chopped	3 cups cider vinegar
	1 cup water
	1-1/2 cups sugar
2 medium green peppers, cored, seeded, and finely chopped	2 teaspoons salt
	2 teaspoons dry mustard
	1 teaspoon turmeric
2 medium ribs celery, trimmed and finely sliced	2 teaspoons celery seed
	2 teaspoons mustard seed

Combine all the ingredients in a large saucepot. Bring to a boil over medium-high heat, stirring often. Reduce the heat to low and simmer, uncovered, for 20 minutes, stirring occasionally.

Immediately ladle the mixture into prepared hot jars (see below), leaving about 1/4 inch of headspace, and vacuum seal according to the jar manufacturer's directions. Place the jars in a boiling water bath for 15 minutes. Remove with tongs and cool to room temperature on wire racks covered with kitchen towels. Makes about 14 cups.

Some useful canning tips:

1. Wash your jars and lids in warm, soapy water and rinse thoroughly.
2. Simmer the lids and screw bands for 6 minutes, then add the rinsed jars to the simmering water. Keep all in the water until you are ready to fill the jars.
3. Fill the jars leaving the recommended headspace. If any air bubbles appear probe down the side of the jar with a wooden or plastic chopstick to release them.

4. Wipe the top edge of each jar with a damp cloth before sealing and screw the band on firmly by hand.
5. Use a water-bath canner with a rack or substitute a large stock pot fitted with a rack. The jars should be covered with 1 to 2 inches of water with an additional 1 to 2 inches of space for the water to boil. Leave ample space between the jars. Place the lid on the pot and start timing when the water comes to a boil. The water should boil gently and steadily for the time required.
6. Remove the jars with tongs to wire racks covered with kitchen towels. You should hear a "ping" as they cool, indication that a seal has formed. When completely cool remove the screw bands and store the jars in a cool, dark place. For best flavor, wait about 10 days before using.

FISH SOUFFLÉ WITH MUSTARD SAUCE
(An Elegant Aftermath)

While working at Cuisinarts, we were frequently asked for ways to use leftover fish to make it appealing. Thanks to the late Helen McCully, the longtime food editor of *House Beautiful* who graciously helped us in our effort to adapt some of the recipes from her book (*Waste Not, Want Not*—published by Random House back in the '70s) to the food processor, one of our favorite adaptations was this Fish Soufflé. It utilizes a good 1-1/2 cups of leftover flaked fish (we recommend mild white fish such as sole, orange roughy, snapper, or tilapia, for instance) in addition to some leftover mashed potatoes. Served with a delicious Mustard Sauce, your friends and family will be delighted with this elegant way to use that leftover fish. You can call it an "elegant aftermath."

Soufflé:

- 2 small yellow onions, peeled and quartered
- 3 tablespoons butter
- 1 cup cold water
- 1 clove garlic, peeled
- 1-1/2 cups leftover flaked mild fish (see introduction)
- 2 cups leftover mashed potatoes
- 4 large eggs, separated
- Salt and fresh-ground pepper to taste
- 2 large egg whites
- Mustard Sauce (recipe given)

Preheat the oven to 375 degrees. Butter a 1-1/2 quart soufflé dish well and refrigerate it while preparing the soufflé.

In a food processor fitted with the metal blade, process the onions until finely chopped. In a skillet, melt the butter over medium-high heat. Add the onions and water and bring to a boil. Continue boiling until all the water has evaporated and the onions are very soft.

Again in the food processor fitted with the metal blade, fine-chop the garlic. Add the fish, potatoes, cooked onions, egg yolks, and seasonings. Process until pureed. Transfer to a large mixing bowl.

In a clean bowl, beat the egg whites (all 6) with an electric mixer until they hold firm, shiny peaks. Using a wire whisk, beat about a third of the egg whites into the fish mixture. Spoon over the remaining whites and fold in gently with a spatula. Transfer to the prepared soufflé dish. Place on a baking sheet in the center of the oven and bake for 30 to 40 minutes or until the soufflé has risen and is firm. Serve at once with the mustard sauce.

Makes 6 servings.

Mustard Sauce:

1 tablespoon butter	1 tablespoon Dijon mustard
1 tablespoon flour	salt and fresh-ground pepper
1 cup whole milk	to taste

In a heavy saucepan, melt the butter over low heat. Stir in the flour and cook, stirring constantly until the mixture froths (about 2 minutes) without browning. Remove from the heat and add the milk. Beat well with a wire whisk to incorporate the roux. Beat in the mustard. Place over medium heat and cook, still whisking, until the sauce comes to a boil. Boil for about 1 minute, whisking constantly. Remove from the heat and season to taste.

Makes about 1 cup.

Gorgonzola
Polenta

GORGONZOLA POLENTA

From a popular restaurant in Florida comes this Gorgonzola Polenta, which has been described as "out of this world." Polenta, originally an import from northern Italy, is also known in the South (and elsewhere) as cornmeal mush. It can be served as a side dish, as it is in the restaurant, or as the base of a main dish served with spaghetti or mushroom sauce, or layered with cheese and sausage and baked, or chilled until firm, cut into shapes then fried until brown and served with molasses, jam, maple syrup or sour cream as a breakfast or brunch dish. (And it is now available ready made.) It is versatile! Depending on the coarseness of your polenta (cornmeal) you may have to adjust the amount of chicken broth. The finer the grind, the more liquid it absorbs.

- 2 tablespoons unsalted butter
- 1 medium clove garlic, chopped
- 2 to 3 cups chicken broth (we used 3 teaspoons instant chicken bouillon granules dissolved in 3 cups hot water)
- 1 cup instant polenta
- 1 teaspoon kosher salt
- 1/2 teaspoon fresh-ground black pepper
- 1/4 cup crumbled Gorgonzola cheese (extra for garnish, if desired)
- 3 tablespoons chopped scallions (white and some green part)

In a large saucepot, melt the butter over medium heat. Add the garlic and cook, stirring for about 2 minutes, or until the garlic becomes fragrant and turns translucent. Add 2 cups of the chicken broth and bring to a boil. Slowly whisk in the polenta and season with the salt and pepper. (Watch the salt since the chicken broth and cheese will add to the saltiness.)

Continue to stir the polenta for about 5 minutes, or until it has thickened. If the polenta seems too thick (it should be the consistency of a serving of grits or cream of wheat), add the additional chicken broth until it reaches the desired consistency. Remove from the heat, and stir in the Gorgonzola cheese and chopped scallions. (You can garnish the polenta with additional Gorgonzola cheese if you wish.)

Makes 6 servings.

HAM AND MAC BAKE

This is a recipe that has survived several generations. We attribute Ham and Mac Bake's survival to the fact that it is an easy, inexpensive way to serve six or more hungry people. Thanks to our thrifty grandmother, we could always count on enjoying it soon after a Sunday dinner of baked ham. (We never referred to it as having leftovers.) We are sure many grandmothers had this comforting oldie in their repertoires.

1 cup (about 3-1/2 ounces) uncooked elbow macaroni
1/4 cup plus 2 tablespoons butter, divided
1/4 cup all-purpose flour
2 tablespoons packed light brown sugar
1 tablespoon or to taste, prepared mustard (grandma used yellow, we prefer Dijon)
2 cups whole milk
1/2 cup shredded Cheddar cheese, optional but highly recommended
salt and fresh-ground black pepper to taste
2 cups diced, fully cooked ham
2 cups thin-sliced peeled apples
1-1/2 cups fresh bread crumbs

Cook the macaroni according to package directions. Drain well and reserve.

Preheat the oven to 350 degrees. In a large saucepan, melt 1/4 cup of the butter over medium heat. Stir in the flour, brown sugar and mustard. Slowly add the milk, stirring or whisking constantly, until the mixture thickens and bubbles.

Stir in the cheese and add salt and pepper. Stir in the cooked macaroni, ham and apples. Transfer the mixture to a 2-quart casserole.

Melt the 2 tablespoons remaining butter, combine with the bread crumbs and sprinkle evenly over the top. Bake, uncovered, in the center of the oven about 35 to 40 minutes or until bubbly and the topping is slightly brown.

Makes 6 servings.

HASH BROWN CASSEROLE

If you have eaten at any of the Cracker Barrel restaurants, you may have enjoyed something they called Potato Breakfast Casserole. Chains are not likely to want to share their recipes, but a traveling friend and fellow cook who always "pigged out" on that casserole came up with what we decided was a good clone. The Colby cheese is a must. It is a soft, mellow orange Cheddar that adds loads of wonderful flavor to the recipe.

- 1 bag (about 24 to 26 ounces) frozen hash brown potatoes
- 2 cups shredded Colby cheese
- 1/2 cup minced onions
- 1 cup milk
- 1/2 cup beef broth (we use a generous 1/2 teaspoon of Better Than Bouillon beef base and 1/2 cup warm water)
- 4 tablespoons melted butter, divided
- 1/2 teaspoon coarse-ground garlic powder (try Lawry's Coarse Ground with Parsley)
- 1 teaspoon salt
- fresh-ground black pepper, to taste

In a large bowl, combine the potatoes, cheese, and onions. Toss to mix. In another bowl, whisk together the milk, beef broth, 2 tablespoons of the butter, the garlic powder, salt, and pepper. Pour this mixture over the potato mixture and toss well.

Preheat the oven to 400 degrees.

In a large oven-going skillet*, heat the remaining butter over medium-high heat. Add the potato mixture and cook, stirring occasionally until heated through and the cheese has melted. Place the skillet in the oven and bake for about 45 to 50 minutes, or until the top is a dark brown. You can run under the broiler, if necessary.

Makes 6 servings.

*If the handle of your skillet cannot withstand the oven heat, wrap it well with several layers of aluminum foil.

Italian Easter Pie (Pizza Rustica)

ITALIAN EASTER PIE (PIZZA RUSTICA)

In spite of the name, we recommend not waiting for Easter to make this delicious dish. When a local restaurant, Lucarella's, shared this recipe, it called for basket cheese, which is not generally available for the home baker. One of our Italian baker friends told us that you can substitute any semihard or fresh cheese and suggested provolone, Swiss, Jarlsberg, Gruyere, or mozzarella. With the inclusion of all the other tasty ingredients, this is a recipe that travels well and is a deliciously successful dish to take on picnics or tailgate parties or neighborhood bring-a-dish suppers, or . . . . It is as tasty at room temperature as it is served warm.

pastry for a double-crust pie*
3 large eggs
1-1/2 pounds ricotta cheese (about 3 cups)
6 ounces Italian sausage (hot or sweet—your choice) cut into 1/4-inch dice
6 ounces pepperoni, cut into 1/4-inch dice
1 small chicken breast (about 4 ounces) cut into 1/4-inch dice
2 hard-cooked eggs, diced
2 heaping tablespoons fresh-grated Parmesan cheese
4 ounces provolone (or Swiss, mozzarella, Jarlsberg, Gruyere—your choice) cut into 1/4-inch dice
1/2 teaspoon fresh-ground black pepper
3 ounces thin-sliced prosciutto

Preheat the oven to 350 degrees. Line a 9-inch pie pan with half of the pastry.

In a large mixing bowl, whisk the eggs until light. Whisk in the ricotta cheese. Add the remaining ingredients except the prosciutto, mixing well. Ladle half of the mixture into the prepared pie pan. Layer half the prosciutto over the top. Ladle in the rest of the mixture, spreading evenly, then cover with the remaining prosciutto.

Place the rest of the pastry over the top, crimping the edges well. Cut several decorative slashes in the top crust to allow steam to escape. Because the pie is very full, we advise you to place it on a baking sheet to catch any bubbling over as it bakes and expands.

Bake in the center of the oven for 1-1/2 hours or until a knife inserted in the center comes out clean. Remove to a wire rack and let cool for 15 to 20 minutes before slicing. You may even want to bring it to room temperature. Makes it easier to slice.

Makes 12 servings.

*We use the Pillsbury ready-made pie crusts found in the refrigerator section of the market.

KING RANCH CASSEROLE

Back in the early '80s, our friend Anne Greer—cookbook author and cooking teacher who hailed from San Antonio, Texas—was one of the first to champion a hybrid of Mexican and American cooking styles called Tex-Mex cuisine. Of all the recipes for a delicious Tex-Mex dish called King Ranch Casserole that we tried, Anne's was by far the best. It is delightfully spicy (but not overwhelming) with its judicious amounts of fresh chili peppers, chili powder, and a wealth of other savory ingredients and spices. We found, too, that cooked turkey as well as the originally-called-for cooked chicken is most satisfactory. Don't let the long list of ingredients deter you from making this outstanding casserole. Once lined up, it goes together quickly and can be prepared ahead before the final baking.

- 6 tablespoons unsalted butter, divided
- 1 small fresh red pepper trimmed, seeded, quartered and thinly sliced
- 2 small fresh poblano chili peppers (trimmed, seeded, deveined, halved, and thinly sliced)
- 1 medium onion, coarsely chopped
- 8 ounces fresh mushrooms, thinly sliced
- 1 medium clove garlic, minced
- 2 cups canned, diced tomatoes, with juice
- 2 tablespoons all-purpose flour
- 2 tablespoons cornstarch
- 2 cups chicken stock
- 1 cup milk
- 1/2 teaspoon salt
- 1/4 teaspoon fresh-ground white pepper
- 1/2 teaspoon chili powder
- 1 teaspoon dried oregano
- 1/4 teaspoon ground cumin
- dash of Tabasco
- 1/4 cup heavy cream
- 10 eight-inch corn tortillas
- 2 cups diced cooked chicken or turkey
- 3 cups shredded Monterey Jack or Cheddar cheese
- 2 tablespoons minced fresh cilantro, for garnish

In a large skillet, melt 1 tablespoon of the butter over medium-high heat. Add the red and poblano peppers, the onions, mushrooms, and garlic. Cook, stirring, for about 2 minutes. Do not overcook. You want the peppers to remain fairly crisp. Add the tomatoes and juice and stir well. Remove from the heat and reserve.

In a large saucepan, melt the remaining butter over medium heat. Stir in the flour and cornstarch. Slowly add the chicken stock and milk, stirring constantly.

Continue cooking and stirring until the sauce has the consistency of heavy cream. Stir in the seasonings and heavy cream. Continue cooking and stirring for 1 minute more. Remove from the heat.

Preheat the oven to 350 degrees. Butter an 11 by 9 by 2-inch baking pan. Layer half of the tortillas on the bottom. Put half the chicken on top, then spoon over about a third of the sauce. Add half the cheese, then half the vegetable mixture and another third of the sauce. Repeat with the remaining tortillas, chicken, sauce, and vegetables, ending with cheese. The casserole can be prepared ahead to this point, covered and refrigerated.

Bake in the center of the oven for 30 to 35 minutes, or until heated through and bubbly. If it has been refrigerated, add about another 10 minutes to the baking time. Garnish with minced cilantro before serving.

Makes 8 servings.

MACARONI CROQUETTES

It has always amazed us how often good recipes keep resurfacing over the years. Our great-aunt Annie Gustafson would be pleased to know that her recipe for Macaroni Croquettes, which she served every Sunday night for years, was recently resurrected when some friends mentioned remembering it. After twenty-five years, we tracked the recipe down. Retesting and sampling it with our friends was most enjoyable. We had almost forgotten how comforting this combination of cooked macaroni, chopped ham, and simple seasonings bound with a perfectly flavored thick white sauce could be. The simple Tomato Sauce with fresh basil adds another dimension to your enjoyment of these croquettes. We won't wait another twenty-five years to make these again!

Croquettes:

- 3 tablespoons unsalted butter
- 1 small shallot, minced
- 5 tablespoons all-purpose flour
- 1 teaspoon dry mustard
- 1 cup milk
- 3 tablespoons fresh-grated Parmesan cheese
- salt and white pepper, to taste
- 2 cups cooked macaroni, well-drained
- 1-1/2 cups medium-chopped cooked ham
- 1 large egg
- 2 teaspoons water
- 1 cup dry bread crumbs
- vegetable oil for frying

Tomato Sauce:

- 1 cup tomato sauce
- 2 teaspoons sugar
- 2 tablespoons julienned fresh basil
- salt to taste

Melt the butter in a medium saucepan over medium heat. Sauté the shallot until soft—about 2 minutes. Stir in the flour and let bubble, stirring for 1 minute. Stir in the mustard then the milk and Parmesan cheese. Stir rapidly and thoroughly while the mixture thickens. It will be very thick and come away from the sides of the pan just like chou paste. Season to taste. Remove from the heat and stir in the macaroni and chopped ham. Make sure the ingredients are well distributed. Spread the mixture in a pie plate and refrigerate until well chilled, about 2 hours.

To complete the croquettes (they can be made several hours ahead and refrigerated until ready to fry), beat the egg with the water in a small bowl until foamy. Place the crumbs in another bowl. Shape the macaroni mixture into 8 discs, about 1/2 to 3/4 inch thick. Dip each in the egg mixture, then the crumbs. Place on a plate and refrigerate until ready to finish cooking.

To make the tomato sauce, in a small saucepan, stir all the ingredients together and heat through over medium heat. Keep warm until serving.

To finish the croquettes, heat about 1/2 inch of vegetable oil in a large skillet over medium heat. Fry the croquettes until golden brown on both sides, about 3 minutes a side. Transfer to paper towels to drain.

To serve, divide the croquettes among 4 warm serving dishes and spoon about 1/4 cup tomato sauce over each serving. Makes 4 servings.

"NO CREAM" CREAM

This is a great "No Cream" Cream mixture you can add to all kinds of savory soups and sauces to simulate the richness and "mouthfeel" of heavy cream. We like to use it in lieu of heavy cream, for instance, when making creamed vegetables. You will find many other uses for this creamy mixture. It makes about 2-1/2 cups and keeps well refrigerated for up to a week. You can thank the Fetzer wine people for first introducing this low-fat "No Cream" Cream years ago.

2 teaspoons olive oil
1/2 cup chopped onions
1/3 cup short grain rice
1 cup chardonnay wine

3 cups chicken or vegetable stock or broth (preferably low-fat, such as the Swanson brand)
salt and fresh-ground pepper to taste

In a heavy saucepan, heat the oil over medium heat. Add the onions and sauté for about 3 minutes, or until soft but not brown. Stir in the rice and wine and bring to a boil. Reduce the heat to low, cover, and simmer about 25 minutes or until the liquid is absorbed. Cool slightly.

Transfer the mixture to a food processor fitted with the metal blade. With the motor running, pour the stock or broth slowly through the feed tube until the mixture reaches a "creamy" consistency. (You may not need all the broth.) Season to taste. Keep refrigerated until using.

Makes about 2-1/2 cups.

ONION SHORTCAKE

From a Connecticut neighbor years ago comes this Onion Shortcake—which could also be called Shortcake Pie, with its shortcake dough patted onto the bottom of a pie dish and the onion-egg mixture over the top. Whatever you wish to call it, it can be served on its own, as a nice luncheon or supper dish, or as a side dish with grilled meats or fish. The buttermilk makes a nice soft "crust."

Shortcake Crust:

1 cup all-purpose flour
2 teaspoons baking powder
1 teaspoon salt

3 tablespoons cold butter
1/4 to 1/3 cup buttermilk

Filling:

3 cups sliced onions
1 large egg
1/2 cup sour cream

1/2 teaspoon ground mace
salt and fresh-ground pepper
to taste

To make the crust, in a mixing bowl, whisk together the flour, baking powder and salt. Work in the butter with (clean) fingertips until the mixture resembles coarse meal. Add the buttermilk gradually, mixing just until a slightly sticky dough is formed. Turn out onto a floured surface and knead briefly until smooth. Pat the dough into a round about 1/2-inch thick and just large enough to fit into an 8-inch pie dish. Set aside.

To make the filling, preheat the oven to 400 degrees. Place the onions in a large saucepan and just cover with water. Bring to a boil over medium-high heat, reduce the heat to medium-low and simmer for about 8 minutes or until they are soft but not mushy. Drain well.

Place the onions over the dough, covering it completely. In a small bowl, whisk together the egg, sour cream, mace, and salt and pepper. Pour over the onions. Bake in the center of the oven for about 25 to 30 minutes or until set.

Makes 4 servings.

RICHARD SAX'S COMFORTING CAFETERIA-STYLE MACARONI AND CHEESE

It seems as if someone is always looking for a "good and easy" recipe for Macaroni and Cheese. There are as many variations on the subject as there are cookbooks and cooks. (And don't forget all those boxed and bagged versions too.) Our choice for one of the best and easiest, since it does not require making a white sauce, is a recipe from a friend—the late Richard Sax (cook, food writer, and teacher extraordinaire). He called his recipe a Comforting Cafeteria-Style Macaroni and Cheese, and indeed, it is comforting. For a change of taste, you might try substituting part of the Cheddar cheese with some jalapeno-spiked Jack cheese or other semisoft cheese of your choice. It's fun to vary the flavor.

1-1/2 cups milk
1-1/2 teaspoons dry mustard
1 teaspoon Worcestershire sauce
3/4 teaspoon salt
dash hot pepper sauce
8 ounces elbow macaroni
3-1/2 tablespoons unsalted butter, divided
1 large egg, lightly beaten
3-1/2 cups grated sharp Cheddar cheese
1/2 cup fresh bread crumbs
1/2 teaspoon paprika

Preheat the oven to 350 degrees. Butter a shallow 2-quart baking or gratin dish.

In a small heavy saucepan, bring the milk to a simmer over moderate heat. Remove from the heat and stir in the mustard, Worcestershire sauce, salt, and hot pepper sauce. Set the seasoned milk aside.

In a large pot of boiling salted water, cook the macaroni until tender but still firm, about 8 minutes. Drain well. Transfer to a medium bowl. Add 1-1/2 tablespoons of the butter and the egg and mix well. Stir in 3 cups of the Cheddar cheese.

Spread the macaroni evenly in the buttered baking dish. Pour the reserved seasoned milk over the macaroni and sprinkle with the remaining ½ cup cheese.

In a small skillet, melt the remaining 2 tablespoons butter over moderate heat. Stir in the bread crumbs until well coated. Scatter the buttered crumbs evenly over the macaroni and sprinkle with the paprika.

Bake in the center of the oven for about 30 minutes, or until the macaroni is bubbling and lightly colored. If you wish to brown the crumbs further, heat the broiler and broil the mixture about 6 inches from the heat for a minute or two.

Makes about 6 servings.

SPAGHETTI PIZZA PIE

If you have teenagers, or even if you don't, we guarantee this Spaghetti Pizza Pie will please all takers. (A husband who always claimed he disliked any form of pasta cleaned his plate and asked for seconds!) The unlikely source of this recipe was in our doctor's office where we began a conversation with another patient over food, of course. The conversation ended with him scribbling this "pizza pie" recipe down for us just before he left. Once you cook your pasta and the ground beef, it takes just a minute to assemble, 30 minutes to bake, and dinner is ready. Just remember the green or fruit salad and some crisp Italian bread.

8 ounces spaghetti, cooked and well drained
1/2 cup fresh-grated Parmesan cheese
2 large eggs, lightly beaten

1 pound lean ground beef, cooked and well drained
3 cups pasta sauce, divided (we use the Ragu brand)
8 ounces shredded mozzarella cheese (about 2 cups)

Preheat the oven to 350 degrees. Lightly grease a 9-inch pie plate

In a large bowl, combine the spaghetti, Parmesan cheese, and eggs. Spread over the bottom and up the sides of the prepared pie plate. Mix the cooked beef with 2 cups of the pasta sauce and spoon over the spaghetti. Sprinkle with the mozzarella cheese.

Bake in the center of the oven for about 30 minutes, or until bubbling and thoroughly cooked through. Let stand for about 5 minutes before cutting and serving.

To serve, place about 2 tablespoons of the remaining pasta sauce on each of 8 serving dishes. Place a slice of the pizza pie on each.

Makes 8 servings.

MAIN DISHES
(RED MEAT)

Book's Veal Stew

BOOKS' VEAL STEW

Notice the first ingredient called for is veal cheeks. Chef/co-owner Jon Howe told us that beef cheeks could also be substituted, but not to even think about substituting stew meat. You won't come close to the same tender and tasty results. It is the fatty, gelatinous nature of these cheeks that make it the perfect meat for braising. Back in the '80s when we at Cuisinarts needed beef cheeks to test a recipe called Daube de Joue de Boeuf (Braised Beef Cheeks), we had to order them from somewhere in the Midwest. Cheeks and lips of livestock were usually considered meat byproducts and were mainly used ground for sausage, franks, etc. Even though they have now moved more into the mainstream of innovative restaurants, you may still have to deal with your local meat purveyor rather than the supermarket, however.

3 pounds veal cheek meat
kosher salt and fresh-ground
    black pepper
3 tablespoons olive oil, divided
2 large garlic cloves, peeled
    and crushed
1 medium onion, peeled and
    diced
1 large carrot, peeled and
    diced
1 large celery rib, diced
2 large shallots, peeled and
    diced
1 cup dry white wine

3 tablespoons tomato paste
3 cups chicken broth (we
    used 3 heaping teaspoons
    Better Than Bouillon
    chicken base and 3 cups
    hot water)
3 cups additional water
1 whole clove
1 whole bay leaf
1 large sprig fresh thyme
2 tablespoons unsalted butter
1/2 cup chopped fresh flat leaf
    parsley

Preheat the oven to 350 degrees.

Trim the excess fat from the veal cheeks and cut each piece into 1 to 1-1/2-inch cubes. In a heavy ovenproof pan, heat 2 tablespoons of the olive oil over medium-high heat. Sprinkle the veal cubes with salt and pepper and brown them in the hot pan. (You can do them all at once, just keep rotating them frequently.) Remove with a slotted spoon to a platter.

Add the remaining tablespoon of oil, the garlic, onions, carrots, celery, and shallots. Cook, stirring frequently, for about 10 minutes, or until the vegetables are soft. Remove to the same platter with the veal.

Deglaze the pan with the white wine and reduce by half. Stir in the tomato paste, chicken broth, and water. Return the veal and vegetables to the pan; add the clove, bay leaf, and fresh thyme sprig; and bring to a simmer on the stove top. Transfer the pan, uncovered, to the center of the oven and let it simmer gently for 2-1/2 to 3 hours, or until the meat is fork tender. Stir the mixture about every 30 minutes.

The broth should be reduced by about half at this point and have some body to it. Remove the bay leaf and thyme sprig. Stir in the butter and parsley and serve. (We like to serve it over cooked rice, which is the perfect vehicle with which to soak up the marvelous broth.)

Makes 8 servings.

BRANDY BURGERS

Years ago, our cul-de-sac neighborhood in Connecticut held periodic cookouts or impromptu potlucks during the summer months. One of the favorite foods contributed by a neighbor was her Brandy Burgers. We were delighted to add the recipe to our files. We like to serve this combination of beef and ham, with other savory ingredients, in the sautéed burgers, drizzled with a heady apricot brandy sauce when we want to add some class to a hamburger dinner. You can serve the burgers as is, of course, or in a bun.

4 tablespoons unsalted butter, divided
2 small shallots, finely chopped
1 pound lean ground beef
1/4 pound cooked ham, finely ground
1/4 cup fresh bread crumbs
1/4 cup ice water
1 large egg, slightly beaten
1/4 teaspoon dried thyme, crushed before adding
fresh-ground pepper, to taste
1/4 cup all-purpose flour
2 tablespoons vegetable oil
1/4 cup beef stock (we use 1/4 teaspoon Better Than Bouillon base and 1/4 cup hot water)
1/4 cup apricot flavored brandy
2 tablespoons cold butter, cut into 4 pieces
chopped parsley, for garnish

Melt 2 tablespoons of the butter in a medium skillet, preferably nonstick. Sauté the shallots for about 2 minutes or until soft. Transfer with a slotted spoon to a large bowl. Let cool for 10 minutes. Wipe out the skillet with paper towels and set aside.

Add the remaining 2 tablespoons butter, beef, ham, bread crumbs, ice water, egg, thyme and pepper. Combine well. Wet your hands and shape the mixture into 4 patties. Place on a plate lined with wax paper and refrigerate for 1 hour.

When ready to cook, dust the patties with the flour. In the reserved skillet, heat the vegetable oil over medium heat. Cook the patties for about 3 minutes a side, or until nicely browned and cooked through. Transfer to a heated serving platter and cover loosely with foil.

If necessary, remove all but 1/2 tablespoon of the oil from the skillet and discard. Stir in the beef stock and brandy. Add the butter, one piece at a time, stirring constantly. To serve, pour the brandy sauce over the patties, sprinkle with parsley, and serve hot.

Makes 4 servings.

BURGER BUNDLES

We don't know if these are a Midwestern innovation, but our introduction to this easy supper dish was many years ago in Indiana. Like a giant meatball with a savory stuffing in the middle and baked under a delicious "gravy," they are a favorite with kids of all ages (including the over-fifty crowd).

1 cup herb stuffing mix (we like the Pepperidge Farm mix, if available)
1-1/2 pounds lean ground beef
1/4 cup evaporated milk
1 tablespoon minced onions
1 can (10-3/4 ounces) cream of mushroom soup
2 teaspoons Worcestershire sauce
1 tablespoon ketchup
chopped parsley, for garnish

Preheat the oven to 350 degrees.

Prepare the stuffing mix according to the package directions. In a large bowl, mix the ground beef with the milk and minced onions. Divide the mixture into 6 patties and flatten each to form 6- to 7-inch circles. Divide the prepared dressing into the middle of the patties. Draw the edges over the stuffing and seal. Shape roughly into balls and place in a 1-1/2 quart casserole. Combine the soup, Worcestershire sauce and ketchup in a saucepan and heat until bubbly over medium heat. Pour over the meat and bake uncovered in the center of the oven for about 50 minutes. Serve warm garnished with the parsley.

Makes 6 servings.

DOUBLE CUT PORK CHOPS WITH COUNTRY APPLESAUCE

Double-Cut Pork Chops with Country Applesauce

Do visit your local butcher shop to order your double-cut pork chops (also called French cut or rib chop with bone) to be assured of quality. After marinating overnight, the chops are simply broiled to the desired doneness and served with what the kind chef called his Country Applesauce. Be warned, this is unlike any applesauce you have eaten during your lifetime. It is the ultimate of its genre with dried cranberries, golden raisins, red peppers, red onions, and of course, the Golden Delicious apples, along with lots of butter, sugar, and cinnamon, all cooked to a thick and exquisite culinary offering. Do make the applesauce several hours or up to a day ahead to allow the flavors to peak. You can reheat it in the microwave or over low heat. You will have leftovers, fortunately, to be eaten straight from the refrigerator or reheated. Delicious with more pork or poultry.

Pork Chops

> 4 double-cut bone-in pork chops, about 1-1/2 inches thick each
> 1-1/2 cups water
> 3 tablespoons sugar
> 1 small red onion, diced
> salt

Country Applesauce, recipe given

The day before serving, pat the chops dry with paper towels. In a large heavy plastic storage bag placed in a mixing bowl, mix the water, sugar, and onions. Submerge the chops in the marinade and seal the bag. Leave the bag in the bowl and refrigerate overnight. At least twice during the marinating, turn the bag with the chops to ensure they are each well covered with the marinade.

When ready to serve, preheat the oven broiler. Remove the chops from the marinade and discard the marinade. Pat the chops dry and sprinkle both sides lightly with salt. Place on a broiler rack and broil the chops about 4 inches from the heat source for about 10 minutes a side. They should register 160 degrees on an instant reading meat thermometer. Serve at once with about 1/2 cup each of the Country Applesauce.

Makes 4 servings.

Country Applesauce:

- 2 sticks (1 cup) butter
- 6 large Granny Smith apples, halved, peeled, cored, and cut into 3/8-inch slices
- 2 cups dried cranberries
- 2 cups golden raisins
- 2 tablespoons firm-packed light brown sugar
- 1 tablespoon ground cinnamon
- 1/2 large sweet red pepper, cut into small dice
- 1 small red onion, diced

In a large sauté pan or skillet, melt the butter over medium heat. Stir in the remaining ingredients one by one so you can be sure they are thoroughly mixed. Bring to a boil, then reduce the heat. Partially cover and simmer for about 12 to 15 minutes or until the apples are tender. Stir the mixture several times during the simmering. Remove from the heat and let cool to room temperature. Transfer to a covered bowl to refrigerate until ready to serve. You can, of course, serve the applesauce immediately, but it is even better if it sits for several hours or overnight. If refrigerated, place the desired amount in a saucepan and reheat over low heat, stirring frequently until hot through. Or reheat in the microwave.

Makes about 6 cups.

HAM PATTIES

When asked how to deal with leftover ham tastefully when one tires of sandwiches, we often suggest making these tasty Ham Patties. The recipe originated back in those BC (before Cuisinart) days when we were dealing with the Harrington's of Vermont hams in their gourmet food and cookware shop, which we managed. We also give you a simple sauce recipe of yogurt, mayonnaise and a dollop of Dijon mustard to enhance the patties even further.

2 cups ground cooked ham
1-1/2 cups cooked long-grain rice
4 tablespoons vegetable oil, divided
1/4 cup fine-chopped celery
2 tablespoons fine-chopped green pepper
2 tablespoons fine-chopped onion
2 tablespoons all-purpose flour
1 teaspoon dry mustard
1/2 cup tomato juice
1 large egg, lightly beaten
1 tablespoon water
3/4 cup dry bread crumbs
1/2 cup mayonnaise
1/2 cup plain yogurt
1 tablespoon fine-chopped fresh parsley
2 teaspoons Dijon mustard

In a large mixing bowl, combine the ground ham and rice.

Heat 2 tablespoons of the oil in a medium skillet over medium heat. Cook the celery, green pepper and onion for about 2 minutes, or until very tender. Blend the flour and dry mustard into the vegetable mixture and stir in the tomato juice. Cook, stirring constantly, until very thick and bubbly. Let cool slightly. Add to the ham-and-rice mixture and mix well. Refrigerate for about an hour, or until chilled.

Combine the beaten egg and water. Form the ham mixture into 8 patties, about 1/2-inch thick. Dip in the egg mixture then the crumbs.

In a large skillet, preferably nonstick, heat the remaining oil over medium heat. Cook the patties for about 2 minutes a side, or until well browned and hot through.

Make a sauce by combining the mayonnaise, yogurt, parsley, and Dijon mustard and serve with the hot patties.

Makes 4 servings, 2 patties each.

Henry's Beef Stroganoff

HENRY'S BEEF STROGANOFF

Several things make Henry's version of Beef Stroganoff remarkably different from many traditional recipes. There is no tomato sauce, ketchup, puree, or paste flavoring the sauce, nor any of the usual Worcestershire sauce as one of the ingredients. Instead of sherry wine, Cabernet Sauvignon is the wine of choice, giving the dish a remarkably rich flavor. Homemade Veal Stock is most highly recommended, and the beef called for—cut into nontraditional cubes—is not the usual fillet or top sirloin cut into thin strips. Yes, you could substitute chicken stock, but be assured, the easy veal stock recipe given here, though a tad time-consuming, is one of the significant ingredients in this dish. Remember, any leftover stock can be frozen and is one of those culinary "aces in the hole" when next a recipe calls for it. You will want to make the stock a day ahead so any fat can be removed from the surface after it has been refrigerated.

Veal Stock:

- 3-1/2 pounds (about) raw veal shanks, meat cut into cubes (ask the butcher to crack the bones)
- 2 medium carrots, washed, unpeeled, and cut into 1-inch pieces
- 2 medium onions, peeled and halved
- 2 medium celery ribs, cut into 1-inch pieces
- 2 medium leeks, white and 1 inch of green, trimmed and cut into 1-inch pieces

Seasonings—tie in rinsed cheesecloth:

- 1/2 teaspoon dried thyme leaves
- 1 large bay leaf
- 6 fresh parsley sprigs
- 2 unpeeled garlic cloves
- 2 whole cloves

Because veal gives off an excessive amount of scum, you want to blanch it first. In a large pot, cover the veal meat and bones with cold water. Bring to a boil over medium-high heat. Reduce the heat to medium-low and simmer for about 5 minutes. Drain, discarding the water and rinse the bones and meat well under cold water to remove all the scum. Rinse out the pot.

Place the meat, bones, all the vegetables and the seasonings in the pot. Cover with cold water by one inch. Bring to a boil over medium-high heat. If need be skim again as the mixture comes to a boil. Reduce the heat to medium-low, partially cover, and simmer gently (the French call it "au riant") for about 4 hours. If the water appears to be evaporating too much, add enough hot water to keep it above the ingredients. Taste the liquid to make sure you have simmered the most flavor from the ingredients. If necessary cook an additional 30 minutes.

Strain the stock, discarding the solids and seasoning packet. Cool slightly, then refrigerate uncovered until any fat congeals and can be scraped off the surface.

Makes about 2-1/2 quarts.

Beef Stroganoff:

- 1/4 cup all-purpose flour
- salt and fresh-ground black pepper
- 2 pounds trimmed chuck underblade steak, bottom chuck steak, or round tip roast (cut into 2-inch cubes)
- 1/4 cup vegetable oil
- 8 ounces small button mushrooms, stems trimmed and discarded
- 2 medium onions, peeled and diced
- 3 medium bay leaves
- 1-1/4 cups cabernet sauvignon wine
- 2-1/2 cups Veal Stock, recipe given
- 1/3 cup heavy cream
- kosher salt and fresh-ground pepper
- 2 sprigs fresh thyme, leaves removed and chopped
- 12 ounces fettuccine pasta, cooked according to package directions
- 2 tablespoons unsalted butter
- 1 cup sour cream

Combine the flour, salt, and pepper in a bowl. Dredge the beef cubes in the mixture. In a large sauté pan, heat the oil over medium-high heat until almost smoking. Brown the seasoned beef well, turning as necessary to brown all sides. Drain off any excess oil. Stir in the mushrooms, onions, bay leaf and wine, scraping up any nice browned bits from the bottom of the pan. Simmer over medium heat until almost all the wine has evaporated.

Preheat the oven to 350 degrees.

Stir in the veal stock and bring just to a simmer. Cover with a lid or heavy foil and cook in the oven for 1 hour and 20 minutes, or until the meat is fork tender. Remove from the oven. Now if your pot had a tight cover, you might want to reduce the liquid a bit. Or if your lid was not tight and the mixture seems almost dry, add additional veal stock and simmer briefly. Stir in the heavy cream, and season to taste. Add half the chopped thyme.

In a large bowl, toss the fettuccine with the butter and remaining thyme, adding salt if desired. Arrange the pasta on four heated plates. Stir the sour cream into the meat mixture; stir gently and serve over the pasta.

You can make this dish several hours ahead or even the day before you plan to serve it. However, do not add the sour cream until the last minute. Slowly reheat the stroganoff over low heat and when it is piping hot but not boiling, stir in the sour cream and serve.

Makes 4 servings.

JEAN-LOUIS' LAMB STEW

There are countless recipes for lamb stew: from Irish Stew to the French Navarin to the Lancashire Hot Pot and on to ragouts. Ingredients and methods vary, and deciding which is the one for you can be mind-boggling. However, after tasting the Lamb Stew at Restaurant Jean-Louis in Greenwich, Connecticut, several years ago, we asked for the recipe. Owner/chef Jean-Louis Gerin not only shared the recipe but came to our kitchen to help translate his flavorful restaurant-size Lamb Stew into a family-size amount. He prefers tender lamb shoulder for the stew and purees the savory vegetables and seasonings cooked with the lamb, making a delicious vegetable-thickened sauce that is perfect served over rice or couscous. This stew keeps and reheats well for several days and can be frozen.

4 tablespoons olive oil, divided
1 tablespoon unsalted butter or margarine
salt and fresh-ground pepper, to taste
3 pounds boned (save bones) and trimmed lean shoulder of lamb, cut into 1-1/2 inches
1 large onion, peeled and coarsely diced
3 medium carrots, halved lengthwise and cut into ½-inch slices
4 medium celery ribs, cut into ¼-inch slices

6 large garlic cloves, unpeeled
1 whole clove
1/2 teaspoon dried thyme
1/4 teaspoon dried basil
1/4 teaspoon dried rosemary
4 coriander seeds
2 bay leaves, broken in 4 pieces
1/2 cup dry white wine
6 large plum tomatoes, peeled, seeded, and coarsely chopped
1 can (10-1/2 ounces) beef broth (or the equivalent in homemade stock)
1 cup water

Heat 2 tablespoons of the olive oil and the butter in a large oven-going sauté pan over medium-high heat. Sprinkle the lamb with salt and pepper and cook in one layer, without crowding, turning to brown on all sides. Repeat as necessary, transferring the meat to a plate as it is browned.

Add the remaining 2 tablespoons olive oil and any bones to the pan. Stir in the onions, the carrots and celery. Cook, stirring, for 1 minute to temper (mix properly) the vegetables.

Preheat the oven to 400 degrees.

Add the garlic cloves, the seasonings, and the wine to the pan. Return the meat and any juices that have accumulated on the plate to the pan and stir to mix. Add the tomatoes, broth, and water. Season to taste with salt and pepper. Bring to a boil on top of the stove, stirring occasionally. Cook, uncovered, in the center of the oven until the meat is very tender—about 1 hour. Stir several times during the cooking to keep all the pieces of lamb moist.

Remove the meat to a plate with a slotted spoon. Remove and discard any bones. Retrieve the garlic cloves and reserve. Transfer the vegetables with a slotted spoon to the work bowl of a food processor fitted with the metal blade or the container of a blender. Squeeze in the flesh from the garlic cloves, then puree the mixture. Whisk the puree back into the remaining liquid in the cooking pan. Stir in the meat and any liquid from the plate. Heat through before serving. This is delicious served over rice or couscous.

Makes 8 servings.

MEAT LOAF

There are those of us who believe there can never be enough good Meat Loaf recipes, so we are sharing this one along with its delicious accompaniment of Our (easy) Bordelaise Sauce. The beef marrow called for is optional, although a traditional bordelaise sauce will include it. Ask your butcher if he/she can supply you. One seasoning this meat loaf includes that is not often associated with beef will keep some tasters puzzled. It is the addition of rubbed sage. There is just enough to creep onto your taste buds past the Dijon mustard and hot sauce and leave you trying to identify the flavor. This loaf is dense in texture, and any leftovers make next-day sandwiches a tasty treat. The jury is still out as to whether a good meat loaf makes a better original meal or better leftovers.

Meat Loaf:

- 1 cup medium-chop chopped onions
- 1/2 cup dry bread crumbs
- 1/2 cup whole milk
- 1 tablespoon Dijon mustard
- 1/2 teaspoon salt
- 1 heaping teaspoon rubbed sage
- 1/2 teaspoon hot sauce (we used Tabasco)
- 1/8 teaspoon fresh-ground black pepper, or to taste
- 2 pounds ground beef (we used ground round)
- Our Bordelaise Sauce (recipe given)

Preheat the oven to 350 degrees. Spray a 9 by 5 by 3-inch loaf pan with no-stick vegetable spray.

In a large mixing bowl, mix together all the ingredients, except the beef and Our Bordelaise Sauce. Crumble in the beef, and with clean hands, combine the ingredients lightly but thoroughly.

Transfer the mixture to the prepared loaf pan, pressing it in evenly and into the corners. Bake in the center of the oven for about 1 hour, or until an instant-reading meat thermometer registers 160 degrees. Remove from the oven and let sit in the pan for 10 minutes. Transfer the loaf to a warm serving platter. Cut into 8 even slices and serve with Our Bordelaise Sauce on the side.

Makes 8 servings. (Do make sure to save some for sandwiches!)

Our Bordelaise Sauce:

1-1/2 tablespoons butter	1/2 cup dry red wine
1-1/2 tablespoons all-purpose flour	1/4 teaspoon chopped fresh tarragon
2 cups beef bouillon (we used 2 teaspoons instant beef bouillon granules dissolved in 2 cups hot water)	Few drops fresh lemon juice
	2 tablespoons small diced and poached beef marrow*

In a small saucepan, melt the butter over medium-low heat. Stir in the flour and cook the roux slowly, stirring constantly, until it is the color of a brown paper bag. Add the beef bouillon, and bring to a boil, stirring. Lower the heat to low and let the mixture simmer slowly for about 25 minutes. Remove from the heat. You should have about 1-1/2 cups of brown sauce.

In a medium skillet, stir together the shallots and wine. Over medium heat cook, stirring occasionally, until the wine is reduced by 3/4. Stir in the brown sauce and simmer for 10 minutes. At this point, you can strain the sauce, if desired. Just before serving stir in the tarragon, lemon juice and poached marrow, if using.

Makes about 1-1/2 cups.

*To poach the beef marrow, remove it (or have your butcher do it) from a split beef bone and cut it into small dice. Poach in boiling salted water for 1 to 2 minutes and drain well.

Meat Loaf with Mushroom Sauce

MEAT LOAF WITH MUSHROOM SAUCE

As we have mentioned before, many of us believe that there can never be enough good Meat Loaf recipes. Thanks to the chef at the popular Bimini Boatyard Bar and Grill in Fort Lauderdale, this version will become a favorite. The addition of Italian sausage, a healthy dose of Worcestershire sauce, and some aromatic vegetables gives this Meat Loaf—with its intense mushroom flavor of the Mushroom Sauce—a distinct culinary personality. You can vary this personality by the kind of heat-intense Italian sausage you choose to use. We opted for a hot Italian sausage that gave the loaf a wonderful spicy flavor. You can prepare the Meat Loaf early in the day and refrigerate it, covered. Just take it out of the refrigerator about 30 minutes before baking. The Mushroom Sauce can also be prepared an hour or so before serving. Just reheat it gently. Again, make sure to save a slice or two for tomorrow's sandwiches!

Meat Loaf:

- 1/2 cup fine-diced celery
- 1/2 cup fine-diced onions
- 1 teaspoon fine-chopped garlic
- 2 tablespoons chopped parsley
- 2 pounds lean ground beef
- 1 pound ground Italian sausage (we used Roman brand hot Italian sausage—casing removed)
- 1/2 cup dry bread crumbs
- 3 large eggs
- 2 tablespoons Worcestershire sauce
- salt and fresh-ground pepper, to taste

Preheat the oven to 375 degrees. Spray a 9 by 5 by 3-inch loaf pan with no-stick vegetable spray.

In a large mixing bowl, combine all the ingredients, working them well with your clean hands until thoroughly mixed. This will take a bit of time since the sausage tends to be somewhat firm and not easily incorporated with the other ingredients. (Consider this excellent hand and arm muscle building.) Pack well into the prepared pan. (Can be made several hours ahead, covered and refrigerated. Remove from the refrigerator at least 30 minutes before baking.)

Bake in the center of the oven for 1-1/2 hours or until the interior temperature reads 145 degrees on an instant-reading meat thermometer. Transfer to a serving platter with slotted spatulas. Let sit about 10 minutes before slicing and serving.

If necessary, use paper towels to blot up any liquid that may accumulate as the loaf sits. Serve with the Mushroom Sauce.

Makes 10 servings. (Remember leftovers for sandwiches.)

Mushroom Sauce:

- 3 tablespoons unsalted butter
- 1 large shallot, finely diced
- 2 medium garlic cloves, finely diced
- 7 ounces shiitake mushrooms, stems removed and discarded, caps cut into just under 1/4-inch slices
- 8 ounces white domestic mushrooms, cut into just under 1/4-inch slices
- 2 cups beef broth or bouillon (we used 2 teaspoons beef bouillon granules dissolved in 2 cups hot water)
- 1/4 cup red wine (we used a Riunite Cabernet Red Table Wine)

Beurre Manie:

- 3 tablespoons softened unsalted butter mixed well with 3 tablespoons all-purpose flour, for thickening
- salt and fresh-ground pepper, to taste

Melt the butter in a large heavy skillet over medium heat. Sauté the shallots and garlic about 2 minutes or until softened. Add the mushrooms and continue cooking, stirring constantly for about 5 minutes, or until the mushrooms are limp and the mixture is just moist. Stir in the beef broth and wine and bring to a boil.

To thicken the sauce, stir in the beurre manie a teaspoon at a time, making sure it has been incorporated before adding the next. Continue adding the beurre manie until the desired consistency has been reached. Season to taste. (You can make this an hour or so before serving, but it will thicken a bit on standing. If upon reheating it is a bit too thick, add some additional beef bouillon.)

Makes about 5 cups.

OSSO BUCO

Osso Buco

According to chef/owner Jean Bert, who kindly shared this recipe with us, the best veal shanks to buy are the hind shanks to make his savory Osso Buco. They are meatier and less tendinous than the fore shanks and contain more of the flavorful marrow that enriches the final sauce. You will want them to be about 1-1/2 inches thick with lots of meat and a marrow bone chock full of marrow. As opposed to many Italian-inspired Osso Buco recipes, Chef Bert does not include tomatoes in any form. His flavorfully inspired recipe is based on the aromatic ingredients of onions, carrots and garlic, bay leaves, and lots of fresh thyme. This is a dish of incredibly tender veal in an incredibly tasty sauce.

3 tablespoons olive oil
4 veal hind shanks, 1-1/2 inches thick each (about 24 ounces total)
salt and fresh-ground pepper
1 large Spanish onion, finely chopped
2 medium carrots, minced
2 medium garlic cloves, minced
8 to 10 sprigs fresh thyme
2 medium bay leaves
2 cups chicken stock (we used 2 heaping teaspoons Better Than Bouillon chicken base and 2 cups hot water)
1/4 cup dry white wine
4 small white-skinned potatoes, peeled and halved

In a heavy skillet, just large enough to hold the veal shanks in a single layer without crowding, heat the oil over medium-high heat. Season the shanks on both sides with salt and pepper and brown them on both sides, turning once. Remove the shanks to a warm plate. Preheat the oven to 350 degrees.

Reduce the heat under the skillet to medium and add the onions, carrots, and garlic. Cook the vegetables, stirring occasionally, for about 4 minutes, or until the onions are slightly caramelized. Return the veal shanks to the skillet, pressing them into the cooked vegetables. Add the thyme, bay leaves, chicken stock, and white wine. Bring the mixture to a simmer, cover tightly, and cook in the oven for about 2-1/2 hours. (N.B. Check after about 20 minutes. If the liquid seems to be simmering at too rapid a rate, reduce the oven to 325 degrees. You just want it to simmer at a leisurely pace or, as the French say, "en riant." Too hard a simmer or a boil and it could toughen rather than tenderize the veal.) Add the potatoes, re-cover, and continue cooking for another hour.

Remove the shanks to two warm serving dishes with the potatoes around them. Remove the thyme stems and bay leaves. Over high heat, reduce the cooking juices until golden and slightly thickened. Correct the seasoning and pour over and around the veal. We like to serve these with rice to enjoy all the delicious sauce.

Makes 2 servings.

REUBEN CROQUETTES

For anyone who likes those famous Reuben sandwiches, these croquettes are a surprisingly delicious alternative. What's more, everything you need to make them can be found on your pantry shelf and in your refrigerator. Once the rice is cooked, the rest is easy. These make a great luncheon or supper dish.

Croquettes:

- 1/2 cup uncooked rice (not instant)
- 1 can (16 ounces) sauerkraut
- 1 can (12 ounces) corned beef
- 1/4 cup chopped onions
- 3 large eggs, divided
- 1 cup shredded Swiss cheese
- 1 teaspoon salt, or to taste
- 1/4 teaspoon fresh-ground pepper, or to taste
- 2 tablespoons water
- 1-1/2 cups fine dry bread crumbs

Sauce:

- 1 cup real mayonnaise
- 1/3 cup milk
- 3 tablespoons (or to taste) prepared mustard (try the stone ground variety)
- 1 tablespoon fresh lemon juice

Cook the rice according to package directions. Transfer to a large bowl and let cool.

Drain the sauerkraut very well, pressing out as much liquid as possible. Chop the sauerkraut and corned beef very fine and add with the chopped onions to the cooled rice. Lightly beat 2 of the eggs and add them and the cheese, salt, and pepper to the rice mixture. Mix well. Shape into 18 croquettes (we like them in hamburger shapes) using about 1/4 cup mixture for each.

Combine the remaining egg and water and beat lightly. Roll each croquette in crumbs, then the egg mixture, and again in the crumbs. Place on a wire rack and let dry for about 10 minutes.

In a large skillet, heat enough vegetable oil to reach 1-inch in depth over medium-high heat. Fry the croquettes for about 5 minutes a side, or until nicely browned and crisp. Serve with about 1 tablespoon of the sauce for each croquette.

Makes 6 servings.

To make the sauce, if you want to serve it warm, mix all the ingredients together in a saucepan and heat over low heat just until warm. Or it is equally good served at room temperature, simply mixed in a bowl.

The sauce makes about 1-1/2 cups.

RIGATONI BOLOGNAISE

Rigatoni Bolognaise

By the time the savory ingredients of carrots, celery, and garlic are sautéed; the beef added; the thyme, tomatoes, red wine, and marinara sauce are stirred in; and the mixture simmering—your taste buds are on high alert. We can thank Chef Oliver Wolf at one of the Marriott Harbor Beach Hotels in Florida for this outstanding Rigatoni Bolognaise recipe. Although this is not a difficult recipe, Chef Wolf told us that what makes it special is swirling in the fresh butter at the end of the simmering time. This technique is usually associated with making a beurre blanc and ensures a sauce that is deliciously creamy. We used the rigatoni pasta for our testing, but other tubular pasta or rotelle or fusilli can be substituted.

2 tablespoons vegetable oil (canola oil recommended)
1 small onion, chopped
2 small carrots, diced
2 small celery ribs, diced
1 medium garlic clove, minced
1 pound lean ground beef (we used ground sirloin)
1 teaspoon dried basil, crushed
1 teaspoon dried thyme leaves, crushed
salt and fresh-ground black pepper

3 tablespoons red wine (we used a merlot)
1/3 cup marinara sauce (we used Paul Newman's)
4 ounces (1 stick unsalted butter, cut into tablespoon size pieces)
1 pound rigatoni pasta, cooked according to package directions
fresh-grated Parmesan cheese, optional

In a large skillet or sauté pan, heat the oil over medium heat. Sauté the onions, carrots, celery and garlic for about 2 minutes or until softened and fragrant. Add the beef. Cook the beef, breaking it apart with your spoon, for about 4 minutes or until no pink remains. If too much accumulated fat cooks out, drain off all but a tablespoon or so. Add the basil and thyme, and salt and pepper to taste.

Stir in the red wine and marinara sauce and bring to a simmer. Reduce the heat and let cook for about 10 to 12 minutes, or until thickened. Stir in the butter, a tablespoon at a time, letting each just about melt before adding the next.

To serve, you can add the pasta to the cooking pan and toss well, or we decided to divide the pasta among 4 warmed serving bowls and divide the Bolognaise Sauce among them. Each tossed his or own and added however much Parmesan cheese they wished—probably about a tablespoon per serving.

Makes 4 servings.

SALISBURY STEAK WITH MUSHROOM GRAVY

We are always reminded of occasional complaints heard when a diners' order for Salisbury Steak (with or without Mushroom Gravy) arrives to find to their consternation that the "steaks" were in fact embellished "hamburgers." Salisbury steaks have been around since the nineteenth century and have been attributed variously to a Dr. J. H. Salisbury, a physician who recommended them as a cure for many ailments, and to the Marquis of Salisbury, an English statesman from 1830 to 1903. Whatever their beginnings, they can be a most delicious entrée, made even more palatable with a good mushroom sauce.

The "Steak":

- 1-3/4 pounds lean ground beef
- 2 tablespoons minced onion
- 3 tablespoons fine-chopped green pepper
- 1 tablespoon fine-chopped fresh parsley
- 1 tablespoon fine-chopped chives
- 1/2 teaspoon dried thyme leaves, crushed
- 1/2 teaspoon dried marjoram, crushed
- 1/4 teaspoon paprika
- salt and fresh-ground black pepper to taste
- 1 teaspoon olive oil
- Mushroom Gravy (recipe given)

To make the "steaks" mix all the ingredients except the olive oil and gravy in a large mixing bowl. Clean hands are best here. Shape into 6 individual patties about 3/4-inch thick. Brush both sides lightly with the olive oil.

Preheat the broiler. Broil the patties 3 to 4 inches from the heat for about 5 to 6 minutes a side or until the desired doneness. Serve each with some of the Mushroom Gravy.

Mushroom Gravy:

3 tablespoons butter	1/2 tablespoon Dijon mustard
1 cup sliced mushrooms	dash Tabasco sauce
1 teaspoon all-purpose flour	dash ground mace
1/3 cup tomato ketchup	salt and fresh-ground pepper to taste
1 tablespoon lemon juice	
1 teaspoon Worcestershire sauce	2 tablespoons dry sherry wine

In a medium skillet, melt the butter over medium heat. Add the mushrooms and sauté for about 5 minutes or until tender. Sprinkle with the flour and stir well. Add the remaining ingredients except the wine and blend well. Stir in the sherry and bring almost to the boil.

Makes about 2/3 cup.

SHEPHERD'S PIE

Shepherd's Pie

There are many versions of Shepherd's Pie, but we were impressed not only with the overall flavor and appetizing appearance of this particular "pie" but also with its wonderfully thick and hearty filling the first time we tasted it. We could also mention the heady aroma filling the house as it undergoes its final baking. The original recipe from the talented chef who shared it called for their version of "thick brown gravy." We were granted permission to substitute a shortcut brown stock we learned some years ago from Julia Child, which uses canned beef bouillon (or bouillon cubes or granules mixed with water). You will like the fact that both the filling and mashed potato topping can be made early in the day.

Quick Brown Sauce and Gravy:

- 3 cups water
- 4 beef bouillon cubes or 4 teaspoons beef bouillon granules
- 1 small carrot, finely chopped
- 1 medium celery rib, finely chopped
- 1/2 small onion, finely chopped
- 1 small bay leaf, halved
- 1/4 teaspoon dried thyme leaves
- 2 tablespoons fresh parsley sprigs
- 4 tablespoons unsalted butter
- 6 tablespoons all-purpose flour
- 1/4 cup dry Madeira wine (optional but highly recommended)

Pie Filling and Topping:

- 1 tablespoon vegetable oil
- 2 pounds ground round steak
- 1 large onion, cut into 1/4-inch dice
- 2 medium garlic cloves, finely chopped
- 2 large carrots, cut into 1/4-inch dice
- 1/2 tablespoon dried basil
- 1/2 tablespoon dried oregano
- 1/4 tablespoon dried thyme
- 2 cups Quick Brown Sauce and Gravy (recipe given)
- salt and fresh-ground black pepper
- 4 large Idaho potatoes (about 8 ounces each)
- 4 tablespoons unsalted butter
- 1/2 cup whole milk (may need a bit more)
- 2 tablespoons fresh-grated Parmesan cheese, for garnish
- 1/2 teaspoon paprika for garnish (optional)

To make the Quick Brown Sauce and Gravy, in a large heavy saucepan, bring all the ingredients except the butter, flour and wine to a boil over medium-high heat, stirring occasionally to dissolve the bouillon cubes or granules. Reduce the heat to low and simmer slowly, uncovered for 30 minutes, stirring occasionally. When done, strain the mixture into a large measuring cup, discarding the solids. You should have about 2 cups, or just a tad more is fine. Wipe out the pan with paper towels.

To finish making the gravy, in the same saucepan melt the butter over medium heat. Stir in the flour and let it simmer for 3 to 4 minutes, or until it just begins to color. Do not let it get too brown or it won't thicken properly. Whisk in the brown sauce and keep whisking until the mixture thickens. Taste for seasoning. Remove from the heat and reserve.

To make the pie filling and topping, preheat the oven to 350 degrees. Heat the oil in a large skillet or sauté pan over medium-high heat. Cook the beef, stirring occasionally, to break it up and until it is nicely browned and all the fat has been rendered out. Drain the meat in a colander and discard the liquids.

In the same pan, sauté the onions and garlic for about 3 minutes or until golden. Add the carrots and herbs and sauté for 2 minutes. Add the reserved gravy and the meat and mix well. Taste for seasoning. Cover and cook in the oven for about 20 minutes or until the carrots are tender. Remove from the oven and let rest for 30 minutes. Spoon into a 1-1/2 quart gratin dish (we use our 10 by 7 by 2-inch dish).

Meanwhile, peel, chunk, and cook the potatoes until soft. In a large bowl, add the potatoes, butter, and milk and mash on the medium speed of an electric mixer. Taste for seasoning. Spread the potatoes over the top of the meat mixture and sprinkle with the Parmesan cheese and paprika, if desired. The pie can be assembled up to this point and refrigerated for several hours. Remove from the refrigerator at least 30 minutes before the final baking.

Preheat the oven to 400 degrees. Bake the pie for about 15 to 20 minutes or until heated thoroughly and golden brown on top.

Makes 4 hearty servings.

SWEDISH MEATBALLS (KJOTTBOLLAR)

When asked for a good recipe for Swedish Meatballs, we immediately reach for the recipe you find here, handed down through many years from our grandmother, Christine Swenson Person Floden, who immigrated to Chicago from Southern Sweden in 1884. It has passed the test of time innumerable times, as have many of her other recipes. We found we could reduce the calories a bit and save some time by baking these savory meatballs instead of frying them before adding them to the Madeira-flavored brown sauce for a final simmer. What we now call chopped or ground meat, Grandmother used to call minced, and the combination of beef, veal, and pork she called meat farce or *kjottfars*. By whatever name, these make a delicious buffet or supper dish.

Meatballs:

- 1 tablespoon unsalted butter
- 2 tablespoons minced onions
- 1 pound lean ground beef
- 4 ounces ground veal
- 4 ounces ground pork
- 3/4 cup dry bread crumbs
- 1 large egg, lightly beaten
- 1/2 cup milk
- 1/4 teaspoon fresh-grated nutmeg
- 1/4 teaspoon ground coriander
- 1/4 teaspoon grated lemon rind
- 1 teaspoon salt
- 1/8 teaspoon fresh-ground black pepper
- Quick Brown Sauce (recipe given)

Melt the butter in a small skillet over medium heat. Sauté the onions for about 3 minutes, or until softened but not brown. Let cool.

In a large bowl, mix all the ingredients together, including the cooked onions. Spray a large baking sheet with no-stick vegetable spray. Shape the meat mixture into 24 balls and place on the baking sheet. These can be shaped ahead and refrigerated until ready to bake.

When ready to bake, preheat the oven to 400 degrees. Bake the meatballs in the center of the oven for 20 to 25 minutes, or until firm and an instant-reading meat thermometer registers 160 degrees when inserted into the center of a ball. These can be served with sauce on the side, but we prefer to add them to the sauce and let them simmer for a few minutes. We like to serve these with rice to soak up the savory sauce.

Makes 6 to 8 servings.

Quick Brown Sauce:

- 1-1/2 tablespoons unsalted butter
- 1-1/2 tablespoons all-purpose flour
- 2 cups beef bouillon (we use 2 heaping teaspoons Better Than Bouillon beef base and 2 cups hot water)
- 1/4 cup dry Madeira wine

In a medium skillet, melt the butter over medium-low heat. Stir in the flour and cook slowly, stirring constantly for about 4 minutes, or until it just begins to take on color. Whisk in the beef bouillon and continue whisking until the sauce is smooth and has thickened. Stir in the Madeira. Bring to a boil, stirring constantly. Lower the heat and let it simmer for about 3 minutes, stirring.

Makes about 2 cups.

Texas Chili

TEXAS CHILI

Chili's origin is not really known for certain, although it has been a part of the American diet for a long time. According to a Southwestern historian named Frank Tolbert, chili was invented in the late nineteenth century almost certainly in Texas, probably near San Antonio. Although popular, one preacher equated chili's fiery properties with the flames of perdition and called it "the devil's soup." One of the hottest debates among chili lovers, who are often an opinionated lot, arises as to whether beans should be included or served on the side. This outstanding Texas Chili recipe from a popular restaurant, complete with its own Texas chili seasoning, does not include beans. It is thick, rich, and hearty without a bean in sight and never missed. (See p. 137 for the chili bread recipe we developed using leftover chili during the time the Cuisinart test kitchen worked on the article we published on chili.)

Texas Chili Seasoning:

- 2 tablespoons chili powder
- 1 teaspoon dried oregano
- 1/2 teaspoon kosher salt
- 1/4 teaspoon Hungarian paprika
- 1 teaspoon ground cumin
- 1 teaspoon ground cayenne pepper

In a small bowl combine all the ingredients and mix together well. Store tightly covered in the refrigerator. This amount makes just enough for the recipe given here. However you can easily double or triple the ingredients to have on hand. It can be made days ahead and stored tightly covered in the refrigerator. Makes about 3 tablespoons.

Texas Chili:

- 1 tablespoon vegetable oil (we used canola)
- 2-1/2 pounds ground beef (we used ground chuck)
- 2 medium Spanish onions, cut into 1/4-inch dice
- 1 large green pepper, seeded and cut into 1/4-inch dice
- 1 medium red pepper, seeded and cut into 1/4-inch dice
- 4 large garlic cloves, coarsely chopped
- 1/4 medium jalapeño pepper, seeded and minced
- 1-1/4 cups water
- 2-1/4 cups crushed tomatoes (we suggest Hunt's Crushed Tomatoes in Thick Tomato Puree, undrained)
- 1 tablespoon beef base (we used Better Than Bouillon beef base)
- 1-1/2 teaspoons kosher salt, or to taste
- 3 tablespoons Texas Chili Seasoning (recipe given)

In a large sauté pan or skillet, heat the oil over medium-high heat. Sauté the beef, breaking it up as much as possible, for about 7 to 8 minutes, or until no pink remains. Add the onions, green and red peppers, garlic and jalapeno pepper, and cook, stirring for about 7 minutes, or until the vegetables are tender. Add the remaining ingredients except the Texas Chili Seasoning. Partially cover the pan, reduce the heat until the mixture is just simmering and let simmer for 50 minutes. Stir in the chili seasoning, mixing well, and simmer for an additional 15 minutes. Remove from the heat. Can be served at once or cooled and refrigerated for up to three days. Reheat over low heat before serving.

The restaurant serves the bowls or cups of chili garnished with mozzarella and/or Cheddar cheese, chopped green and red onions, and the essential saltines.

Makes 8 servings.

MAIN DISHES (POULTRY)

Anthony's Chicken Al

ANTHONY'S CHICKEN AL

From a popular restaurant in Fort Lauderdale, Florida, comes Anthony's Chicken Al recipe. You will find this dish a remarkable medley of an aromatic, picturesque, and highly flavorful production. The portions of an entire half a small chicken immersed in a lemony, rosemary, garlic bath, are more than generous, served on a bed of wilted fresh garlic-infused spinach and surrounded by the vegetables that have been roasted with the chicken. Should you have any leftovers from the generous servings, pile them on the bottom of a good sandwich roll, top with shredded Gruyere cheese, spread the upper portion of the roll with Dijon mustard, wrap in foil and heat in a 350 degree oven until the cheese melts. You will be happy the original portions were so generous.

Chicken:

- 1 whole chicken, about 3-1/2 to 4 pounds
- 1/3 cup olive oil
- 2 tablespoons fresh-squeezed lemon juice
- 2 teaspoons crushed dried rosemary
- 4 large garlic cloves, minced
- salt and fresh-ground black pepper, to taste

Vegetables:

- 1/3 cup olive oil
- 2 teaspoons crushed dried rosemary
- Salt and fresh-ground black pepper to taste
- 1 large baking potato (about 12 ounces), peeled, sliced lengthwise, then crosswise, each section cut into 3 wedges
- 1 small red pepper, seeds and ribs removed, cut into 1/4-inch julienne strips
- 1 small yellow pepper, seeds and ribs removed, cut into 1/4-inch julienne strips
- 1 medium onion, peeled and thinly sliced

Spinach Garnish:

2 tablespoons olive oil
1 medium garlic clove, minced

1 pound fresh spinach, tough stems removed, washed and dried thoroughly
salt and fresh-ground black pepper, to taste

Preheat the oven to 425 degrees.

Have the butcher cut the chicken into two halves—discarding the backbone, tail, and first section of the wings. (You can do the job yourself if you have strong poultry shears and a good cleaver.)

In a large bowl, mix together the oil, lemon juice, rosemary, garlic, and seasonings. Immerse the chicken halves, one at a time, and completely cover with the oil mixture. Place in a roasting pan skin-side up, large enough to hold the vegetables around the chicken. Tuck the wings under—using a skewer, if necessary—and skewer the legs to the breast portion to prevent the chicken halves from spreading too much as they roast.

To prepare the vegetables, in another bowl, mix together the oil, rosemary, and seasonings. Immerse the potato wedges in the mixture, making certain all surfaces are covered, and place around the chicken halves. Roast in the center of the oven for 30 minutes. Meanwhile, immerse the julienned peppers and onion slices in the remaining oil mixture and sprinkle around and over the chicken. Continue roasting until the chicken is nicely browned and the vegetables are soft and beginning to take on color—about 20 minutes more. The chicken should register 145 degrees on an instant-reading meat thermometer.

Meanwhile, in a large skillet, prepare the spinach garnish. Heat the oil over medium-high heat and sauté the garlic just until softened, but not brown—about 45 seconds. Add the spinach and sauté 3 to 4 minutes. Make sure to keep turning the spinach so it wilts evenly.

To serve, divide the spinach between two large serving dishes (we used 2 white platters, each about 14 by 10 inches). Place a chicken half on top of the spinach and divide the roasted vegetables between them. Serve immediately.

Makes 2 generous servings.

AWESOME TURKEY LOAF

Awesome Turkey Loaf

Not just another turkey loaf but an Awesome Turkey Loaf which—according to the Executive Director of Food for all the Gardner's Markets in Miami—has been a hit in all their locations from the very first day it was offered. It is visually appealing with flecks of carrot and green spinach throughout. The remaining savory ingredients, including prepared horseradish, are sure to tempt your taste buds on its own, in sandwiches, or even on salads. Just make sure your ground turkey is very lean. Some preground packages include some skin and fat.

- 1 medium carrot, finely chopped
- 1 medium onion, finely chopped
- 1 celery rib, finely chopped
- 2-1/2 pounds lean ground turkey
- 1 large egg white, lightly beaten
- 1 cup herb stuffing mix, crushed
- 1 tablespoon prepared horseradish, undrained
- 6 ounces frozen chopped spinach, defrosted (a 10-ounce box when defrosted and squeezed almost dry gives you exactly 6 ounces)
- 1/2 teaspoon salt
- 1/2 teaspoon fresh-ground black pepper
- 1/4 cup plus 2 tablespoons ketchup, divided

Preheat the oven to 350 degrees. Spray a 9 by 5 by 2-3/4-inch loaf pan with vegetable spray.

Vegetables may be chopped in a food processor fitted with the metal blade. In a large mixing bowl, thoroughly mix all the ingredients except 2 tablespoons of the ketchup. (Your clean hands are the best utensils for this job.) Pack the mixture into the prepared pan and spread the top with the remaining ketchup.

Bake in the center of the oven for 50 to 60 minutes, or until the temperature of the loaf reaches 160 degrees on a meat thermometer. Let cool in the pan for 10 minutes, then transfer the loaf to a serving platter. Let cool another 5 minutes for easier and neater slicing.

Makes 8 servings.

CAP'N CRUNCH CHICKEN WITH CREOLE MUSTARD SAUCE

Cap'n Crunch Chicken with Creole Mustard Sauce

If you aren't young enough to have small children at home still begging for Cap'n Crunch cereal, you might have forgotten how crunchy it is. You will enjoy eating the leftovers for breakfast after using the amount called for in the breading for these Cap'n Crunch chicken tenders. The Creole Mustard Sauce benefits from being made ahead so all the ingredients have a chance to become fully acquainted. And you will be happy you have sauce left over! Use it in sandwiches and on salads. You can also prepare the breading and seasoned flour ahead as well as remove any tendons from the tenders.

Creole Mustard Sauce:

- 1 piece green pepper (about 2 by 5 inches, cut into 3 pieces)
- 1 small rib celery cut into 1-inch lengths
- 6 scallions, white and 2 inches of green, cut into 1/4-inch lengths
- 2 medium garlic cloves
- 1 cup mayonnaise
- 1 tablespoon creole mustard
- 2 teaspoons yellow mustard
- 2 teaspoons prepared horseradish, drained
- 1 tablespoon cider vinegar
- 1 tablespoon red wine vinegar
- 1/2 teaspoon Worcestershire sauce
- 1/8 teaspoon Tabasco sauce
- 1 tablespoon water
- dash cayenne
- salt to taste

In a food processor fitted with the metal blade, puree the green pepper, celery, scallions, and garlic. Add the remaining ingredients and process until smooth, scraping down the side of the bowl as necessary. Cover and refrigerate for several hours or overnight.

Makes about 1-1/2 cups.

Cap'n Crunch Breading:

- 3 cups Cap'n Crunch cereal
- 1-1/2 cups corn flakes

In a food processor fitted with the metal blade, process the cereals until fine crumbs are formed. Place in a shallow dish.

Makes about 1-1/3 cups breading.

Seasoned Flour:

- 3/4 cup all-purpose flour
- 1 tablespoon dry minced onions
- 1 tablespoon coarse ground garlic (we used Lawry's Coarse Ground with Parsley)
- 1/2 teaspoon fresh-ground black pepper

Use a fork to combine all the ingredients well in a shallow bowl

Egg Wash: 2 large eggs lightly beaten with 2 tablespoons milk, placed in a shallow bowl
16 fresh or defrosted chicken tenders (tendons removed)
vegetable oil for frying

When ready to serve, line up the bowls of breading, flour, and egg wash, with the egg wash in the middle.

Pat the chicken tenders dry with paper towels.

In a large heavy skillet, heat 1/4 inch of vegetable oil over medium-high heat. Dip each tender first in flour, then in egg wash, then in the breading. Place on paper towels as you coat the remaining tenders. (These can be done about 30 minutes ahead to allow the coating to dry a bit.)

Fry the tenders in a single layer for about 1 to 1-1/2 minutes a side, or until a golden brown and just cooked through. Do not overcook. Transfer to paper towels to drain. Repeat until all are cooked.

To serve, arrange 4 tenders on each of 4 warm serving plates with a small ramekin of Creole Mustard Sauce. (We used about 1/4 cup for each serving.)

Makes 4 servings.

Chicken Asiago Pasta

CHICKEN ASIAGO PASTA

Once tasted, you will agree that Chicken Asiago Pasta is a deliciously rich and eminently filling dish that will stay with you for a long time. The Asiago Cream Sauce is what you might term a culinary coup. Asiago cheese—sometimes described as a straw-colored, waxlike Italian cheese—melts easily when stirred into sauces and gives the sauce a velvety texture and a pleasantly rich, sweet, and salty flavor. The pancetta called for, usually sold sliced from a tightly rolled sausage shape, is best purchased for this recipe in one piece, not sliced, since you can then unroll it and cut it into the 1/4-inch strips, then the 1/4-inch dice you need. For the most convenient execution of the recipe, we suggest having all the ingredients for the chicken/pasta mixture ready to cook, then make the Asiago Cream Sauce and keep warm while preparing the chicken mixture. A warning here: this is not a dish for anyone watching calories!

Chicken/Pasta Mixture:

- 6 tablespoons unsalted butter, divided
- 3 ounces pancetta, cut into 1/4-inch dice
- 4 large skinless, boneless chicken breast halves, about 6 ounces each
- 3/4 cup diced red onions
- 2 large cloves garlic, coarsely chopped
- 4 scallions, white and 1-inch green, sliced 1/4-inch thick
- 1 cup heavy cream
- 9 ounces farfalle (bowtie) pasta (about 4 heaping cups dry), cooked according to package instructions
- Asiago Cream Sauce, recipe given
- chopped parsley for garnish (optional)

In a large nonstick sauté pan, melt 1 tablespoon of the butter over medium-high heat. Cook the pancetta, stirring, for 1 minute. Remove with a slotted spoon to drain on paper towels. Reserve.

Pound the chicken breasts between pieces of wax paper until they are all about the same thickness. Cook the chicken breasts in the sauté pan over medium heat, turning once until just cooked through, about 4 minutes a side. Remove from the heat, cool slightly, and slice on the diagonal (about 1/2-inch slices). Reserve.

Melt the remaining 5 tablespoons butter in the sauté pan over medium-high heat. Add the red onions and cook, stirring until soft but not brown, about 20 seconds. Add the reserved pancetta and chicken, the garlic and green onions. Cook, stirring until heated through. Stir in the hot pasta and the Asiago cream sauce.

To serve, divide the mixture among 4 heated serving plates of bowls. Garnish with chopped parsley if desired.

Makes 4 servings.

Asiago Cream Sauce:

2 cups heavy cream
6 ounces shredded Asiago cheese, about 2-1/4 cups

2 tablespoons cornstarch
2-1/2 tablespoons cold water

In a heavy saucepan, heat the cream to about 160 degrees over medium heat. Whisk in the Asiago cheese, whisking constantly until completely melted. Stir together the cornstarch and cold water and whisk into the cream/cheese mixture. It should be the consistency of a good hollandaise sauce. Keep warm while cooking the chicken/pasta mixture.

Makes about 2-1/2 cups.

CHICKEN SAN REMO

Chicken San Remo

Chicken San Remo, from a popular restaurant in Florida, is a flavorful variation on Chicken Florentine and a delicious way to get your spinach! This egg-battered, sauced, boneless chicken breast topped with a fresh spinach and wine-laced cream sauce as well as melted mozzarella cheese is a culinary triumph. Be sure to pound your chicken breasts to an even quarter-inch thickness. Pounded thin, these floured and battered breasts brown quickly and beautifully. The only time-consuming part of the recipe is reducing the sauce. Your guests won't mind the short wait after they take the first bite.

Chicken:

- 3 tablespoons olive oil
- 4 large boneless and skinless chicken breast halves (ours weighed about 7 ounces each) trimmed and pounded to an even 1/4 inch thick
- 1/4 cup all-purpose flour
- salt and fresh-ground pepper to taste
- 1 large egg, beaten lightly with 1 tablespoon water

Sauce:

- 2 tablespoons olive oil
- 2 medium shallots, minced
- 10 ounces fresh baby (important) spinach, rinsed and dried well
- 3/4 cup chicken stock (we used a scant teaspoon of the Better Than Bouillon chicken base and 3/4 cup warm water)
- 1/4 cup dry white wine
- 1 cup heavy cream
- cayenne pepper to taste
- salt to taste
- 4 ounces mozzarella cheese, shredded (about 1 cup) or cut into 16 thin slices

To make the chicken, heat the oil in a large heavy skillet over medium-high heat. Mix the flour with salt and pepper and dredge the chicken in it. Shake off the excess and dip each side in the egg wash. Sauté to a golden brown, turning once. This should take just a minute or two on each side. Transfer to a baking pan just large enough to hold the chicken in a single layer. Tent with foil to keep warm.

Wipe out the skillet and make the sauce. Heat the oil over medium heat. Sauté the shallots with the spinach until the spinach is completely wilted. (Your pan will be heaped with the spinach, but will soon reduce to a manageable amount.) Stir in the chicken stock, wine and cream. Bring to a boil and let the mixture reduce by half. This took us about 12 minutes. Season to taste with the cayenne pepper and salt.

Meanwhile preheat the broiler. Spoon the sauce over the chicken breasts and divide the Mozzarella cheese over the tops of each. Broil the chicken 4 to 5 inches from the heat source for about 2 to 3 minutes or until the cheese bubbles and is a light golden brown. Serve at once with angel hair or linguini pasta.

Makes 4 servings.

CHICKEN SILANA

From a popular Italian restaurant called Rosa's and Pasquale's comes this delightful blend of flavors called Chicken Silana. The prep time (without a sous chef or two) is a bit time-consuming; but most of the chopping, slicing, roasting, and blanching can be done ahead so final assembly and cooking goes quickly and smoothly. The ingredient amounts given are for two generous servings. However, this is an easily expandable recipe, the kind where very exact measurements are not critical. If you love artichoke hearts, add a couple more, or if you are inordinately fond of broccoli, stir in a few extra florets. Just include some crusty Italian bread to soak up every bit of the savory sauce.

- 2 large boneless, skinless chicken breast halves, about 8 ounces each
- 3 tablespoons all-purpose flour
- 3 tablespoons extra virgin olive oil
- 5 medium garlic cloves, peeled and thinly sliced
- 1 small onion, peeled and thinly sliced
- 3/4 cup chicken stock (we used a scant teaspoon instant chicken bouillon granules dissolved in 3/4 cup hot water)
- 1/4 cup dry white wine
- 4 ounces fresh mushrooms, cut into slices just under 1/4-inch (about 1 heaping cup)
- 3 canned artichoke hearts, drained and quartered (not marinated)
- 1-1/2 cups broccoli florets, blanched for 3 minutes
- 1 small red pepper, seeded, roasted*, peeled and cut into 1 by 1/4-inch julienne strips
- 2 tablespoons chiffonade** of fresh basil
- 3 tablespoons cold unsalted butter
- salt and fresh-ground black pepper, to taste

Trim the chicken breasts and pound them briefly between pieces of plastic wrap to an even thickness. Place the flour in a shallow dish and dip the chicken breasts in it, shaking off the excess.

In a large skillet, preferably nonstick, heat the oil over medium-high heat. Sauté the chicken for about 2 minutes a side, or until nicely browned and just barely cooked through. Remove to an oven proof dish and keep warm in a low (about 200 degrees) oven while making the sauce.

In the same skillet, over medium heat, add the garlic and onions. Sauté them for about 1 minute, or until fragrant. Stir in the chicken stock and wine, scraping up the browned bits in the bottom of the pan. Bring to a boil, lower the heat to medium-low, and simmer for about 7 minutes to reduce slightly.

Add the remaining ingredients except the basil, butter and seasonings. Let cook briefly, about 5 minutes, over medium-low heat, stirring occasionally. Remove from the heat, and stir in the basil and butter one tablespoon at a time. Wait until each pat of butter is almost melted before stirring in the next. Season to taste.

To serve, place a chicken breast on each of two warm serving plates. Divide the vegetable mixture between them.

Makes 2 generous servings.

*To roast the pepper, preheat the broiler. Cut the pepper in half, remove the seeds, and place cut-side down in a broiler-proof pan. Press firmly to flatten the pepper halves. Broil 5 inches from the heat source for about 5 to 7 minutes or until the skins are charred. Remove from the oven, cover with plastic wrap, and let cool to room temperature. Peel off the charred skins and cut into julienne strips.

**To chiffonade the basil, pile 3 or 4 leaves approximately the same size on top of each other. Roll tightly and cut crosswise into strips a bit less than 1/4 inch.

CHICKEN WELLINGTON

The original recipe for this Chicken Wellington came from the Pepperidge Farm people who make the required frozen puff pastry sheets. (If you have ever struggled through making puff pastry from scratch, you will thank Pepperidge Farm for their excellent ready-to-use frozen dough.) Once you try the recipe with the ingredients listed here, you will see how easy and impressive it is. The chicken breasts can be cooked several hours ahead or even the day before since you want them well-chilled. (See p. 311 if you would like to substitute the make-ahead Tender Poached Chicken Breasts.)

4 tablespoons unsalted butter, divided
4 boneless and skinless chicken breast halves, about 4 ounces each
salt and fresh-ground black pepper
1/2 cup fine-chopped onions
1/2 cup coarse-chopped mushrooms
2 tablespoons chopped fresh parsley
1 sheet (half a 17-1/4 ounce package) Pepperidge Farm frozen puff pastry sheets
4 ounces cream cheese, at room temperature
1 teaspoon dried thyme leaves, crushed
1 tablespoon Dijon mustard
1 large egg beaten with 1 teaspoon water, for egg wash

In a heavy skillet, melt 2 tablespoons of the butter over medium-high heat. Season the chicken breasts with salt and pepper. Add the chicken to the skillet and sauté for about 3 minutes on each side, or until nicely browned and just cooked through. Cool the chicken and refrigerate for at least 30 minutes or up to 24 hours.

In the same skillet melt the remaining butter over medium-high heat. Add the onions and mushrooms and sauté for about 8 minutes, or until soft and the liquid has evaporated. Stir in the parsley and let cool.

Thaw the pastry at room temperature for 30 minutes. Preheat the oven to 400 degrees. On a lightly floured surface, roll the pastry into a 14-inch rectangle and cut into 4 equal (7-inch) squares.

In a small bowl, combine the cream cheese, thyme, and mustard. Spread the mixture over the chilled chicken breasts. Divide the onion mixture over the center of the pastry squares and top with a chicken breast. Brush the edges of the pastry with the egg wash. Fold each corner to the center on top of the chicken and seal the edges well. Place seam side down on an ungreased baking sheet and brush with the egg wash. Bake in the center of the oven for about 25 minutes or until golden.

Makes 4 servings.

CHICKEN WITH FORTY CLOVES OF GARLIC

The original dish of Chicken With Forty Cloves of Garlic, French in origin, was popularized years ago by the late James Beard and Julia Child. Over the ensuing years, dozens of variations have surfaced thanks to innovative chefs who added their own favorite herbs, some broth and/or wine, and slightly different ways of prepping the chicken for the oven. We were pleased when our staff at Cuisinarts came up with their own recipe using legs and thighs in lieu of a whole chicken. This meant you could up or down the recipe to suit the number of people you intended to serve, and the dark chicken meat did not dry out like white meat often tends to do in a long cooking process, even though we suggest removing the skin before baking. The heady aroma of baking garlic with a hint of tarragon will awaken your taste buds in anticipation.

2 large heads of garlic
4 chicken legs (this includes thighs and drumsticks)
2 teaspoons vegetable oil
2 medium celery ribs, sliced
1/2 teaspoon dried tarragon
salt and fresh-ground black pepper
1/3 cup dry vermouth

Preheat the oven to 350 degrees.

Separate the garlic cloves, counting out approximately 40 of the best. In a saucepan simmer the cloves in a pot of boiling water to cover for about 1 minute. Drain and rinse under cold water. Slip off and discard the skins, reserve the cloves.

Separate the thighs and drumsticks and remove the skin and any visible fat. Rub the chicken with the vegetable oil. Place the chicken in a lightly oiled baking dish, just large enough to hold it in one layer with sides just touching. Add the celery and sprinkle with the seasonings. Distribute the garlic over the chicken and add the vermouth. Cover and bake in the center of the oven until both chicken and garlic are tender, about 1-1/2 to 1-3/4 hours.

Makes 4 servings.

Dragon Palace Mango Chicken

DRAGON PALACE MANGO CHICKEN

A good friend who has traveled widely and admits to eating at some of the finest Chinese restaurants in New York, Boston, San Francisco, and Vancouver claims this Mango Chicken from the Dragon Palace restaurant in Lauderdale Lakes, Florida, exceeds any dish he had ever eaten in the above cities. You will agree with this assessment once you experience the extraordinary flavors and visually enjoy the colorful presentation of the combination of vegetables. We suggest serving this with rice and a sprinkling of crunchy chow mein noodles.

Chicken:

- 1 large egg white
- 1 teaspoon cornstarch
- 1 tablespoon water
- pinch white pepper
- pinch salt
- 3 skinless, boneless chicken breast halves (about 14 ounces total), cut diagonally into slices a bit smaller than 1/2 inch

Sauce:

- 1/2 teaspoon salt
- 2 teaspoons sugar
- 1 teaspoon white vinegar
- 1 teaspoon cornstarch
- 2 teaspoons ketchup
- 1 tablespoon water

Vegetables:

- 2 cups water
- 12 snow peas
- 1 medium carrot, sliced on the diagonal (about 1/4-inch slices)
- 3/4 medium green pepper (cut vertically into 1-inch strips, then cut the strips into triangles)
- 3/4 medium red pepper, cut the same as the green pepper
- pinch salt

Mango:

- 1 large semiripe mango
- 1 teaspoon salt
- 2 cups water

Aromatics:

> 1 teaspoon fresh minced ginger
> 1 teaspoon minced garlic
> 4 scallions, white part only, coarsely chopped
> 5 tablespoons vegetable oil, divided
> 1 tablespoon dry sherry
> 2 teaspoons sesame oil

To prepare the chicken, whisk all the ingredients except the chicken in a medium bowl until well mixed. Add the chicken and swoosh around with your fingers to make certain all the chicken is completely covered. (If you are going ahead with the rest of the preparation now, you can leave the chicken out—but no longer than 30 minutes. Otherwise, cover and refrigerate until ready to use.)

To prepare the sauce, whisk all the ingredients together in a small bowl. Set aside.

To prepare the vegetables, bring the water to a boil in a medium saucepan. Add the remaining ingredients and bring back to a boil; lower the heat and let cook for one minute. Drain well and reserve.

To prepare the mango, peel and cut into 1-inch chunks. Stir together the water and salt until the salt has dissolved. Add the mango chunks and set aside.

To complete the Mango Chicken, in a large heavy skillet (preferably nonstick), heat 3 teaspoons of the oil over medium-high heat. Remove the chicken from the marinade and stir-fry the chicken just until no pink remains—about 1-1/2 minutes. Remove to paper towels with a slotted spoon.

Drain and dry the mango chunks on paper towels. Add 1 teaspoon of oil to the skillet and sauté the mango just until some of the chunks begin to take on some color—about 1-1/2 minutes. Add to the reserved chicken.

Add the remaining teaspoon of oil to the skillet and stir-fry the ginger, garlic, and scallions until softened but not brown—about 1 minute. Return the chicken and mango chunks to the skillet, then the blanched vegetables. Stir in the sauce and cook until slightly thickened. Drizzle in the wine and sesame oil and toss well.

Serve over rice and sprinkle with some crunchy chow mein noodles.

Makes 2 hearty or 4 moderate servings.

EASY, EASY CHICKEN

Over the years there have been a number of recipes appearing combining various preserves, such as apricot or orange, with other ingredients such as Russian dressing, Wish-Bone Italian dressing, and various dry soup mixes, among others. We have probably tried most of them. Each was fairly tasty but not memorable. Then a Connecticut neighbor passed on the one published years ago by the A.1. Steak Sauce people. That was voted the best by far, and we named it our Easy, Easy Chicken. We did opt to remove the skin on the chicken and found the flavor even better since the sauce penetrated the flesh more readily. You will be glad we included this recipe as a reminder of the old saying "simplest is sometimes best."

6 large skinned and boned chicken breast halves (about 6 ounces each)
1 teaspoon garlic salt
1/2 cup orange marmalade
1/4 cup A.1. Steak Sauce
1/2 cup ketchup

Preheat the oven to 375 degrees. Spray a shallow baking pan with no-stick vegetable spray.

Sprinkle the chicken breast with the garlic salt and place in the baking pan in one layer. Combine the remaining ingredients well in a small bowl and spread over the chicken. Cover the pan with foil and bake in the center of the oven for 30 minutes. Remove the foil and continue baking for another 30 minutes, or until the chicken is tender and well glazed.

Makes 6 servings.

GROUND TURKEY STROGANOFF

A few years ago, we were asked if it would be possible to substitute ground turkey in a recipe that originally called for ground beef, as well as using fat-free sour cream in place of the real stuff. We gladly made a few adjustments to our original ground meat stroganoff recipe calling for hamburger and were pleased with the lower-calorie version, which we called (of course) Ground Turkey Stroganoff. We like to serve this on some plain rice.

- 2 tablespoons butter or margarine
- 1/2 cup fine-chopped onions
- 1 clove garlic, minced
- 1 pound lean ground turkey
- 2 tablespoons all-purpose flour
- 1 can (3.5 ounces) stems and pieces of mushrooms, drained (chop any large pieces)
- 1 can (10-3/4 ounces) Campbell's Condensed Healthy Request Cream of Mushroom Soup
- 1/4 cup skim milk
- 1/4 teaspoon paprika
- 1 cup imitation (fat-free) sour cream
- salt and fresh-ground pepper to taste

In a large, heavy nonstick skillet, melt the butter over medium heat. Sauté the onions until golden, about 3 minutes. Add the garlic and turkey and cook, breaking up the turkey and stirring until no pink remains, about 4 minutes. Sprinkle the flour over the turkey mixture, then stir in the mushrooms, soup, skim milk, and paprika. Simmer uncovered for 10 minutes. Add the sour cream and heat through—do not boil. Season to taste. Good served on some plain rice.

Makes 4 servings.

HENRY'S COQ AU VIN

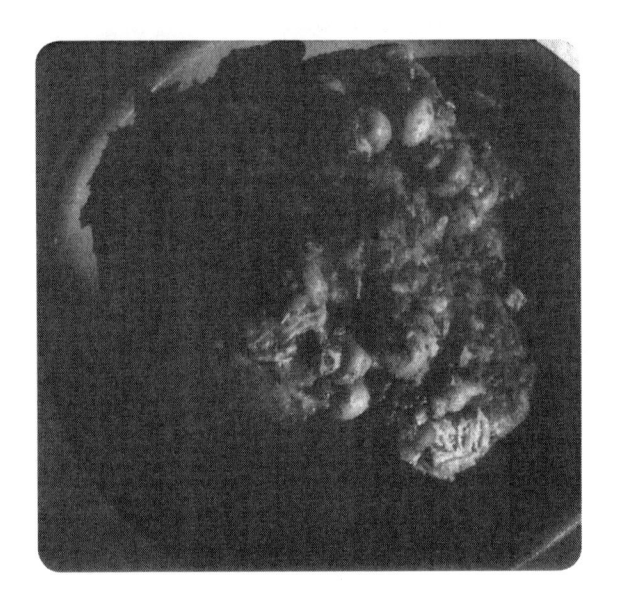

Henry's Coq Au Vin

Plan your time ahead for Henry's (restaurant) Coq Au Vin. Between the veal stock's long simmer one day and the cooking of all the bacon and savory vegetables as well as the wine and stock reductions and the final baking the next day, be prepared for your house (or apartment) to be filled with incredibly tantalizing aromas. However, eating this dish is the best treat of all. The Veal Stock, which we recommend you make a day ahead, yields about 6 cups. The recipe requires four, so you will have two cups to freeze as a bonus. The classic Coq Au Vin is usually made with whole chickens, but Chef Grant recommended using already-cut-up chickens. You can choose only white or dark meat or a combination. The chef prefers boneless thighs since the dark meat not only retains its moisture during the long cooking, but adds flavor to the resulting sauce.

The Sauce:

- 4 strips lean bacon, diced
- 3/4 cup diced carrots
- 3/4 cup diced onions
- 3/4 cup diced celery
- 2 cups peeled, seeded and diced tomatoes
- 1 tablespoon each chopped fresh thyme, parsley and oregano
- 2 tablespoons light brown sugar
- 8 ounces small button mushrooms, cleaned
- 2 cups red wine, either Pinot Noir or Cabernet Sauvignon recommended
- 4 cups Veal Stock (recipe given)
- salt and fresh-ground pepper

The Chicken:

- 8 large boneless, skinless chicken thighs
- 1/3 cup all-purpose flour
- 1 tablespoon chopped fresh thyme
- salt and fresh-ground pepper
- vegetable oil for frying

To make the sauce, in a large skillet or sauté pan, sauté the bacon over medium heat until light brown. Add the carrots, onions, and celery; and cook, stirring for about 3 minutes or until these begin to soften. Add the tomatoes, herbs, brown sugar, and mushrooms; and continue cooking and stirring until the vegetables are tender and there is little liquid left. Add the wine, bring to a simmer, and reduce by half. Add the stock and reduce the mixture by a quarter. Season to taste.

While the sauce is cooking, prepare the chicken. Trim any excess fat from the thighs. Roll the flaps together so they resemble thighs with the bone in. With a fork, stir together the flour, thyme, salt, and pepper in a flat bowl.

In a large skillet or sauté pan, add enough oil to measure 1-1/2 inches. Heat the oil over medium-high heat to a temperature of 400 degrees. Dredge each thigh in the flour mixture. Shake off any excess and place flap side down in the heated oil. Cook for about 2 minutes or until nicely browned. Turn and brown the second side. Remove to some paper towels to drain briefly.

Preheat the oven to 330 degrees. Place the chicken flap side down in a shallow baking pan. Spoon the sauce evenly over the chicken, making sure everything is well covered. Cover with heavy aluminum foil or a tight-fitting lid and bake for 1 hour and 45 minutes.

Makes 8 servings.

Veal Stock:

- 2 pounds veal knuckles (hock or heel) cracked into 2-inch pieces
- 2 pounds thick slices veal shank with large bones, cracked
- 6 ounces chicken backs and necks
- 3 quarts water
- 4 parsley sprigs
- 1/4 teaspoon dried thyme
- 1/4 teaspoon dried marjoram
- 1 small bay leaf, crumbled
- 1 large carrot, roughly diced
- 3 large celery ribs, roughly diced
- 1 medium onion, roughly diced
- 3 whole cloves
- 6 black peppercorns
- 2 teaspoons salt

Put all ingredients into a large (at least 5-quart) pot. Bring slowly to a boil over medium heat, skimming foam from liquid as necessary. When the liquid begins to boil, reduce heat so that it retains a good simmer. Partially cover and cook for 4 hours. You might stir it a time or two.

Remove from the heat and let sit 30 minutes. Line a large strainer or colander with cheesecloth and strain the stock into a large bowl. Press solids to extract all the good stuff. Cool quickly and refrigerate. Fat will solidify on top when cool and can be removed easily.

Makes about 6 cups.

Palm Chicken

PALM CHICKEN

Like many other outstanding recipes, the ingredients in Palm Chicken are all readily available. Again, it is the chef's skillful use of those ingredients which guarantees a delectable dish like this that, once tried, will remain high on one's "make again" list. The canned hearts of palm, which always remind one of white asparagus, have a flavor similar to the artichoke and a texture that is silky and tender, giving this dish its special appeal. It is comforting to know that there are now varieties of palm trees that sprout up many separate shoots that can be harvested without having to kill the entire tree. That makes fresh hearts of palm, with their crisp texture and a slightly woody flavor, more available to chefs and home cooks to use in a variety of ways, including deep frying. Make sure you serve this dish with rice or pasta (such as fettuccine) to help you enjoy the deliciously rich sauce.

4 large (about 6 ounces each) skinless, boneless chicken breast halves
1 large egg, lightly beaten
1/4 cup all-purpose flour
2 medium garlic cloves, finely chopped
8 ounces fresh mushrooms, cleaned, stems trimmed, and cut into 1/4-inch slices
1-1/2 cups heavy cream
3 tablespoons unsalted butter
2 tablespoons fresh-grated Parmesan cheese
4 to 6 stalks canned hearts of palm, cut into 1/2-inch slices
2 tablespoons sliced almonds, toasted*

Dip the chicken breasts in the beaten egg, then the flour. Heat the oil in a large heavy skillet over medium-high heat. Brown the chicken on both sides, about 1 minute per side, and remove to paper towels. (This is not long enough to cook the chicken through, but because it will be simmered later, this ensures the chicken will not be overcooked.)

Add the mushrooms and garlic and sauté for just a few minutes, about 2. Drain off any excess oil if any. Cut the chicken diagonally into 1/2-inch strips and return to the pan with the remaining ingredients except the almonds. Stir well to mix and reduce, uncovered, over medium heat until the desired thickness. Ours took about 6 minutes. Stir in the almonds and serve hot over rice or pasta.

Makes 4 servings.

*To toast the almonds, spread in a single layer in a baking pan and bake in a 350-degree oven until lightly browned—about 6 to 8 minutes.

Pete's Chicken Pecan

PETE'S CHICKEN PECAN

From Pete's—a popular restaurant in Boca Raton, Florida—comes the best Chicken Pecan dish we have ever eaten. Not only is the chicken tender and flavorful with its crust of bread crumbs and pecans, but the apricot-chutney mustard sauce is absolutely ambrosial. The optional toasted coconut sprinkled over each serving adds yet another dimension to the visual appeal of this delicious dish. The sauce can be made about an hour ahead. It will thicken a bit on standing but will loosen up perfectly when reheated slowly.

Apricot Mustard Sauce:

- 2 cups heavy cream
- 4 large canned apricot halves, drained
- 1/2 cup mango chutney
- 1 tablespoon Dijon-style mustard
- 2 tablespoons dry white wine
- 1 tablespoon honey
- 1 tablespoon red wine vinegar
- 1 tablespoon arrowroot, mixed with 1 tablespoon water

In a large heavy saucepan, bring the heavy cream slowly to a boil and reduce by 1/3 at a comfortable simmer. Measure the depth on the handle of a wooden spoon and check periodically until the proper reduction has been reached.

In a food processor fitted with the metal blade, or a blender, puree all remaining ingredients except the arrowroot. Whisk the mixture into the reduced cream and simmer gently for 2 minutes. Whisk in the arrowroot and cook, stirring, until thickened. Reserve while fixing the chicken. Makes about 2 cups.

Chicken:

- 4 large boneless, skinless chicken breast halves, about 6 to 7 ounces each
- 1/4 cup all-purpose flour
- 1 large egg, lightly beaten
- 1-3/4 cups fresh bread crumbs (about 4 slices firm white bread, crusts removed)
- 1/2 cup coarse-chopped pecans
- 3 tablespoons vegetable oil
- 1/2 cup loose-packed, flaked coconut, toasted* optional

Pound the chicken breasts between pieces of wax paper to an even thickness of about 1/4 inch. Dip each breast in flour, then the beaten egg. Pat both sides of the breasts with the bread crumbs and pecans.

In a large nonstick skillet, heat the oil over medium-high heat. Sauté the prepared breasts until golden brown on both sides and just cooked through. This should take no more than 1-1/2 minutes a side. Remove to paper towels.

To serve, reheat the sauce if necessary and divide among 4 warmed serving plates. Place a chicken breast on the sauce and sprinkle with the toasted coconut.

Makes 4 servings.

*To toast the coconut, preheat the oven to 350 degrees. Spread out the coconut in a single layer in a baking pan and bake for 7 to 8 minutes, stirring once, or until the coconut is a toasty brown.

POTTED TURKEY LEGS

Potted Turkey Leg

You will need to check with your butcher before you make these outstandingly delicious Potted Turkey Legs because whole fresh turkey legs are not always available. The restaurant and deli owner who kindly shared this recipe with us said it was a very popular dish, and we can attest to that. Served in its entire tender splendor and masked with the most flavorful gravy—a reduction of the strained roasting ingredients—it will become a favorite anywhere. Our turkey legs were so meaty that we cut off the remaining meat and served it the following day over lightly buttered homemade whole wheat toast covered with the leftover gravy.

2 jumbo fresh turkey legs, about 1 pound each
1 teaspoon paprika
2 large garlic cloves, smashed
1/2 medium onion, diced
2 large celery ribs, cut into 1/4-inch slices
1 medium carrot, scrubbed (no need to peel) and diced
3 tablespoons tomato juice
1 teaspoon granulated garlic
1 teaspoon fresh-ground white pepper
3 chicken bouillon cubes dissolved in 4 cups hot water
1/4 cup (1 stick) unsalted butter
1/3 cup all-purpose flour

Preheat the oven to 450 degrees.

Rinse the turkey legs and pat dry with paper towels. Place them in a shallow roasting pan with a tight fitting lid. Add all the ingredients in the order listed, except the butter and flour, distributing them evenly over and around the turkey. Lift the turkey legs to allow some liquid underneath to prevent them from sticking to the pan. Bring the mixture to a boil on top of the stove. Cover and place in the center of the preheated oven.

Bake the turkey for about 45 to 50 minutes, or until fork tender and the thickest part of the legs register 170 degrees on an instant-reading meat thermometer. Remove the legs to a platter and cover loosely with foil to keep warm while making the gravy.

Strain the liquid remaining in the roasting pan and reserve. (We had about 3-1/2 cups.) Press firmly on the vegetables to extract as much flavor as possible. Discard the solids. In a heavy saucepan melt the butter over medium heat. Stir in the flour and cook, stirring, until the roux is just beginning to take on color. Remove from the heat and whisk in the reserved strained liquid. Return to medium heat, bring to a boil, then reduce to medium-low and let simmer until reduced by about half. (This took about 30 minutes.) Stir frequently, especially as the gravy reduces, to prevent it from sticking to the bottom of the pan. You will have about 1-2/3 cups.

To serve, place a turkey leg on each of two large serving platters and cover with the gravy. Make sure you have lots of crusty bread to help you enjoy every bit of that delicious and aromatic gravy.

Makes 2 generous servings.

PRETZEL CHICKEN WITH BEURRE BLANC SAUCE

Pretzel Chicken with Beurre Blanc Sauce

Once you taste this Pretzel Chicken with Beurre Blanc sauce—with its unusual coating combination of pretzels, bacon bits, Parmesan cheese, and fresh parsley—you may never go back to plain or even Italian-flavored bread crumbs to coat any food. And you can thank the owner and chefs at the Big Bear Brewing Company restaurant further for the unique dipping batter made from McCormick's Golden Dipt Fish 'n Chips mix, which they combine with beer instead of water. That and the accompanying Beurre Blanc Sauce enhanced with grainy mustard served once the crumb-coated chicken is sautéed until golden brown, all contribute to the many delicious flavor dimensions.

Crumb Mixture:

- 1 cup pretzel crumbs (we used about 2 cups of Snyder's Butter Snaps in the food processor)
- 1/4 cup bacon bits (we used Betty Crocker brand Bacos)
- 1 cup fresh-grated Parmesan cheese
- 1/4 cup fresh-chopped parsley
- 1/2 teaspoon salt
- 1/4 teaspoon fresh-ground pepper

Batter:

    1 cup McCormick Golden Dipt Fish 'n Chips batter mix*

    3/4 cup (or more) red beer

Chicken:

    3 tablespoons unsalted butter
    3 tablespoons vegetable oil
    6 boneless, skinless chicken breast halves (about 5 ounces each)
    Beurre Blanc Sauce (recipe given)

To make the crumb mixture, stir all the ingredients together well in a bowl large enough in which to dip the chicken breasts. Set aside.

In another bowl large enough to dip the chicken breasts in, whisk together the batter mix and beer. If the mixture seems too thick—it should be the consistency of very lightly whipped cream—add a little more beer a tablespoon at a time.

To prepare the chicken, preheat the oven to 375 degrees. Heat the butter and oil together in a large heavy skillet or sauté pan over medium-high heat. Dip each piece of chicken in the batter, letting excess drip off, then cover well with the crumbs. Sauté the chicken for about 2 minutes a side, or until golden brown and not quite cooked through. Transfer to a baking sheet and finish cooking them in the oven—about 5 to 7 minutes more. Serve at once with the Beurre Blanc Sauce.

Makes 6 servings.

*Available in most supermarkets in the baking products aisle.

Beurre Blanc Sauce:

    2 tablespoons butter
    1 large shallot, finely chopped
    1/3 cup dry white wine
    2 teaspoons chicken base (we used the Better Than Bouillon chicken base)
    1-2/3 cups heavy cream
    3 teaspoons cornstarch
    3 teaspoons water
    1 teaspoon grainy mustard (this is optional but highly recommended)

In a heavy saucepan, melt the butter over medium heat. Add the shallots and sauté for 2 minutes. Add the white wine and chicken base. Stir to dissolve the base. Let come to a simmer and cook for about 5 to 7 minutes, or until most of the liquid has evaporated. Stir in the heavy cream and bring back to a simmer.

Mix the cornstarch and water together to make what the restaurant calls a "slurry." Slowly stir this into the cream mixture and continue cooking and stirring until the mixture thickens and coats the back of a spoon. Let simmer for another minute or two. If using the mustard, stir in the last minute of simmering.

Makes about 1-3/4 cups.

Stuffed Chicken Breasts

STUFFED CHICKEN BREASTS

Of all the Stuffed Chicken Breasts recipes we have enjoyed, this from a delightful restaurant in Davie, Florida, is one of our favorites. The stuffing of fresh spinach, zucchini, mushrooms, and shredded mozzarella combined with an incredible sauce of more sautéed mushrooms, brandy, Marsala wine, and marinara sauce makes a perfect culinary marriage. You can make the stuffing several hours or even a day ahead (refrigerated, covered) since it needs to be cooled completely before stuffing the chicken breasts. You will enjoy the chef/owner Fulvio's comments on how to tell when the chicken is done: "Poke it with a fork. If it leaks, it's done!" He was referring, of course, to the stuffing with its mozzarella cheese—which turns that stuffing into a soft, succulent mixture.

Stuffing:

- 3 cups (about 2-1/2 ounces) loosely packed, washed and stemmed fresh spinach leaves
- 8 medium mushrooms, cleaned, stems removed, quartered
- 1 small zucchini, ends trimmed, cut into 1-inch pieces
- 2 tablespoons olive oil
- salt and fresh-ground black pepper
- 3/4 cup shredded mozzarella cheese

The Stuffed Chicken:

- 4 large boneless, skinless chicken breast halves (about 6 ounce each)
- 1/4 cup all-purpose flour
- 1 large egg, beaten with 2 teaspoons cold water
- 3/4 cup dried bread crumbs
- 3 tablespoons unsalted butter
- 8 medium mushrooms, cleaned, stems removed and thinly sliced
- 1/4 cup brandy
- 1/4 cup Marsala wine
- 1/4 cup marinara sauce
- 1/4 cup chicken broth

To make the stuffing, in a food processor fitted with the metal blade or a blender, process the spinach, mushrooms, and zucchini to a chop somewhere between medium and fine.

In a medium nonstick skillet, heat the oil over medium-high heat. Cook the processed vegetables, stirring frequently until soft but not brown and most of the moisture has evaporated. This will take about 8 minutes. Season to taste and set aside to cool completely. (Can be covered and refrigerated overnight.) When cool, stir in the mozzarella cheese. Reserve.

To make the stuffed chicken breasts, pound the breasts between pieces of wax paper to an even 1/4-inch thickness. Divide the stuffing into four compact balls about 1-1/2 inches in diameter. Place a ball in the center of each chicken breast and bring up the sides to completely enclose the stuffing. Use toothpicks to hold it all together. (This takes a bit of maneuvering.)

Dredge each breast in the flour; dip in the egg wash and then in the bread crumbs. Set aside to dry while you cook the mushrooms.

In a large nonstick skillet, melt the butter over medium-high heat. Sauté the mushrooms until just limp—about 2 minutes. Add the stuffed chicken breasts, brown nicely on all sides, reduce heat to low, cover, and cook about 10 minutes. Uncover; stir in the brandy, Marsala, marinara sauce, and chicken broth. Re-cover and continue cooking for about 5 minutes more or, to quote Fulvio, "When you poke it with a fork, it leaks." The stuffing, of course.

To serve, place each stuffed breast on a warm serving plate and drizzle with an equal amount of the aromatic sauce.

Makes 4 servings.

TENDER POACHED CHICKEN BREASTS

This is an easy method of cooking chicken breasts to retain their tenderness and moistness for use in any recipe calling for cooked chicken. You can adjust the ingredients to poach as many or as few as you wish.

4 whole boned and skinned chicken breasts, split
1/4 cup chicken bouillon (we use a heaping 1/4 teaspoon Better Than Bouillon chicken base dissolved in 1/4 cup hot water)
1/2 cup dry white wine
1/2 teaspoon crushed dried rosemary leaves
fresh-ground black pepper

Preheat the oven to 400 degrees. Tuck the narrow or thin ends of the chicken breasts under and place the breasts side by side in a baking dish just large enough to hold, snugly, however many you are poaching.

Combine the bouillon and wine and pour over the breasts. Insert a knife between all the breasts to be sure the liquid reaches between them. Sprinkle with the rosemary and pepper. Cover with a tight-fitting lid or a double thickness of aluminum foil and bake in the center of the oven for about 25 minutes, or until just cooked through and no pink remains.

Makes 8 poached chicken breast halves.

TURKEY LOAVES WITH APRICOT GLAZE

We use the plural "loaves" here since this recipe—for what was described by those who tasted it as "divine"—calls for shaping the turkey mixture into two free-form loaves. Each loaf serves 4 to 6, but if you don't plan to serve 8 or more, the baked loaves can be frozen, well wrapped, for up to 4 months. (Of course, leftovers can also be savored in cold or warm sandwiches for the next few days.) Just defrost overnight in the refrigerator, cut into serving slices, and reheat briefly in the microwave. They are guaranteed to taste as fresh as the day they were originally baked. The sliced loaves are appealingly colorful with their diced bits of carrot and red pepper, and there is just enough hint of sage to add interest to each bite. This is indeed comfort food at its best.

Turkey Loaves:

- 1/4 cup plus 2 tablespoons olive oil
- 4 medium garlic cloves, finely chopped
- 1 large onion, cut into small dice (about 1/4 inch)
- 2 medium carrots, cut into small dice (about 1/4 inch)
- 1/2 a medium sweet red pepper, cut into small dice (about 1/4 inch)
- 5 slices firm white bread (we used Pepperidge Farm Original White bread), cut into small dice (about 1/4 inch)
- 3/4 cup milk
- 2-1/2 pounds lean (important) ground turkey
- 4 large eggs, lightly beaten
- 1/4 cup fine-chopped fresh sage leaves (can substitute 1 tablespoon dried rubbed)
- 1/3 cup chopped fresh parsley
- salt and fresh-ground black pepper, to taste
- apricot glaze, recipe given

In a large skillet, heat 2 tablespoons of the olive oil over medium heat. Sauté the garlic, onions, carrots, and pepper for about 3 minutes, or until soft. Remove from the heat and cool to room temperature.

Soak the bread cubes in the milk until the milk is absorbed.

In a large mixing bowl combine all the ingredients, including the remaining 1/4 cup olive oil, well. (Clean hands work best here.) Shape the mixture into two free-form loaves and place side by side in a lightly oiled 9-inch square baking pan. The loaves can be made ahead to this point, covered loosely with plastic wrap and refrigerated for several hours. Remove from the refrigerator 35 to 40 minutes before baking.

To bake, preheat the oven to 375 degrees and cook the loaves in the center of the oven for 1 hour, or until internal temperature has reached 145 degrees. Drain off any scum (protein) and grease and transfer the loaves to heated platters. Brush liberally with the apricot glaze.

Makes 2 loaves, each serving 4 to 6.

Apricot Glaze:

1/3 cup apricot preserves
1 teaspoon Dijon mustard

1 teaspoon whole grain mustard (we used Grey Poupon Country Mustard)
dash fresh-ground black pepper

Warm the preserves in a small saucepan over low heat. Press through a sieve into a small bowl and stir in the mustards and black pepper.

Makes about 1/3 cup.

MAIN DISHES (SEAFOOD)

Atlantic Salmon with Sun-Dried
Tomato Vinaigrette

ATLANTIC SALMON WITH SUN-DRIED TOMATO VINAIGRETTE

This is guaranteed to become your favorite way to serve fresh salmon. We strongly urge you to buy your fish from a reliable source where freshness and full flavor are a given and you won't be disappointed with less than the best. The Sun-Dried Tomato Vinaigrette is a true culinary coup. The mélange of strong flavors (sun-dried tomatoes, balsamic vinegar, fresh basil, garlic, shallots, and olive oil) come together in a most delightfully tangy, tasty sauce that compliments the full-flavored salmon fillets perfectly. Should you be fortunate enough to have any leftover vinaigrette as we did, it is delicious over other seafood, to marinate chicken breasts before baking, and even drizzled over a bowl of pasta.

Sun-Dried Tomato Vinaigrette:

1/2 cup sun-dried tomatoes (not in oil), reconstituted* (about 14 halves)
1 medium clove garlic, peeled and halved
1 medium shallot, peeled and quartered

1/2 cup loosely packed fresh basil leaves
3/4 cup balsamic vinegar, divided
1-1/4 cups extra virgin olive oil
salt and fresh-ground black pepper to taste

Salmon:

6 salmon fillets, about 8 ounces each, skin removed

2 tablespoons olive oil

To make the vinaigrette, in a food processor fitted with the metal blade or a good blender, puree the tomatoes, garlic, shallot, basil, and 2 tablespoons of the vinegar. Add the remaining vinegar and, with the motor running, pour the olive oil in slowly. Season to taste with salt and pepper. This can be made several hours or a day ahead. Refrigerate, covered, but bring to room temperature before using.

To prepare the salmon, preheat the oven broiler. Brush the salmon on both sides with olive oil and place skinned side up on a broiler pan. Broil the salmon about 4 to 6 inches from the heat source for about 4 minutes. Turn carefully and continue cooking for an additional 4 to 5 minutes or until the flesh is just opaque throughout. Remember, cooking time is generally about 10 minutes per inch of fish.

To serve, place the fillets on warmed serving dishes and top with about 1/4 cup of the vinaigrette.

Makes 6 servings.

*To reconstitute the dried tomatoes: cover with water, bring to a boil over medium-high heat, then lower the heat and simmer for about 4 minutes. Remove from the heat and let cool in the water. Drain well.

BAKED BEER BATTER SHRIMP

For anyone who loves fried beer batter shrimp but whose physician may have recommended avoiding fried foods, this Baked Beer Batter Shrimp is the answer. We have managed to fool family and guests alike who swear the shrimp is fried. There are a number of good coating mixes on the market now, but we found making our own was simple, fast, and could be tailored to this specific dish. Serve these crispy mouthfuls with chili sauce or tartar sauce.

1/3 cup all-purpose flour
1/4 cup dark beer
1 large egg white
1/2 teaspoon salt, divided
3/4 cup dry unseasoned bread crumbs
1/4 cup fine-chopped pecans (we also tried cashews and liked them)
fresh-ground black pepper to taste
1 pound medium shrimp, peeled and deveined with tails left on
lemon wedges

Preheat the oven to 450 degrees. Spray a wire rack large enough to hold the shrimp in a single layer with no-stick vegetable spray. Place the rack on a baking sheet. Set aside.

In a medium bowl, whisk together the flour, beer, egg white, and half the salt until creamy and smooth. In another bowl, combine the bread crumbs, nuts, pepper, and remaining salt. Dip the shrimp first in the bread-crumb mixture, then the egg-white mixture, and again in the bread crumbs. Turn them with a fork to make sure they are well coated. Place without touching on the prepared rack. Bake in the center of the oven for 12 to 15 minutes or until golden brown. Serve immediately with a lemon wedge or two. (Also good with some chili sauce or tartar sauce.)

Makes 4 servings.

Dolphin Zingara

DOLPHIN ZINGARA

Our experience with the sauce known by the name *zingara* had been with foods other than seafood—primarily poultry or veal. One bite of Dolphin Zingara will convince you that, with minor variations, this sauce is a perfect partner for seafood as well. Some of the so-called original recipes included chopped ham, tongue, Belgian endives, and even truffles; but thanks to innovative chefs, this thoroughly flavorful, tomato-based wine sauce has been modified now and then to be the perfect accompaniment to almost any meat, seafood, or even pasta dishes. You can adjust the heat of your sauce by the amount of cayenne pepper you choose to use. Be prepared to savor every bite.

- 2 dolphin fillets, each about 8 ounces, skinned and boned
- 5 heaping tablespoons all-purpose flour, divided
- 2 tablespoons olive oil
- 2 tablespoons plus 1 teaspoon butter, divided
- 6 large mushrooms, stems trimmed and thinly sliced
- 6 quartered marinated artichoke hearts (we like Vigo's Imported and Quartered)
- 4 halves sun-dried tomatoes (either dried and reconstituted or in oil, both drained) cut into 1/4-inch julienne strips
- 5 ounces dry white wine
- 1-1/2 cups chicken broth
- 2 heaping teaspoons your choice marinara sauce
- pinch cayenne pepper (or to taste)
- salt and fresh-ground pepper

Dredge both sides of the dolphin fillets in 2 tablespoons of the flour. Shake off any excess.

Heat the olive oil in a large nonstick skillet over medium-high heat. Brown the fillets, turning once for about 2 minutes per side. Set aside and discard any oil remaining in the skillet.

Add 2 tablespoons of the butter to the skillet and melt over medium heat. Add the mushrooms, artichoke hearts, and sun-dried tomatoes; and sauté for about 1 minute just to soften the mushrooms. Stir in the remaining 3 tablespoons flour, then add the wine and chicken broth and seasonings. Stir over low heat until slightly thickened, about 3 minutes. Bring to a boil and simmer over low heat until reduced to your desired consistency, about 15 minutes. Halfway before the sauce is done, return the dolphin fillets to the skillet and simmer in the sauce, turning once, for 4 minutes a side.

To serve, add 1/2 teaspoon butter on top of each fillet and let it melt into the sauce. Transfer the fillets to warmed individual serving dishes and divide the sauce between them.

Makes 2 servings.

GRILLED LOBSTER CLUB SANDWICH

Grilled Lobster Club Sandwich

Providing your taste buds are in working mode, just reading through the list of ingredients (applewood-smoked bacon, vine-ripe tomatoes, arugula, Cajun Remoulade, and of course, lobster) will convince you how special and delicious this sandwich is going to be. Once you taste the Cajun Remoulade, you won't relegate it to this outstanding sandwich only. Try it with other seafood and/or chicken. Just FYI, that *hogie* (hoagie) roll—whose original Italian contents consisted of prosciutto, salami, and provolone cheese—was named after Italian immigrants who worked on the shipyards of Hog Island and bought these for lunch. The workers were nicknamed "hoagies" and, over the years, the name was given to the sandwich but under a different spelling.

Cajun Remoulade:

- 2 teaspoons brandy
- 2 teaspoons wasabi powder*
- 1 teaspoon chopped capers
- 2 teaspoons chopped fresh dill
- 1/8 teaspoon Tabasco sauce
- 1/8 teaspoon Worcestershire sauce
- 1 teaspoon fresh lemon juice
- 1/2 teaspoon prepared horseradish
- 1/3 cup mayonnaise
- 1/4 cup cocktail sauce
- 1/4 teaspoon salt or to taste
- 1/4 teaspoon fresh-ground black pepper or to taste

In a medium bowl, stir the brandy and wasabi powder together to form a paste. Add the remaining ingredients. (We used a whisk to beat the ingredients well.) Refrigerate until ready to use, stirring again.

Makes about 1/2 cup plus 1 tablespoon.

Lobster Club Sandwich:

2 slices thick cut applewood-smoked bacon**
1 cornmeal-dusted hogie roll
8 medium arugula leaves
2 small broiled Maine lobster tails
4 slices medium ripe tomato

Cook the bacon until crisp. Drain on paper towels. Slice the roll lengthwise and lightly toast the cut surfaces. Spread about 2 heaping tablespoons of the Cajun Remoulade on each side. Top with arugula leaves.

Remove the lobster meat from the shells and pound slightly. (This is so they fit nicely on the lower half of the roll.) Place the lobster flesh on the arugula, then the strips of bacon, then the tomato slices, and cover with the top half of the roll. (You might want to stick a small skewer or two through the sandwich to hold it nicely together.)

Makes 1 serving.

*Available in some supermarkets and specialty shops.
**Available in some supermarkets and your favorite meat market

LA COQUILLE SHRIMP PASTA

La Coquille Shrimp Pasta

We had to translate one of our familiar American slang expressions, "this dish literally knocked our socks off," for French owner/chef Jean Bert of La Coquille restaurant when we asked if he would be willing to share his recipe for Shrimp Pasta requested by one of our readers. You will agree with that expression when you taste the superb flavors of the dish, thanks to the savory sauce that is worth every minute of the time it involves in the making. The hint of red from the delicate saffron threads and the green of the chopped fresh basil add to the perfect culinary painting on each serving plate.

36 large uncooked, unshelled shrimp (10 to 15 to a pound)
5 tablespoons olive oil, divided
1 large, sweet onion, minced
3 large leeks, white part and 1 inch of light green, trimmed, washed and minced
6 medium garlic cloves, minced (reserve 1 teaspoon to sprinkle over shrimp later)
1 tablespoon Cognac
1/4 cup plus 2 tablespoons dry white wine
2 large garden ripe tomatoes (about 1 pound), diced
6 cups water
salt and cayenne pepper to taste

Bouquet Garni:

1 large bay leaf, 1 sprig fresh thyme (or 1/2 teaspoon dried), and 2 large fresh basil leaves, tied in rinsed cheesecloth—leave about an 8-inch end on the string to drape over the side of the pan

1 large pinch saffron threads, not powder*
1 tablespoon minced fresh basil
12 ounces angel hair pasta, cooked
6 fresh basil leaves or sprigs, for garnish

Peel and devein the shrimp and reserve the shrimp and shells separately.

In a large heavy sauté pan, heat 3 tablespoons of the oil over medium heat. Add the onions, leeks, and garlic (except for the 1 teaspoon kept in reserve). Cook—stirring until softened, but not brown—about 3 to 4 minutes. Add the reserved shrimp shells and stir until they turn red. Add the Cognac, white wine, and diced tomatoes. Stir in the water, salt, and cayenne pepper. Submerge the Bouquet Garni. Bring to a boil, reduce the heat, and cook at an energetic simmer for 10 minutes.

In a food processor fitted with the metal blade, or in a blender, puree the contents of the sauté pan in batches. (Remember to remove the bouquet garni first.) Press the pureed mixture through a fine strainer into a large bowl then return to the sauté pan. Bring to a boil, reduce the heat, and simmer the sauce until it coats the back of a spoon. This took me about 25 minutes. Stir in the saffron threads and keep warm. This makes about 4-1/2 cups.

Heat the remaining 2 tablespoons oil in a large skillet. Sauté the reserved shrimp until they have turned red and are just cooked through—do not overcook. Sprinkle with the remaining 1 teaspoon minced garlic and minced fresh basil.

To serve, divide the sauce around the edge of 6 warmed serving plates. Place a mound of pasta in the center. Arrange 6 shrimp on the sauce on each plate. Garnish the pasta with fresh basil leaves.

Makes 6 servings.

*Saffron threads, though more expensive than the powdered, are preferred by most chefs. There is always a chance that the powdered saffron, particularly if it seems a bargain, is adulterated with other ingredients, such as turmeric.

MAHI MAHI MANGO MANGO

Mahi Mahi Mango Mango

Owner Johannes of a popular restaurant in Boca Raton, Florida, told us he works with mostly local Florida and Caribbean ingredients to create a cuisine that is fun, interesting, and creative. His recipe for Mahi Mahi Mango Mango is a perfect example. The presentation of this dish is outstanding with its riot of color contrasts and the myriad of flavors introduced in both the Black Bean Salsa and Mango Mango sauce. We liked the fact that there were no "hot" ingredients in either sauce—making it light, refreshing, delicate, and fairly bustling with tropical flavors. Both sauces can be made several hours in advance and refrigerated, covered. Just stir well before using. And, FYI, both sauces are delicious with other seafood and poultry.

Mahi Mahi:

4 mahi mahi (dolphin) fillets, about 7 ounces each

salt, fresh-ground black pepper and paprika
1 tablespoon olive oil

Black Bean Salsa:

3/4 cup tender cooked black beans (We used the canned Goya brand, which we rinsed and drained. Save the remaining for a future salad or a salsa repeat.)
1 medium yellow pepper, coarsely chopped
1 small red pepper, coarsely chopped
2 scallions, coarsely chopped
2 tablespoons rice wine vinegar
3 tablespoons extra virgin olive oil
1/4 teaspoon ground cumin, or to taste
salt and fresh-ground pepper to taste

Mango Mango:

1/2 medium green pepper, cut into ¼-inch dice
1/2 medium red pepper, cut into ¼-inch dice
4 tablespoons diced red onion
1 ripe mango, peeled and coarsely chopped
2 tablespoons fresh cilantro, chopped
1/4 cup fresh-squeezed lime juice

To prepare the Mahi Mahi, remove the skin and any bones you can feel. Cover with wax paper and refrigerate until ready to cook.

To prepare the Black Bean Salsa, combine all the ingredients, toss well, and refrigerate, covered until serving time. Stir a time or two while everything is melding. Makes about 2 cups.

To prepare the Mango Mango, combine all the ingredients, toss well and refrigerate, covered until serving time. Stir a time or two while everything is melding. Makes about 2-1/2 cups.

Preheat the oven to 350 degrees. Lightly salt and pepper the dolphin fillets on each side and dust with paprika for color.

In a skillet—preferably nonstick and large enough to hold the fillets in one layer—heat the oil over medium-high heat. Pan sear the fillets, about 1 minute on each side or until nicely browned. If the skillet is not oven-going, transfer the fillets to a baking dish and bake in the center of the oven until just cooked through, about 10 minutes.

Place the fillets in the center of 4 warmed serving plates. Alternate small mounds of the two sauces, about 1/4 cup each, around the fillets. We used two mounds of each. Serve immediately.

Makes 4 servings.

MONKFISH WITH PRUNES

One of our favorite recipes using prunes (after we got weary of stewed prunes and the old-fashioned prune whip Grandmother forced on us) is this delicious Monkfish With Prunes. Prunes have never had the kind of status they enjoyed in France over the years, where prunes were paired with different kinds of meat, poultry, fish, and game and appear as the dominant flavor in many tempting desserts. Several years ago, the California Prune Board asked the FDA for permission to change the name "prune" to "dried plum" to give it an improved image. Considering prunes come in at about the top of the list (ahead of even such greens as kale and spinach) by the amount of antioxidants they contain, we welcomed their emerging popularity.

2 pounds monkfish, cut into serving pieces*	1/2 teaspoon salt
5 ounces lean slab bacon, cut into 1/4-inch dice	1/4 teaspoon fresh-ground black pepper
1/4 cup Cognac	1/2 cup crème fraîche **
16 whole, moist pitted prunes (cut in half)	2 tablespoons Dijon mustard
	4 tablespoons unsalted butter, cut into 4 pats

Pat the fish dry with paper towels and set aside.

Cook the bacon in a large skillet over medium-high heat, stirring, for about 5 minutes or until the bacon is nicely browned. Remove to paper towels with a slotted spoon. Drain off all but 4 tablespoons of the fat.

Add the fish to the skillet in a single layer without crowding and sear each side for about 30 seconds or until lightly browned. (If necessary, do this in batches.) Return all the fish and any accumulated juices to the skillet and reduce the heat to low. Add the Cognac, warm the mixture for 2 minutes, then carefully ignite it. Shake the skillet back and forth until the flames die out, about 1 minute.

Add the prunes, salt, and pepper; cover the skillet; and simmer for 15 minutes. Turn the fish and simmer, covered, for 10 minutes more.

Transfer the fish and prunes to a warm serving platter. Whisk the crème fraîche and mustard into the remaining pan juices and stir in the bacon. Heat the mixture, but do not let it boil.

Just before serving, whisk in the butter one pat at a time and pour the mixture over the fish and prunes.

Makes 6 servings.

*If you can't find monkfish, substitute tuna or swordfish since they are firm-fleshed like the monkfish, although monkfish is milder.

**To make crème fraîche, whisk together 3 tablespoons buttermilk with 2 cups heavy cream (preferably non-ultrapasteurized) in a glass jar. Cover the jar loosely and set aside in a warm place until the mixture becomes very thick—about 24 to 36 hours. Chill overnight in the refrigerator. Makes about 2 cups.

OUT OF DENMARK SNAPPER EN PAPILLOTE

Out of Denmark Snapper

When you see "papillote" on a menu, you can assume it describes a dish served in an envelope, usually of parchment paper. Folded and sealed correctly, no steam can escape and the food inside bakes in its own juices. When opening the papillote, the escaping aroma will put your taste buds on alert. This Snapper en Papillote recipe was created by Monica, the wife of the owner of the Out of Denmark restaurant in Delray Beach, Florida, Jorgen Moller. The flavorful combination of savory vegetables cooked in a mixture of red and white wine and butter, placed on top of perfectly seasoned fish and adorned with fresh mushrooms, bakes to an awesome culinary experience in its envelope of parchment paper, affecting all the senses the minute it is open. You can make the papillotes up to two days ahead, but be certain you have purchased your snapper from a reliable fishmonger to ensure its freshness.

- 3 medium carrots, peeled and cut into 2-inch long fine julienne strips
- 2 fine-sliced small red onions
- 1 large leek, white and 1-inch of green, cleaned and cut into fine julienne strips
- 1/3 cup dry vermouth
- 1/3 cup sweet vermouth
- 10 tablespoons unsalted butter, divided
- 6 pieces parchment paper 15 by 12 inches (the standard roll is 15 inches wide)
- 6 yellowtail snapper fillets (about 7 ounces each), skinned and boned
- salt and fresh-ground black pepper
- 2 fine-diced large shallots
- 12 large wild mushrooms (we like shiitake) cleaned and sliced

In a large pot, place the carrots, onions, leeks, dry and sweet vermouth, and 4 tablespoons of the butter. Bring to a boil over medium-high heat. Reduce the heat, cover, and simmer for about 4 minutes, or until half done (al dente). With a slotted spoon remove the vegetables to a bowl, reserving the liquid. Let both cool completely.

Preheat the oven to 375 degrees. Melt the remaining 6 tablespoons butter.

Fold the pieces of parchment paper in half from the 15-inch side. Start cutting from the folded side, ending up with what looks like half a heart shape. They will measure roughly 10-1/2 inches long and about 7 inches at the widest part.

Unfold the hearts and brush all over liberally with the melted butter. Place a snapper fillet on half of each near the fold. Season with salt and pepper and sprinkle each with the shallots. Divide the vegetable mixture on top of the shallots, then the sliced mushrooms. Fold the second side of the heart over the ingredients and, starting at the rounded end of the fold, pleat the edges and crimp them to make an airtight seal. When you get to the tip (or top) of the "bag" add about 3 tablespoons of the cooled vegetable liquid. Twist the top several times and fold it under the envelope. Place the envelopes on a large baking sheet.

Bake in the center of the oven for 17 to 20 minutes, or until the paper turns a golden brown. Serve the papillotes in their paper envelopes and let each guest cut them open to get the full benefit of the heady aroma.

Makes 6 servings.

PAN-SEARED SCALLOPS IN MUSHROOM CREAM SAUCE

Pan-Seared Scallops In Mushroom Cream Sauce

Once you taste these Pan-Seared Scallops in Mushroom Cream Sauce, you will understand why tasters have called it a "scrumptious" dish. It is not a difficult recipe to make but will take some time. The rich Portobello Mushroom Sauce can be made several hours (or even a day ahead) and reheated when you finish the dish, just before serving. The portobello mushrooms used in both the sauce and the final scallop preparation add a savory dimension. Your palate will be pleased with the elusive taste the abundant fresh thyme has left behind in the sauce reduction.

Portobello Mushroom Cream Sauce:

- 4 ounces large portobello mushrooms
- 3 cups heavy cream
- 10 sprigs fresh thyme
- 1 teaspoon kosher salt
- 1/8 teaspoon fresh-ground black pepper

Remove and discard the brown gills from the underside of the mushrooms. This is easily done with the tip of a teaspoon. Cut the mushrooms into 1-inch cubes. In a large heavy saucepan, bring all the ingredients to a simmer over medium heat, stirring occasionally. Watch closely as it may boil up and over once it reaches a simmer. Reduce the heat to keep it at a low simmer, stir occasionally, and reduce the mixture by half. This took about 45 minutes. When reduced, strain the sauce and discard the solids. May be made ahead to this point and refrigerated, covered, for up to a day.

Makes about 1-1/2 cups.

Scallops:

- 1/4 cup vegetable oil (we use canola)
- 12 sea scallops (10 to 15 size) about 1 pound
- 1/2 cup seasoned flour*
- 2 large garlic cloves, chopped
- 3 ounces portobello mushrooms (3 medium), gills removed and julienned
- 3 ounces dry white wine
- 2 cups baby spinach leaves
- 1-1/2 cups Portobello Mushroom Cream Sauce
- 1 tablespoon each chopped fresh parsley and basil
- 10 ounces fresh-cooked linguine pasta (can substitute cooked rice)

Heat the oil over medium-high heat in a large skillet or sauté pan. Dredge the scallops in seasoned flour just enough to coat, shaking off any excess. Sear the scallops in the oil on all sides, about 40 seconds a side. Remove to a warm plate.

Stir in the garlic and mushrooms and sauté for about 2 minutes, or until the garlic just begins to take on color and the mushrooms have wilted. Deglaze the pan with the wine. Stir in the spinach, the mushroom cream sauce, the parsley, and the basil. Add the browned scallops and toss the mixture to incorporate all the ingredients, and heat the scallops through.

Divide the pasta between two large serving bowls. Pour half the scallop mixture over each and serve.

Makes 2 servings.

*Seasoned flour is made with the 1/2 cup all-purpose flour, 1 teaspoon salt, 1/4 teaspoon fresh-ground pepper, and 1/4 teaspoon garlic powder.

SALMON QUICHE

As we have mentioned before, one never knows where one might stumble over a good recipe. This Salmon Quiche recipe came from one of those unlikely places—the nurse in our former (Greenwich, Connecticut) dentist's office. This makes a delicious luncheon or light supper dish with just a nice green or fruit salad. To make this dish even easier to execute, we like to use the Pillsbury ready-made pie crusts rolled to fit the 10-inch pie pan, and all the other ingredients can be found in your cupboard or refrigerator.

1 10-inch unbaked pie shell*
1 can (15-1/2 ounces) pink salmon (Bumble Bee brand recommended)
1 package (10 ounces) frozen chopped spinach
1-1/2 cups shredded Monterey Jack cheese or Muenster cheese
1 package (3 ounces) cream cheese at room temperature
1/2 teaspoon salt
1/2 teaspoon dried thyme, crushed
4 large eggs, lightly beaten
1 cup whole milk

Preheat the oven to 375 degrees. Line the pie shell with aluminum foil, and fill with pie weights or dried beans. Bake for 10 minutes or until partially set. Remove the foil with the weights and let cool completely.

Drain the salmon well, discarding the liquid. Flake the salmon, mashing the soft bones with it, and reserve. Cook the spinach according to package directions and drain well. In a bowl, combine the spinach, Jack or Muenster cheese, cream cheese, salt, and thyme. Arrange the salmon and mashed bones evenly in the bottom of the pie shell. Spoon the spinach mixture over the top. Whisk together the eggs and milk and pour carefully over all. Bake in the center of the preheated oven for about 45 minutes or until firm to the touch and nicely browned.

Makes 8 servings.

*We use the Pillsbury ready-made pie crusts, rolled to fit the 10-inch pan. They are available in most supermarkets in the refrigerated section.

SEAFOOD CAKES

These Seafood Cakes, a close relative of the ever-popular crab cakes, are filled with a delectable mixture of fresh fish fillets (we used grouper), fresh shrimp, and sea scallops. Although the list of ingredients may seem long, most of the real work of chopping the fish and vegetables can be done in a food processor or a good blender. The seasonings are perfect, and with each bite, they all affirm their presence. Served with a simple citrus-based sauce or tartar sauce (recipes below), these "cakes" will bring rave reviews.

- 1/2 medium green pepper, seeded and coarsely chopped, about 1/2 cup
- 1/2 medium Spanish onion, peeled and coarsely chopped, about 2/3 cup
- 2 medium garlic cloves, minced
- 8 ounces fresh fish fillets (I used grouper), coarsely chopped
- 4 ounces fresh shrimp, peeled, deveined, and coarsely chopped
- 4 ounces sea scallops, any muscles removed, and coarsely chopped
- 1 small potato, peeled, cooked and mashed, about 2/3 cup (you can substitute a good brand of instant mashed potatoes, if desired)
- 1 large egg, lightly beaten
- 2 tablespoons grated Parmesan cheese
- 1 teaspoon Tabasco sauce
- 2 teaspoons dried basil
- 2 teaspoons dried oregano
- 1-1/2 cups dried bread crumbs, divided
- 1/4 cup minced parsley
- salt and fresh-ground black pepper, to taste
- 1/4 cup canola oil, about
- lemon wedges
- Light Lemon Butter Sauce (recipe given)
- Easy Tartar Sauce (recipe given)

In a large mixing bowl, add the ingredients through the salt and fresh-ground pepper in the order listed, using only 3/4 cup of the bread crumbs. With clean hands, thoroughly blend the mixture. This should be made, covered, and refrigerated for at least an hour before forming the cakes so the flavors can unite.

Line a baking sheet with wax paper. Put the remaining bread crumbs in a shallow bowl. Divide the seafood mixture into 12 equal cakes, about 2-1/2 inches across and about 3/4 of an inch thick. Coat each side of the cakes with the remaining bread crumbs and place on the baking sheet, ready to cook.

Heat 2 tablespoons of the oil in a large no-stick skillet over moderate heat. Cook half the seafood cakes at a time until cooked through and well browned on both sides. This will take about 3 to 4 minutes a side. Remove to a warm platter and cover loosely with foil. Repeat with the remaining oil and cakes. Serve with lemon wedges or the sauce of your choice.

Makes 6 servings.

Light Lemon Butter Sauce: Melt about 1/4 cup butter in a small skillet over medium-low heat. Just when it begins to turn a nutty brown (about 4 minutes), stirring constantly, remove from the heat and stir in a tablespoon of fresh lemon juice and a teaspoon of fresh chopped parsley.

Easy Tartar Sauce: Mix your favorite mayonnaise with about half as much sweet pickle relish. The amounts are your choice. We usually mix about 1/3 cup mayonnaise with about 1/4 cup relish.

Seafood Newburg

SEAFOOD NEWBURG

The combination of mahi-mahi, salmon, and lobster for this savory Seafood Newburg given here is just one of many you can use. According to the former chef of a popular restaurant who shared this recipe, the seafood choices are completely flexible. He informed us he waits to see which seafood will be the freshest on any given day he will be making the dish, adding that there could be a day when only one makes the list. Served on toast points, on a bed of rice, or even in a casserole topped with bread crumbs and butter, we guarantee you will be pleased with any combination once it meets the savory sauce.

6 tablespoons clarified butter*, divided
2 small bay leaves
2 medium shallots, minced
3 tablespoons all-purpose flour
1/8 teaspoon paprika, or enough to make a nice red-hued roux
2 cups heavy cream
1-1/2 teaspoons chicken base (we used the Better Than Bouillon chicken base)
pinch fresh-ground white pepper, or to taste
pinch cayenne pepper, or to taste
8-ounce piece mahi-mahi (dolphin), cut into 1/2- to 3/4-inch cubes
6-ounce piece salmon, cut into 1/2- to 3/4-inch cubes
1 8-ounce uncooked lobster tail, meat removed and cut into 1/2- to 3/4-inch cubes
1/2 cup cream sherry (do not use dry sherry)

Melt 3 tablespoons of the butter in a large saucepan over medium heat. Add the bay leaves and shallots and sauté for about 2 minutes, or until the shallots are fragrant and softened. Stir in the flour and paprika and cook, stirring for about 3 minutes. Slowly add the heavy cream and chicken base. Cook, stirring, until the chicken base has dissolved and the mixture has thickened. Season with the white and cayenne peppers. Keep warm.

In a large skillet melt the remaining 3 tablespoons butter over medium-high heat. Add the seafood and sauté for about 2 minutes, or until just cooked through. Transfer the seafood to the cream sauce with a slotted spoon. Deglaze the skillet with the sherry and stir into the cream sauce. Fish out the bay leaves, or let your guests do the job. Serve over cooked rice or with toast points.

SUZANNE S. JONES

Makes 4 servings.

*To clarify butter, melt it over low heat. Skim off and discard the foam on top. Refrigerate the remaining butter. When it has chilled, remove the solid piece of clarified butter and discard the milky residue on the bottom.

SHRIMP MOUSSE WITH SOLE

A good friend in Connecticut shared this recipe for Shrimp Mousse with Sole a number of years ago. It is the perfect seafood offering to guests (or family) when you really want to impress. It is visually appealing as well as delicious, and everyone will think you spent days preparing it. You can assemble the several parts hours ahead and refrigerate it until just before baking and serving. This is perfect on its own, but to make it even more elegant, fill the center with a green vegetable—such as fresh peas or peas and carrots—and surround it with sautéed mushrooms.

Sole:

- 8 fillets of sole, each weighing about 5 ounces
- 2 tablespoons fresh lemon juice
- salt and fresh-ground white pepper
- 1 tablespoon soft butter

Mousse:

- 1 pound raw shrimp
- 2 large egg whites
- 1 cup heavy cream
- 1 teaspoon salt
- 1 tablespoon ketchup
- 1 tablespoon fresh parsley leaves
- 2 tablespoons dry sherry

Sauce:

- 1/4 cup unsalted butter
- 1/4 cup all-purpose flour
- 1/2 teaspoon salt
- 1 cup light cream or half and half
- 1 tablespoon ketchup
- 2 large egg yolks
- 1/4 cup dry sherry

To prepare the sole, rinse and pat dry the fillets with paper towels. Brush both sides with lemon juice and sprinkle with salt and pepper. Lightly butter a 5-cup ring mold (about 8-1/2 inches across and 2 inches deep). Line the mold with the fillets. With the dark side up, position each fillet so that the narrow end is facing the center hole and each fillet overhangs both the outside and inside rim. You will be folding the overhanging ends over the mousse. Set aside.

To make the mousse, shell and devein the shrimp and rinse under cold water. Pat dry and cut in half. In a food processor fitted with the metal blade (you can still use a good blender, of course), put the shrimp, egg whites, cream, salt, ketchup, parsley, and sherry. Process until the mixture is very smooth, scraping down the side of the bowl as necessary.

Spoon the mousse into the lined mold, smoothing the top. Fold the ends of the sole overlapping over the top of the filling. Spread the soft butter over the top and cover loosely with a square of waxed paper. Can be prepared ahead to this point.

When ready to bake, preheat the oven to 350 degrees. Place the mold in large baking pan and pour enough boiling water around the mold to measure about 1 inch. Bake in the center of the oven for about 30 to 35 minutes, or until just firm. Do not overbake.

While the fish is baking, make the sauce. In the top of a double boiler over direct heat, melt the butter. Stir in the flour and salt, then gradually whisk in the light cream and ketchup. Cook over medium heat, whisking, until the mixture comes to a boil. Remove from the heat. In a small bowl, whisk the egg yolks until well mixed. Gradually whisk in about 1/2 cup of the hot sauce. Stir the yolk mixture back into the sauce and add the sherry. Continue stirring over low heat until very hot and the temperature has reached 140 degrees. You can keep the sauce warm over hot water in the bottom of the double boiler until ready to serve.

To serve, loosen the edge of the mold with a sharp knife. Pour off any accumulated liquid into the hot sauce. Invert the mold onto a warm platter and lift off the ring. Spoon some of the sauce over the ring and pass the remaining sauce in a bowl.

Makes 8 servings.

SNAPPER CALYPSO

Snapper Calypso

This outstanding recipe for yellowtail snapper, with its accompanying savory seafood sauce, is served surrounded by the restaurant's own recipe for their distinctively flavored golden-colored rice. You might want to call your fishmonger ahead to order the yellowtail snapper since it is not always readily available. If it is not at the moment you are determined to share the recipe with your guests, our fishmonger recommended substituting red snapper, tilapia, or grouper. All are fish with medium-firm flesh and a mild flavor—a perfect foil for the rich topping of leeks, mushrooms, and shrimp.

Snapper:

12 tablespoons unsalted butter, divided
1/3 cup all-purpose flour
salt and fresh-ground black pepper
4 yellowtail snapper fillets (about 7 ounces each), skin removed
2 large leeks, white part only, thinly sliced
12 ounces button mushrooms, thinly sliced
8 ounces baby shrimp (also called salad shrimp, 50-60 count) peeled and deveined*
1/2 cup white wine (the restaurant recommends a Chardonnay)
1/2 cup fish stock**
1 tablespoon fresh lemon juice
Yellow Rice, recipe given

Preheat the oven to 200 degrees. In a large skillet, heat 3 tablespoons of the butter over medium-high heat. Mix the flour with some salt and pepper and lightly salt and pepper the snapper fillets. Dredge the fillets in the seasoned flour and place in the heated butter. Cook the fillets for about 2 minutes a side, or until golden brown and just cooked through. Transfer the fillets to a baking dish and place in the warm oven while finishing the sauce.

Melt 3 more tablespoons of butter in the same skillet over medium heat and sauté the leeks and mushrooms for about 3 minutes, or until soft. Add the shrimp, wine, fish stock, and lemon juice and bring to a simmer. Reduce the liquid by half. Reduce the heat to low and swish in the remaining 6 tablespoons butter, one at a time, until each has melted. To serve, place a fillet on each of 4 warmed serving plates and divide the leek/mushroom sauce over the tops of each. Divide the rice alongside of each serving of snapper.

Makes 4 servings.

*If not available fresh, you can use the uncooked frozen salad shrimp.
**We used 1/4 cube of the Knorr fish bouillon 2-cup cubes dissolved in 1/2 cup boiling water.

Yellow Rice:

- 2 tablespoons unsalted butter
- 1/4 cup diced onions
- 1 medium garlic clove, chopped
- 1/4 teaspoon dried oregano
- 1/2 teaspoon yellow rice seasoning (Sazon Goya con Azafran seasoning recommended)
- 2 cups chicken stock (we used the Better Than Bouillon chicken base and 2 cups hot water)
- 1 cup uncooked long-grain rice
- 3 tablespoons diced roasted red peppers (you can use the jarred variety)
- 3 tablespoons sliced scallions, white part only

In a large saucepan, melt the butter over medium heat. Add the onions and sauté until clear. Add the garlic, oregano, and yellow rice seasoning, stirring to blend. Stir in the chicken stock and bring to a boil. Add the rice and bring back to a boil. Cover, reduce the heat, and simmer for 20 minutes or until all the liquid has been absorbed. Just before serving, toss in the red peppers and scallions. Mix well.

Makes 4 servings.

MAIN DISHES (SEAFOOD)

STUFFED SOLE

Stuffed Sole

"Out of this world" is how this Stuffed Sole recipe from a well-known restaurant (Sea Watch) in Florida has been described over and over again. There are several steps to this recipe of fresh sole, but it can all be assembled a few hours ahead and refrigerated until ready to bake. The "stuffing" of flavorful, soft, spreadable Alouette cheese (we opted for the garlic and herb flavor) and fresh shrimp between layers of fresh sole—covered with what the restaurant calls a New England Crumb Topping, bathed in a lemony-wine cooking liquid and baked just until the fish is cooked through and the topping lightly browned—is guaranteed to pleasantly arouse your culinary taste buds with the first bite. A word of caution: you may become addicted.

New England Crumb Topping:

3 cups Ritz Cracker crumbs
6 ounces (2/3 stick) unsalted butter, melted
2 teaspoons paprika
3 tablespoons dry sherry wine
1/8 teaspoon white pepper

Cooking Liquid:

1 cup dry white wine
1/4 cup fresh lemon juice
3/4 cup light fish bouillon (we used 1/2 extra large cube Knorr's fish-flavored bouillon dissolved in 3/4 cup hot water)

Sole:

2 pounds fillet of sole, divided into 8 equal portions of 4 ounces each
8 ounces Alouette cheese (we used the garlic and herb version), removed from the refrigerator 30 minutes before using to soften
8 ounces shelled and cleaned fresh small (125-175 count) shrimp, cut into just under 1/2-inch pieces
8 ounces (1 stick) unsalted butter, melted

To make the New England crumb topping, mix all the ingredients together in a large mixing bowl and set aside.

To prepare the cooking liquid, stir all the ingredients together in a 2-cup measure.

To assemble the sole for baking, use individual ovenproof dishes that have at least a 1/2-inch lip on them and can be served right from the oven. (We use individual ceramic oval gratin dishes that measure 7-1/2 by 4-1/2 by 1-1/4 inches high. These are a bit smaller than those served at the restaurant, so you will have a bit of cooking liquid left. Just refrigerate any leftover to use to poach future fish. It will keep for up to a week.)

In each of four ungreased gratin dishes, lay one piece of sole. Spread each with 2 ounces (about 3 tablespoons) of the Alouette cheese. Divide the shrimp in four and place on top of the cheese. Cover with another piece of sole, sealing in the cheese. Now divide the crumb topping into four portions and cover each entire fish assembly with a portion: it will be about 1/2-inch thick. Drizzle about 1/2 cup cooking liquid over each, or enough to come to just under the bottom of the crumbs. Drizzle 2 tablespoons of the melted butter over each. Can be assembled a few hours ahead and refrigerated. Remove from the refrigerator 30 minutes before baking.

Preheat the oven to 450 degrees. Place the gratin dishes on a sided baking sheet, such as a jelly roll pan, for easy handling. Bake in the center of the oven for about 14 or 15 minutes or until the crumb topping is nicely browned and the fish are just cooked through. Serve immediately in the gratin dishes.

Makes 4 servings.

The Whale's Rib Baked
Dolphin

THE WHALE'S RIB BAKED DOLPHIN

This remarkably easy recipe for Baked Dolphin from the popular Whale's Rib restaurant is guaranteed to become a favorite. You will wonder as we did when reading through the ingredients and instructions, why the topping of Italian bread crumbs, Parmesan cheese, and parsley were all layered separately. But we followed the directions and were amazed and delighted at how your taste buds pick up each layer distinctly from every other even as all the flavors meld into a perfect marriage in the mouth. The layers also keep the fillets moist and tender.

4 dolphin fillets (about 7 ounces each)*
1 medium garlic clove, minced
1/4 cup unsalted butter, melted
1/3 cup plus 1 tablespoon Italian-style bread crumbs
1/4 cup fresh-grated Parmesan cheese
1/4 cup fine-chopped fresh parsley

Preheat the oven to 350 degrees. Prepare a baking pan or dish large enough to hold the fillets in a single layer without touching, with no-stick vegetable spray.

Remove any skin and center boney pieces from the fillets and place on the prepared pan. Stir the garlic into the butter and spread about a tablespoon over each fillet, making sure to cover the entire surface.

Sprinkle about 1-1/2 tablespoons bread crumbs evenly over each fillet and press gently with your fingers so the crumbs adhere to the butter coating. Sprinkle each fillet with about 1 tablespoon of Parmesan, again pressing gently and top each with about 1 tablespoon of the parsley.

Bake in the center of the preheated oven until the thickest part of the fillet is opaque. The usual guideline is approximately 10 minutes per inch of fish.

Makes 4 servings.

*If dolphin is not available, you can substitute other medium-firm fillets, such as pompano, cod, tilefish, tilapia, or grouper.

SUZANNE S. JONES

Tuna Catania

TUNA CATANIA

Even though the short list of ingredients might make you wonder, be assured that this is an outstanding recipe. It is an excellent example of the importance of using top quality seafood, which means buying the tuna from your favorite fishmonger. Add to that the fact that the owner of the restaurant Kitchenetta recommends cooking the tuna either rare or medium rare, so freshness tops the requisite list.

The thick crust of chopped toasted pine nuts and bread crumbs is a culinary delight with each bite of the fresh tuna. If you have a couple spoonfuls of the nut/crumb mixture left over, just grab a spoon and clean the bowl!

You only need some lemon wedges to serve with the fillets. Or you can improvise if a guest asks for tartar sauce or cocktail sauce and you don't happen to have any. Our secret? Mix about 1/2 cup of some good mayonnaise (Hellmann's Real recommended) with about 2 tablespoons of sweet pickle relish for the tartar sauce and 1/4 cup mayonnaise with about 1/4 cup chili sauce and a bit of bottled horseradish for a simulated cocktail sauce.

- 1-1/2 cups pignoli (pine) nuts, toasted
- 1/2 cup plain bread crumbs
- salt and fresh-ground pepper to taste
- 1-1/2 teaspoons extra virgin olive oil
- 2 fresh tuna fillets (about 8 ounces each and 3/4-inch thick)
- 2/3 cup whole milk or half and half
- extra virgin olive oil for frying (you want enough to measure about 60 percent of the tuna height to ensure both sides are evenly and quickly cooked)
- 4 lemon wedges

To toast the nuts, preheat the oven to 350 degrees. Spread the nuts evenly in a baking pan. Bake in the center of the oven for 8 to 10 minutes, stirring once. Watch carefully since they brown quickly. Cool completely.

In a food processor fitted with the metal blade, process the nuts and bread crumbs just until the nuts are coarsely chopped and the mixture is well combined. Transfer to a flat dish such as a pie plate and stir in some salt and pepper.

Rinse the fillets under cold water and pat dry with paper towels. Dip into the milk or half and half, covering well. Press the nut mixture well onto both sides of the fillets. Place on paper towels while heating the oil.

In a heavy skillet, heat the olive oil over medium heat. Fry the fillets about 3 minutes on the first side and about 2 minutes on the second for medium rare. If you want the tuna more well done, place in a 350-degree oven for 4 to 5 minutes more. Just be careful you don't overcook either in the pan or oven since the pignoli nuts burn easily. Serve with lemon wedges.

Makes 2 servings.

DESSERTS

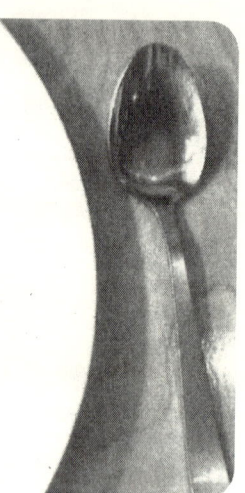

Apple Pound Cake

APPLE POUND CAKE

The recipe for this delectable dessert called Apple Pound Cake comes from a popular restaurant in Fort Lauderdale and was voted even better than a slice of "Mom's" apple pie. What makes this cake so exceptionally good is the large amount of diced apples and nuts in proportion to the small amount of soft cake surrounding those ingredients. It slices like an apple pie without a crust but with the texture of a very moist cake. We found that the cake was easier to cut when completely cooled or refrigerated, but if you want to serve it warm as they do in the restaurant, just pop each serving in the microwave for 30 seconds more or less depending on your oven, before you scoop the ice cream or frozen yogurt on or beside it. (We have to admit sharing the last piece for breakfast right out of the refrigerator.)

3 to 4 medium Granny Smith apples (you need 4 cups diced)
1 tablespoon fresh lemon juice
1 cup all-purpose flour
1-1/2 teaspoons baking powder
pinch salt
2 large eggs
1 cup sugar
1 teaspoon pure vanilla extract
1 stick (4 ounces) unsalted butter, melted and cooled
1/2 cup chopped pecans
3 cups (1-1/2 pints) vanilla ice cream or frozen yogurt

Preheat the oven to 300 degrees. Grease an 8-inch springform pan and line the bottom with parchment paper.

Peel, core, and cut the apples into 1/4-inch dice. Toss with the lemon juice in a large mixing bowl. Set aside.

In a mixing bowl, whisk together the flour, baking powder, and salt. Transfer to a piece of wax paper. In the same bowl, beat together the eggs and sugar on the medium speed of an electric mixer until thick and smooth. Beat in the vanilla and slowly beat in the melted butter.

Fold the dry ingredients gently into the batter, followed by the diced apples and nuts. Mix thoroughly but gently. Transfer the mixture to the prepared pan, place the pan on a baking sheet, and bake in the center of the oven for 50 to 60 minutes, or until a toothpick inserted in the center comes out clean. Transfer the pan to a wire rack and let sit for 10 minutes. Carefully run a knife around the edge of the pan and remove the outer ring. Cool to room temperature for easier slicing.

You can refrigerate the cake at this point. If you wish to serve it warm, zap the individual slices for about 30 seconds in the microwave before adding the 1/4-cup ice cream or yogurt per serving.

Makes 12 servings.

AUNT JEN'S BLACKBERRY JAM CAKE

Our Aunt Jen from West Virginia, long deceased, was an outstanding cook to whom we are grateful for the many wonderful recipes she shared during her lifetime and passed on to us when she died. Blackberry Jam Cake is one of those recipes. The Caramel Frosting, according to Aunt Jen, is a must for a traditional blackberry jam cake. We have been known, however, to substitute a plain buttercream or even serve it without frosting, cutting each plain layer into slices and adding a dollop of whipped cream or ice cream over the top. We guarantee, leftovers will never be a problem.

4 cups all-purpose flour
2 teaspoons ground allspice
2 teaspoons ground cinnamon
2 teaspoons ground nutmeg
1/2 teaspoon ground cloves
2 teaspoons baking soda
1-1/2 cups (3 sticks) unsalted butter, at room temperature
2 cups sugar
6 large eggs
2 cups seedless blackberry jam
1-1/2 cups buttermilk
Caramel Frosting (recipe follows)

Preheat the oven to 350 degrees. Butter and flour three 9-inch round cake pans.

In a large mixing bowl, whisk together the flour, spices, and baking soda. Transfer to a large piece of wax paper.

In the same bowl, beat the butter and sugar together on the medium speed of an electric mixer until light. Beat in the eggs one at a time, then the blackberry jam. On low speed, beat in the flour mixture alternately with the buttermilk.

Divide the batter evenly among the prepared pans and bake in the center of the oven for 35 minutes, or until a toothpick inserted in the center comes out clean. Remove to wire racks and let cool for 10 minutes. Invert the layers onto the wire racks to cool completely.

When cool, place 1 layer on a serving plate and spread about 1 cup of the icing over the top. Top with the second layer and spread another cup of the icing over that. Top with the third layer and spread the remaining icing over the top and sides.

Makes 16 servings.

Caramel Frosting:

2 cups granulated sugar
2 cups firm-packed light brown sugar
1-1/2 cups light cream
1/2 cup (1 stick) unsalted butter, at room temperature, cut into 8 pieces

2 large egg yolks, lightly beaten
1/2 teaspoon pure vanilla extract
1 cup chopped nuts (pecans or walnuts)

In a large saucepan combine the sugars, light cream, butter, and egg yolks. Cook over medium heat, stirring constantly until the sugar is dissolved. Still stirring, bring the mixture to a boil, reduce the heat so the mixture is simmering, and cook, stirring, for about 10 minutes or until thickened. Remove from the heat and stir in the vanilla and chopped nuts. Let icing cool, stirring frequently, until of spreading consistency.

Makes about 4 cups.

BANANA CREAM PIE

Banana Cream Pie

You will agree with the friend who, after the first bite, called this Banana Cream Pie the "best I have ever had." The crust contributes strongly to the uniqueness of the pie, as did the abundance of sliced bananas—about twice as many as in most standard Banana Cream Pie recipes. The crust is closer to a cookie dough and is not as flaky or tender as a typical pate brisee or pie dough. In its favor is the fact that it rolls easily (it is not springy or elastic) and does not get soggy as easily as a standard pie dough. The aroma while baking reminds one of the scent of shortbread, and its crispness when baked marries perfectly with the richness of the filling.

Pie Shell:

- 1-1/4 cups all-purpose flour
- 1/4 cup sugar
- 1/2 cup (1 stick) chilled unsalted butter, cut into tablespoon-size pieces
- 1 large egg yolk, lightly beaten
- 2 tablespoons fresh lemon juice (or enough to moisten the dough)

Filling:

3/4 cup sugar
6 tablespoons cornstarch
1/2 cup cold milk
4 large egg yolks
1-1/2 cups hot milk
2 teaspoons pure vanilla extract

4 or 5 medium bananas (not too ripe) cut into slices a tad over 1/4 inch
1 cup heavy cream
2 tablespoons confectioners' sugar

To make the crust, in a large mixing bowl stir together the flour and sugar. Use a pastry blender to cut the butter into the flour/sugar mixture until it resembles coarse crumbs. With a fork, stir in the egg yolk and just enough fresh lemon juice to hold the mixture together when pinched with your fingers. Transfer to a large piece of plastic wrap and use the wrap to pull the pastry into a compact disc. Wrap well and refrigerate for at least 30 minutes.

To finish the crust, preheat the oven to 350 degrees. On a floured surface, roll out the dough into a circle about 11 inches in diameter. Keep the surface and rolling pin dusted with flour. Carefully roll up the dough around the rolling pin and unroll it into a 9-inch tart pan with a removable bottom. Press the dough onto the bottom and sides of the pan, being careful not to stretch the dough. With sharp scissors, trim the dough to within half an inch of the top of the pan. Turn the half-inch overhang to the inside and press against the side to make a firm edge. Line the shell with aluminum foil and fill with pie weights, dry beans, or rice. Bake in the center of the oven for 15 minutes or until the edges are just beginning to take on color. Remove the pie weights and foil and continue baking until golden brown and the bottom is firm—about 8 minutes more. Remove to a wire rack and cool completely. Can be made a day ahead and stored in an airtight container overnight.

To make the filling, in the top part of a double boiler, whisk together the sugar and cornstarch, then whisk in the cold milk. In a separate bowl, whisk the egg yolks until light. Add to the sugar/cornstarch mixture.

Whisking rapidly, slowly pour the hot milk into the above mixture. Place the top of the double boiler pan over simmering water, making certain the bottom of the top does not touch the water. Whisking constantly, cook the mixture until it thickens (it will be quite thick) and the temperature reaches 160 degrees on an instant-reading thermometer.

Remove the top of the pan to a wire rack to cool. Stir in the vanilla. While it is still just slightly warm (once it cools completely it will be very thick), carefully fold in the sliced bananas—you will have as many bananas as custard. Transfer to the prepared tart pan, smoothing the surface as much as possible. Chill several hours or even overnight.

To finish the pie, whip the heavy cream in a chilled bowl with chilled beaters on the medium speed of an electric mixer until it is foamy. Add the sugar and continue beating until it is stiff, being careful not to arrive at sweet cream butter! Spread the whipped cream over the top of the chilled pie, swirling it decoratively. Before serving, carefully remove the outer rim of the pan.

Makes 8 servings.

Chocolate Almond
Balls

CHOCOLATE ALMOND BALLS

These outrageous chocolate-filled almond butter cookies are one of many we developed in the Cuisinart test kitchen years ago to complete an article scheduled for publication in our bimonthly magazine *The Pleasures of Cooking*. This is a time-consuming recipe, but once tasted, you will admit it is definitely a winner. Make sure to hide the cookie jar. They disappear otherwise.

Almond Balls:

- 1/4 cup blanched almonds
- 1/2 pound (2 sticks) unsalted butter, cut into 16 pieces
- 3/4 cup confectioners' sugar
- 2 cups unbleached all-purpose flour
- pinch salt
- 1-1/2 teaspoons pure almond extract
- Chocolate Filling (recipe given)

Preheat the oven to 350 degrees. Spread the almonds in a pie plate and bake in the center of the oven for about 8 to 10 minutes or until lightly colored. Let cool. In a food processor fitted with the metal blade, chop the almonds finely. Reserve.

With the metal blade still in place, process the butter and sugar until smooth and creamy. Add the flour, salt, and almond extract and pulse until well mixed.

Preheat the oven again to 350 degrees. Roll the dough into balls the size of a marble and place 1 inch apart on ungreased baking sheets. Bake in the center of the oven for about 10 to 12 minutes or until firm but not brown. Transfer to wire racks to cool completely.

To finish, spread about 1/2 teaspoon of the Chocolate Filling on the bottom of one cookie. Place another cookie bottom-side-down on the filling and press lightly. Roll the chocolate edge of the cookie in the reserved chopped almonds.

Makes about 4 dozen cookies.

Chocolate Filling:

- 4 ounces semisweet baking chocolate, broken into 1-inch pieces
- 2-1/2 tablespoons unsalted butter
- 2-1/2 tablespoons heavy cream
- pinch salt
- 1-1/2 cups confectioners' sugar

In a food processor fitted with the metal blade, process the chocolate until finely chopped. Leave in the workbowl.

In a saucepan, bring the butter and cream to a boil over medium heat. With the motor running, pour the butter and cream mixture through the feed tube and process until the chocolate is smooth. Add the remaining ingredients and pulse to combine. Let cool.

Makes about 1 cup filling.

CREAM CHEESE CHOCOLATE CHIP POUND CAKE

Incredible was the word used by our "visiting" tasting panel that consisted of our daughter, husband, and grandchildren when we made this Cream Cheese Chocolate Chip Pound Cake the first time. It was a resounding success, and in no time at all, not a crumb was left (well, there actually were a few on the kitchen floor). We found you could forget any need for icing in this rich cake, though aesthetically, one could cover the top with a light dusting of confectioners' sugar.

- 3 cups all-purpose flour
- 3 teaspoons baking powder
- 1 teaspoon salt
- 1 cup unsalted butter, at room temperature
- 8 ounces cream cheese, at room temperature
- 1-1/2 cups sugar
- 2 teaspoons pure vanilla extract
- 1/2 cup whole milk
- 12 ounces semisweet chocolate chips
- confectioners' sugar for dusting (optional)

Preheat the oven to 325 degrees. Butter and flour a 12-cup Bundt pan. Set aside.

In a large mixing bowl, whisk together the flour, baking powder, and salt. Transfer to a piece of wax paper.

In the same bowl, beat together on the medium speed of an electric mixer the butter and cream cheese until creamy. Gradually add the sugar, beating all the while, then the eggs, one at a time, beating well after each addition. Beat in the vanilla. Stir in the flour mixture alternately with the milk, mixing well. Lastly, stir in the chocolate chips, making sure they are well distributed. Pour the batter into the prepared pan and bake in the lower third of the oven for 55 to 60 minutes, or until a skewer inserted in the center comes out clean.

Cool in the pan on a wire rack for 10 minutes, then invert onto the wire rack to cool completely. If desired, dust with confectioners' sugar just before serving. This keeps, well wrapped and refrigerated, for up to a week. (Ours lasted less than 24 hours!)

Makes 16 servings.

EASY RICE PUDDING

We always thought our mother's rice pudding was the ultimate comfort dessert until we tasted this Easy Rice Pudding courtesy of our good friend and excellent cook, Fran Wool. When we learned how easy it was to make and how extraordinarily creamy and flavorful (not too sweet and not overly spiced), our loyalties shifted. No double boiler needed here, just a good heavy saucepan and about 45 minutes to hover and stir occasionally. It is as good served warm, at room temperature, or right from the refrigerator. It needs no further embellishments, although we have been known to drop a dollop of whipped cream on top for special guests.

1 cup water
1/2 cup rice (not instant)
1/2 cup sugar
pinch salt
1 whole cinnamon stick, broken in half

4 cups whole milk
1/4 cup seedless raisins (optional but recommended)
1 tablespoon butter (optional but recommended)

In a good heavy (important) 1-1/2- to 2-quart saucepan, stir the water and rice together. Bring to a boil over medium-high heat, stirring. Reduce the heat to medium and simmer the rice for about 7 to 10 minutes or until the water has almost evaporated. Stir in the sugar, salt, cinnamon sticks, and milk and raisins, if using. Continue simmering over medium-low to low heat (you want this to barely simmer to avoid scorching) for about 30 to 40 minutes, stirring frequently, until the rice is very soft and the consistency is creamy. Retrieve and discard the cinnamon sticks. Stir in the raisins and butter, if using.

Makes 6 servings.

FROZEN FRUIT YOGURTS

Frozen
Fruit Yogurts

Frozen Fruit Yogurts were one of the many quick, easy, healthful, and delicious desserts that were developed in the Cuisinart test kitchen during my tenure there. We all looked forward to the days of experimentation and the load of necessary tastings required. There are some basic guidelines that you will find below, plus amounts of some of the favorite fruits or combinations. (Do try some of your own.) We did find that bananas alone were not a good idea—they have a tendency to turn into glue. But combined with other fruits, the flavor is delightful.

Frozen Fruit Yogurts:

Except for raspberries, which need to be washed and forced through a strainer to yield about 2 cups of puree, the general directions here will give you a map for making all manner of delicious and refreshing fresh fruit desserts. We give a few specifics. PLEASE NOTE THAT ALL WILL INCLUDE 1 CUP OF VERY COLD PLAIN NONFAT YOGURT. Each makes about 1-1/2 cups.

Peel, core or wash, stem, or hull the fruit and—except for the raspberries and blueberries—cut into 1-inch pieces and freeze in a single layer. (Freeze the raspberry puree and cut it into 1-inch pieces before processing.) A few minutes or up to 2 hours before serving, put half the frozen fruit into the workbowl of a food processor fitted with the metal blade. Pulse a few times, then process to chop into pea-size pieces. Transfer to a bowl and reserve. Chop the remaining frozen fruit pieces to pea-sized bits. Add the yogurt, the sweetening, the reserved pea-size fruit, and any additional ingredients called for (e.g., fresh lemon juice). Process until the mixture is creamy and circulates in the bowl. Taste and, if needed, process in more sweetening. This is best served immediately or stored in the freezer for just up to 2 hours. If you need to freeze for a longer time, cut the frozen mixture into chunks and reprocess just before serving.

1. Pears: 3 large ripe (about 2-1/2 pounds) ones peeled and cored; 2/3 cup confectioners' sugar; 1 tablespoon fresh lemon juice or 1/4 teaspoon vitamin C powder.
2. Strawberries: 1-1/2 pints fresh strawberries, washed and hulled; 1/2 cup confectioners' sugar.
3. Blueberries: 2-1/4 cups fresh blueberries, washed and stemmed (can use already frozen); 1/2 cup confectioners' sugar.
4. Strawberry-Banana: 1 banana (about 3 ounces) peeled; 2-1/2 cups fresh strawberries; 1/2 cup confectioners' sugar.
5. Peaches: 7 ripe peaches (about 1-1/2 pounds total) peeled and pitted, 1/2 cup confectioners' sugar.
6. Raspberries: 2-1/2 pints fresh raspberries (see instructions above); 2/3 cup confectioners' sugar.

FROZEN KEY LIME-GINGER PIE

Frozen Key Lime-Ginger Pie

    You will need to set aside extra time for making, cooling, and chopping the large Gingerbread Cookie that is the basis for the crust of this "amazing, to-die-for" dessert. And you will need additional time for the filling to bake and chill and the ginger cream to complete its infusion. That quote above is from our tasters, members of a musical group where we live, who after several bites sang their praises for a local chef's innovative version of the familiar Key Lime Pie. Even after adjustments for the restaurant's original recipe, the Gingerbread Cookie yielded 4 cups of crumbs. Since you only need 3, consider that extra cup a bonus for the future.

Gingerbread Cookie:

1-1/2 to 1-3/4 cups all-purpose flour	6 tablespoons butter at room temperature
1/2 teaspoon baking soda	1/4 cup firm-packed light brown sugar
1/2 teaspoon ground cinnamon	1 large egg
3/4 teaspoon ground ginger	1/4 cup molasses (robust flavor recommended)
1/4 teaspoon ground allspice	1 stick butter, melted
1/4 teaspoon fresh-ground black pepper	

Preheat the oven to 350 degrees. Line a baking sheet with parchment paper.

In a large mixing bowl, whisk together 1-1/2 cups flour, the baking soda, and the spices. Transfer to a piece of wax paper. In the same bowl, cream the room-temperature butter and sugar until light. Beat in the egg then stir in the molasses, combining well. Stir in the dry ingredients. The dough should be soft but not sticky. If still sticky, add the remaining 1/4 cup flour. Place the dough on the parchment paper and pat out into a rectangle about 1/4 inch thick. Bake in the center of the oven for about 17 to 20 minutes or until firm to the touch. It will firm up more as it cools. Let cool completely.

In a food processor fitted with the metal blade, break up the cooled cookie into chunks and process into crumbs. Makes about 4 cups. Mix 3 cups of the crumbs with the melted butter and press firmly and evenly over the bottom and about 2 inches up the sides of a 9-inch springform pan. (Refrigerate or freeze the remaining crumbs for future use.)

Key Lime Filling:

1 can (14 ounces) sweetened condensed milk	1/2 cup key lime juice
4 large egg yolks	2 teaspoons lime zest

Preheat the oven to 300 degrees. In a mixing bowl, whisk all the ingredients together thoroughly. Pour into a 1-1/2 quart round casserole dish. Place the dish in a larger dish or pan filled with hot water and bake in the center of the oven for about 35 to 40 minutes or until set. Cool completely and refrigerate for at least 6 hours or until firm.

Ginger Cream:

2 cups heavy cream
2-inch piece of fresh gingerroot (1 inch in diameter), peeled and very thinly sliced

1/4 cup sugar

In a mixing bowl, infuse the cream with the ginger and refrigerate overnight.

To finish the pie, strain the ginger from the cream. Whip 1 cup of the cream to soft peaks with 2 tablespoons of the sugar. Reserve the remaining cream and sugar for garnish.

In a large mixing bowl, stir the cold filling to loosen. Stir in about 1/4 of the whipped cream, then fold in the remaining whipped cream. Spoon the filling evenly into the prepared gingerbread crust and freeze for at least 6 hours.

To serve, whip the remaining ginger cream with the remaining 2 tablespoons sugar and place a dollop (about 2 tablespoons) on top of each slice of pie.

Makes 16 servings.

GREEN TOMATO FUDGE CAKE

Green tomatoes—like zucchini or carrots or sauerkraut, for instance—when added to a good cake batter, add moisture and mystery. The moisture part is obvious, and the mystery is just that. Except for the carrots' color, you would not be able to pick out that ingredient since the carrots and the others, particularly in a chocolate cake, simply blend into the whole, and their identity is very much a "mystery" to anyone sampling such a cake.

This recipe for Green Fudge Tomato Cake originated at a luncheon years ago in Connecticut, where the hostess—a displaced lady from Georgia—had all of us trying to guess what was in it. Most guessed zucchini. Do make sure the green tomatoes used are nice and firm since you want them to stand up to grating.

2-1/2 cups all-purpose flour
1/2 cup baking cocoa
2-1/2 teaspoons baking powder
1-1/2 teaspoons baking soda
1 teaspoon salt
1 teaspoon ground cinnamon
1 cup fine-chopped walnuts
3/4 cup butter or stick margarine

1-1/2 cups sugar
3 large eggs
2 teaspoons pure vanilla extract
2 teaspoons grated orange peel
2 cups coarsely grated firm green tomatoes
1/2 cup milk
2 tablespoons confectioners' sugar

Preheat the oven to 350 degrees. Grease and flour a 10-inch Bundt pan. Set aside.

In a large bowl, whisk together the flour, cocoa, baking powder, baking soda, salt, and cinnamon. Stir in the walnuts. Set aside.

In another large bowl, beat the butter and sugar together until light. Add the eggs one at a time, beating well after each addition. Stir in the vanilla, orange peel, and grated green tomatoes. Add the dry ingredients to the tomato mixture alternately with the milk, mixing well.

Pour the batter into the prepared Bundt pan and bake in the lower third of the oven for about an hour, or until a toothpick inserted in the center comes out clean. Cool in the pan for about 15 minutes, then turn out onto a wire rack to cool completely. Just before serving, sprinkle with confectioners' sugar. This is a good keeper when stored in the refrigerator.

Makes 16 servings.

GUINNESS FRUITCAKE

To quote the friend who shared this recipe with us: "On a recent trip to Ireland, I came upon a recipe for Guinness Fruitcake. It is absolutely great, and I don't even like fruitcake. My problem, it calls for mixed spice but no explanation of what that is. Help!" Our Irish cousin, knowledgeable about foods and customs of his native country, informed us that mixed spice was allspice. We tested the recipe and can guarantee that this fruitcake, with its cup of Guinness, will disappear quickly and not be passed on for generations as so many fruitcakes tend to do. (Make sure you put all the Guinness in the cake!)

1 cup Guinness (we used imported St. James's Gate Dublin Guinness Extra Stout, available in most supermarkets), at room temperature
1 cup sugar
4 ounces (1 stick) margarine, cut into 4 pieces
1 pound fruitcake mix (we used Paradise brand Extra Fancy Fruitcake Mix, available now in most supermarkets)*
1 teaspoon baking soda
1 teaspoon fresh-ground allspice (do make sure it is fresh)
2 large eggs, lightly beaten
2 cups all-purpose flour

In a large saucepan, bring the Guinness, sugar, margarine, fruit, baking soda, and allspice to a boil over medium heat. You want to watch this carefully and stir frequently since the baking soda will react with the Guinness, and as it comes to a boil, it will foam up and boil over the side if you turn your back. After it comes to a boil, remove from the heat and let it come to room temperature. To expedite this, place the pan in the sink filled with cold water and stir gently.

Preheat the oven to 325 degrees. Grease well and flour a 9 by 5 by 2-1/2-inch loaf pan.

When the Guinness mixture is cool, stir in the eggs, then the flour. Mix well and turn into the prepared pan. Bake in the center of the oven for 1 hour and 30 minutes. (Your kitchen will smell a lot like Christmas!) The loaf will be firm, slightly cracked, and will have pulled away from the sides of the pan. Let cool in the pan on a wire rack for 10 minutes, then turn out onto the wire rack to cool completely. Wrap well and keep refrigerated. It slices well into thin slices if you wait for 3 to 4 days.

Makes 32 slices.

*We cut the whole cherries in the mix in half to better match the size of the rest of the fruit.

HOLY CROSS HOSPITAL OATMEAL RAISIN COOKIES

Holy Cross Oatmeal
Raisin Cookies

In Fort Lauderdale, we are fortunate to have a heart-healthy café located in one of the hospitals. These "heart-kind" Oatmeal Raisin Cookies are for sale every day for the patients in the Jim Moran Heart Center as well as visitors and employees who take advantage of all the other delicious meal choices the café has to offer. For the heart patients, a nice two-bite-size cookie is baked, but for the café visitors you can count on at least four-biters. The batter for these cookies is thicker than most standard oatmeal cookie recipes. The ratio of oatmeal and raisins to the other ingredients is higher, making each mouthful a healthy and extremely satisfying treat. And they are not too sweet.

1-1/3 cups all-purpose flour	2/3 cup firm-packed light brown sugar
3/4 teaspoon ground cinnamon	1/4 cup granulated sugar
1 teaspoon baking soda	3 large egg whites
3/4 teaspoon salt	1/2 teaspoon pure vanilla extract
1 cup regular margarine (2 sticks) at room temperature	3-1/3 cups oatmeal, regular or quick-cooking
	1-1/4 cups seedless raisins

Preheat the oven to 350 degrees

In a large mixing bowl, whisk together the flour, cinnamon, baking soda, and salt. Transfer to a piece of wax paper.

In the same bowl, cream the margarine with the sugars until light. Add the egg whites one at a time, beating well after each addition. Stir in the vanilla extract. Add the dry ingredients, oatmeal, and raisins, mixing well. The dough will be very thick, so it will take a bit of muscle to get it all together.

If making the small cookies, drop a heaping teaspoon of dough about 1-1/2 inches apart on an ungreased baking sheet. Bake in the center of the oven for about 10 to 12 minutes or until firm and beginning to brown on top. Remove to wire racks to cool and repeat with the remaining dough.

To make the larger cookies, drop by the heaping tablespoons onto the ungreased baking sheets about 2 inches apart. Press down on the dough with the bottom of a glass that has been dipped lightly in flour to flatten. Bake in the center of the oven for about 10 to 12 minutes or until well baked through and lightly brown.

Makes about 140 small cookies and about 42 larger cookies.

MARBLE CAKE (a.k.a. CONDO CAKE)

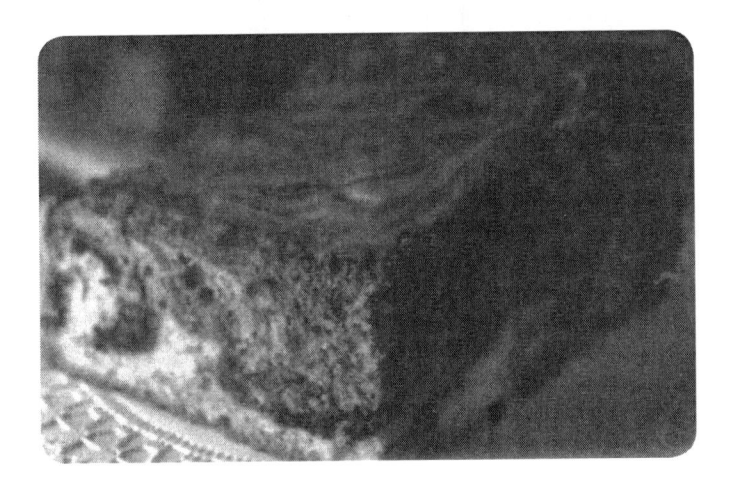

Marble Cake (a.k.a. Condo Cake)

If you have lived in South Florida, you will have noticed a certain cake called the Condo Cake served at many meetings and condo affairs. It is actually a delicious marble cake, which originated at the Family Bakery in Sunrise, who generously shared the recipe with us. You will notice that the recipe reads like a classic chiffon cake recipe, which is usually baked in a tube pan. This cake is perfectly at home in your 13 by 9-inch cake pan. The presence of egg yolks and oil in the batter ensures a tender and moist crumb. The "marble" in this highly addictive cake is from the use of chocolate syrup as the swirled chocolate and not from the more commonly used chocolate batter. You are free to use any icing you wish, but we found it was best just dusted with confectioners' sugar.

2-1/2 cups cake flour
1-3/4 cups sugar, divided
3 teaspoons baking powder
large pinch salt
4 large egg yolks
1/4 cup vegetable oil (we use canola)
2 teaspoons pure vanilla extract
1/3 cup cold water
7 large egg whites
1/2 cup dark chocolate syrup (we use Hershey's brand)
3 tablespoons confectioners' sugar

Preheat the oven to 350 degrees. Grease the bottom only of a 13 by 9 by 2-1/2-inch cake pan.

In a large mixing bowl, whisk together the flour, 1-1/2 cups of the sugar, the baking powder, and salt. Transfer to a large piece of wax paper. In the same bowl, beat the egg yolks on the medium speed of an electric mixer until light. Beat in the oil, vanilla, and water. Add the dry ingredients and mix well.

In a clean bowl with clean beaters, beat the egg whites on medium speed until soft peaks form. Slowly add the remaining 1/4 cup sugar, beating constantly. Change to high speed and continue beating until the egg whites are firm but not dry. With a large spatula, preferably rubber, fold about 1/4 of the egg whites into the egg yolk mixture until no whites remain. Then fold in the remaining whites, making sure the batter is thoroughly mixed but not overmixed. Transfer the batter to the prepared pan. Drizzle the chocolate syrup evenly over the top and swirl it gently into the batter with the blade of a silver knife. Bake in the center of the oven for 50 to 55 minutes or until it is firm to the touch and has begun to pull away from the sides of the pan. Cool completely in the pan. Before serving, dust generously with the confectioners' sugar.

Makes 16 servings.

MOTHER-IN-LAW APPLE CAKE

We often had inquiries about good recipes using black walnuts. Those intensely flavored and aromatic nuts are native to the U.S., with the major growing region formerly in the Appalachia area, and that some say require an educated palate to appreciate their flavor. A dear friend, whose untimely death robbed the world of one wonderful lady and fine cook, shared this recipe with us (with no idea where the name originated) along with a big bag of black walnuts. This extremely moist, fruit-filled apple cake improves in flavor if you can resist eating it for a couple of days. It is a good keeper, covered and refrigerated, for up to a week.

2 cups all-purpose flour
2 teaspoons ground cinnamon
1 teaspoon baking soda
1/2 teaspoon salt
1/2 teaspoon fresh-grated nutmeg
1 cup butter or margarine, at room temperature
1-2/3 cups sugar
2 large eggs, lightly beaten
1-1/2 cups coarse-chopped black walnuts
3 large apples (we like Yellow Delicious)—peeled, seeded, and cut into 1/2-inch chunks
confectioners' sugar, optional
Caramel Icing, recipe given (optional)

Preheat the oven to 350 degrees. Coat a 13 by 9-inch baking pan with no-stick cooking spray. Whisk the flour, cinnamon, soda, salt, and nutmeg together in a large mixing bowl. Transfer to a piece of wax paper. Reserve.

In the same bowl, use a mixer on medium speed to cream the butter and sugar until light. Then, using a wooden spoon, stir in the eggs, mixing well. Stir in the flour mixture in two batches, mixing well after each addition. Stir in the walnuts, then the apples. Let the mixture sit for 10 minutes to blend the flavors. Stir again and spread the thick mixture in the prepared pan. Bake in the center of the oven for 35 to 40 minutes, or until nicely browned on top and a toothpick inserted in the center comes out clean. Remove from the oven and place on a wire rack to cool completely in the pan. Before serving, dust with confectioners' sugar or spread with Caramel Icing.

Caramel Icing:

6 tablespoons butter
3/4 cup firm-packed light brown sugar

2 tablespoons light cream or whole milk
1-1/2 cups confectioners' sugar

Melt the butter in a heavy skillet over low heat. Add the sugar, bring to a boil over low heat, then, stirring constantly, boil for 2 minutes. Add the cream and bring back to a boil over low heat. Remove from the heat and cool to lukewarm. Stir in the confectioners' sugar. Add more, if necessary, to reach spreading consistency.
Makes about 1 cup.

OATMEAL LAYERED BROWNIES

With their layer of oatmeal, you can easily convince yourself these Oatmeal-Layered Brownies are a healthy snack. We featured these absolutely delicious brownies way back in the '70s in a one-page Cuisinart publication we called *Recipes of the Month*. A few years later, due to the volume of requests, we published it again in a Cuisinart Cooking Club publication called *The Cooking Edge*. Once made and tasted, you will know why this recipe deserves to be resurrected frequently. We suggest using the food processor to speed up the preparation, but handmade will taste just as good!

Oatmeal Layer:

- 1/2 cup cold margarine (1 stick, not the soft spread)
- 1/3 cup firm-packed dark brown sugar
- 1/2 cup all-purpose flour
- 1-1/2 cups quick cooking oatmeal
- 1/8 teaspoon salt

Chocolate Topping:

- 3 ounces unsweetened chocolate
- 1-1/4 cups sugar
- 3 large eggs
- 3/4 cup margarine (1-1/2 sticks, not the soft spread)
- 1-1/2 teaspoons pure vanilla extract
- 3/4 cup all-purpose flour
- 3/4 cup chopped walnuts

Preheat the oven to 350 degrees.

To make the Oatmeal Layer, cut the margarine into 1-inch pieces. In a food processor fitted with the metal blade, pulse the margarine and the remaining ingredients until crumbly, about 10 pulses. Press into an ungreased 9 by 9-inch baking pan and bake in the center of the oven for about 10 minutes or until lightly browned. Let cool for about 5 minutes before adding the topping.

To make the Chocolate Topping, cut the chocolate into 1-inch pieces. In a food processor fitted with the metal blade, process the chocolate and sugar until finely chopped. Add the eggs, margarine, cut into 1-inch pieces, and vanilla and process until well combined. Pulse in the flour and nuts until just incorporated.

SUZANNE S. JONES

Spread the mixture evenly over the oatmeal layer and bake in the center of the oven for about 25 minutes or until a toothpick inserted in the center comes out clean. Let cool completely before cutting.

Makes 36 servings.

PARSNIP TART

Vegetable desserts have been around for years, but it never fails to amaze us at how frequently they will turn up on dessert menus. Think Carrot Cake, Zucchini Cake, Pinto Bean Pie, Chocolate Beet Cake, Pumpkin Pie (although pumpkin is really a fruit), Sweet Potato Pie, Spiced Potato Cookies, and a wonderful French Tourtes de Blettes—just to name a few. We can't think of a more tempting way to get your vegetables, if you can ignore the added calories! Just thank your ancestors for teaching us how to turn otherwise plain vegetables into mouthwatering sweets. Here, especially, the parsnip—sometimes called the "garden candy"—gives this dessert a deliciously sweet and somewhat nutty flavor. Just make sure your parsnips are fresh.

Partially-Baked Tart Shell:

2 cups all-purpose flour
3/4 teaspoon salt
12 tablespoons chilled butter
2 tablespoons chilled vegetable shortening (Crisco suggested)
1/4 to 1/3 cup ice water

Lightly oil a 10-inch tart pan. In a food processor fitted with the metal blade, process the flour and salt just to mix. Add the butter and shortening and process on and off until you have pea-size pieces. Add the ice water through the feed tube little by little until the dough just begins to form a mass. Transfer to a floured surface and shape into a disc. Wrap well and chill for two hours. Roll dough out on a floured surface to a circle 2 inches larger than the prepared tart pan. Fit into the pan, pressing excess dough slightly down the inside of the sides to make the sides thicker. Prick all over with a fork and refrigerate for 30 minutes. Preheat the oven to 425 degrees. Line the tin with aluminum foil and fill with pie weights or dry beans. Bake in the center of the oven for 8 minutes. Remove the foil and weights or beans and prick the bottom of the dough again. Bake an additional 4 minutes to just faintly brown and set the dough. Set aside to cool while making the filling.

Filling:

4 tablespoons orange marmalade	1 tablespoon fresh lemon juice
1-1/2 cups pureed cooked parsnips	1 tablespoon grated orange zest
4 large eggs	1 package (3 ounces) cream cheese at room temperature
1/4 teaspoon salt	
1/2 cup heavy cream	6 tablespoons sugar, divided
4 tablespoons fresh orange juice	1/4 cup chopped toasted walnuts*

Preheat the oven to 400 degrees. In a small saucepan, heat the marmalade until softened and coat the inside of the cooled tart shell. Set aside.

In a large mixing bowl, beat together the remaining ingredients, reserving 4 tablespoons of the sugar and the nuts. Pour the mixture into the prepared shell and bake in the center of the oven for 15 minutes. In a small bowl, combine the reserved 4 tablespoons sugar and the nuts and sprinkle over the top of the tart. Bake for an additional 15 minutes or until the filling is set. Cool before serving.

Makes 12 servings.

*To toast the walnuts, preheat the oven to 350 degrees. Sprinkle the nuts in a pie pan and bake in the center of the oven for 8 to 10 minutes or until fragrant and just beginning to color.

POTATO CHIP COOKIES

Potato Chip Cookies are the best way we know to utilize any leftover chips you may have purchased for your party dips and spreads. We made them the first time just as a novelty but discovered they were extremely tasty. The recipe came from a friend in Connecticut many years ago who served them at an afternoon tea. We were intrigued and asked her to share. We did find that you should not use any sodium-reduced or sodium-free chips since the salt from the standard chips are needed for the best flavor. Once you make and taste these cookies, we guarantee you will buy potato chips just to make them again and again.

- 1-1/2 cups butter or stick margarine, at room temperature
- 1/2 cup firm-packed light brown sugar
- 3/4 cup granulated sugar
- 2 large egg yolks
- 2 teaspoons pure vanilla extract
- 3 cups all-purpose flour
- 2 cups crushed potato chips
- 1/2 cup chopped nuts (walnuts, pecans—or try peanuts for fun)

Preheat the oven to 350 degrees

In a large bowl, cream the butter and sugars with an electric mixer on medium until light. Beat in the egg yolks and vanilla. With a spoon, stir in the flour, potato chips, and nuts. The mixture should be quite thick.

Shape into balls the size of a small walnut and place about 2 inches apart on an ungreased baking sheet. Flatten the cookies with a fork dipped in flour in a crisscross pattern. Bake in the center of the oven for 10 to 12 minutes or until firm.

Makes about 60 cookies.

Saquella Chocolate Espresso Cookies

SAQUELLA CHOCOLATE ESPRESSO COOKIES

There is a delightful restaurant in Boca Raton, Florida—called the Saquella Café—known for its amazing line of bakery products. We were fortunate to be able to convince the owner to share the recipe for our very favorite Saquella Chocolate Espresso Cookies. One look at the ingredient list and you will know immediately how appealing these cookies will be to all chocoholics. The mixture of 3-1/2 cups of semisweet chocolate bits, 3/4 cup of bittersweet chocolate bits, and 1-1/2 cups of white chocolate bits are artfully infused with espresso coffee and vanilla extract with just enough flavor to offset what could have been chocolate overload, even for chocolate lovers. Do plan ahead when making these cookies since the dough needs to chill to firm up before baking. Having the dough chilled makes it easier to handle and keeps it from spreading too much as the cookies bake.

3-1/2 cups semisweet chocolate chips, divided
3/4 cup bittersweet chocolate chips
4 ounces (1 stick) butter
1 cup all-purpose flour
3/4 teaspoon baking powder
1/2 teaspoon salt
4 large eggs
1-1/2 cups sugar
1/4 cup strong espresso coffee*
1 teaspoon pure vanilla extract
1-1/2 cups white chocolate chips

In a heavy saucepan, combine 2 cups of the semisweet chocolate chips, the bittersweet chocolate chips, and the butter. Over low heat, melt the ingredients, stirring constantly. Remove from the heat and let cool.

In a large mixing bowl whisk together the flour, baking powder, and salt. Transfer to a piece of wax paper. In the same bowl, beat the eggs on the medium speed of an electric mixer until well mixed. Add the sugar, coffee, and vanilla; and beat well for about 2 minutes. Turn the mixer to low and slowly add the cooled chocolate mixture, mixing well. Add the dry ingredients and mix just until incorporated. Fold in the remaining 1-1/2 cups semisweet chocolate chips and the white chocolate chips. Cover and place in the freezer for about 30 minutes, or refrigerate for about 1-1/2 hours or until firm.

When ready to bake, preheat the oven to 350 degrees. Grease cookie sheets. Using a scoop, portion the dough into about 1/2 cup amounts (3 ounces). With lightly oiled hands, shape into balls and place 3 inches apart on the cookie sheet. Gently flatten the cookies to discs about 3-1/4 inches across and 3/4 inch high.

Bake in the center of the oven for about 19 to 21 minutes or until the edges are firm. The center will be slightly soft but will firm up when the cookies cool. Do not overbake. Let sit on the cookie sheet for a few minutes before transferring to brown paper-covered wire racks to cool completely.

Makes about 20 cookies.

*We used about 1/2 teaspoon of instant espresso coffee (Pilon brand) in 1/4 cup boiling water.

SHORTCUT GINGERSNAPS

We learned the secret for these easy and delicious Shortcut Gingersnaps from one of our Swedish relatives in our hometown of Rockford, Illinois, many years ago. We not only use it during the holidays when time is short but any time during the year when we have a hankering for fresh and crisp gingersnaps. Aunt Annie Gustafson, a baker extraordinaire (from scratch) at any time, admitted she resorted to this recipe when friends were coming for coffee on short notice.

1 box (14.5 ounces) gingerbread mix	1/3 cup lukewarm water 1/8 teaspoon lemon extract

In a large mixing bowl, blend the ingredients together well. Wrap the dough in plastic wrap and refrigerate for several hours (usually 4 to 6) until well chilled.

Preheat the oven to 375 degrees and lightly grease your cookie sheets. Divide the dough in half (keep the other half covered and refrigerated), and on a lightly floured surface, roll it out to about 1/4-inch thick. Cut with floured cookie cutters (any shape will do), measuring around 2 to 2-1/2 inches. Place on the prepared cookie sheets and bake in the center of the oven for about 8 to 10 minutes or until firm. Remove to wire racks to cool. Repeat with the remaining dough. The scraps can be rerolled.

Makes about 3 dozen cookies.

SWEET POTATO CHEESECAKE

This recipe came about as a result of friends and family members asking for a substitute dessert for the ubiquitous pumpkin pie, which was always on the menu during the holidays. Of course, once tasted, you will realize that this rich and rewarding dessert—though holiday oriented with its spicy seasonings (cinnamon, ginger, nutmeg, and cloves)—is a winner any time of the year. We found that occasionally substituting gingersnap cookie crumbs for the original graham cracker crumbs in the crust added even further to the culinary enjoyment of this delicious cheesecake.

Crust:

> 2 cups graham cracker crumbs (you might try gingersnap crumbs for a real treat)
> 1/2 cup melted butter
> 1/4 cup chopped pecans

Filling:

> 3 8-ounce packages cream cheese, at room temperature
> 1 cup sugar
> 4 large eggs
> 3 large egg yolks
> 3 tablespoons all-purpose flour
> 1 teaspoon ground cinnamon
> 3/4 teaspoon ground ginger
> 1/2 teaspoon fresh-grated nutmeg
> 1/4 teaspoon ground cloves
> 1 cup heavy whipping cream
> 1-1/2 cups cooked mashed sweet potatoes

To make the crust, combine all the ingredients together well and press onto the bottom of a 10-inch springform pan. Set aside. Preheat the oven to 425 degrees.

To make the filling, in a large bowl, beat together the cheese, sugar, eggs, yolks, flour, and spices on the medium speed of an electric mixer until well blended. Beat in the heavy cream, then the sweet potatoes on medium speed until well mixed. Pour into the prepared pan. Bake in the center of the oven for 15 minutes. Reduce the heat to 275 and continue baking for another hour or until just firm in the center. Remove to a wire rack to cool completely.

Makes 16 servings.

TOURTES DE BLETTES
(Swiss Chard and Apple Pie)

Another tempting way to get your vegetables! We found that you can substitute spinach for the Swiss chard in this unusual dessert, but be sure to call it Tourte d'Epinards instead. (We give you the amount of spinach to substitute.) Again, thank your ancestors for thinking of so many ways to turn otherwise plain vegetables into delicious sweets.

Pastry:

- 3 cups all-purpose flour
- 2 sticks (1 cup) cold unsalted butter, cut into tablespoon-size pieces
- 5 tablespoons confectioners' sugar
- 1/4 teaspoon salt
- 1 large egg yolk
- 4 to 5 tablespoons ice water

In a food processor fitted with the metal blade, process the flour, butter, sugar, and salt until the mixture resembles coarse meal. Lightly beat the egg yolk with 3 tablespoons of the ice water. With the motor running, pour the liquid through the feed tube and process until the liquid is absorbed, but the dough does not form a ball. If it seems too dry, add more ice water a couple teaspoons at a time just until the dough begins to form a mass. Remove from the workbowl and shape into disc. Wrap well and refrigerate for 30 minutes.

Roll out 2/3 of the dough on a lightly floured surface to fit into a 10-inch pie pan with a 1/2-inch overhang. Turn the overhang to the inside and press against the edge of the pan. Prick with a fork and chill for 15 minutes or until firm. Preheat the oven to 400 degrees. Line the pastry with parchment paper or aluminum foil and fill with pie weights or dried beans. Bake for 15 minutes or until the pastry edges are set and lightly browned. Remove the paper and weights or beans. Reduce the heat to 375 and bake for another 4 or 5 minutes or until the base is firm. Set aside to cool while making the filling.

Filling:

- 1/2 cup raisins
- 1/3 cup milk
- 3 pounds Swiss chard (or substitute 13 ounces fresh spinach)
- 2 medium apples (about 13 ounces total)—peeled, seeded, and cut into slices just short of 1/4-inch thick (we like Golden Delicious)
- 1/2 cup pine nuts
- 2 tablespoons red currant jelly
- 1/2 cup plus two tablespoons firm-packed light brown sugar
- 3/4 cup grated mild Dutch cheese, such as Gouda
- 2 large eggs, lightly beaten
- 2 teaspoons grated lemon rind
- 1 tablespoon dark rum
- confectioners' sugar for dusting

In a small saucepan, soak the raisins in the milk for 30 minutes, then simmer them in the milk for 10 minutes or until very soft. Drain well and discard the milk. Reserve.

Discard the ribs from the chard and use only the leaves. (If using spinach, trim away the large stems.) Add the leaves to a large pot of boiling water and boil for 3 to 4 minutes. (If using spinach, about 1 minute is enough.) Drain under cold running water. Drain again and squeeze out all excess liquid.

Preheat the oven to 375 degrees.

Chop the chard (or spinach) and in a large bowl mix it well with the raisins and the remaining ingredients except the sugar. Spoon the filling into the baked shell. Roll out the remaining dough on a lightly floured surface into a thin layer and use a pan lid to cut out a circle a little larger than the diameter of the top of the baked pie shell. Set the circle on top of the filling and press it against the edge of the baked shell. Cut a few decorative slits in the top crust. Bake in the center of the oven for about an hour or until the dough is golden brown.

Cool the tourte in the pan. Best served at room temperature, with confectioners' sugar sifted over the top.

Makes 8 servings.

VEGETARIAN KEY WEST LIME CHEESECAKE

Vegetarian Key West Lime Cheesecake

According to the owner of a popular vegetarian restaurant, everyone who tastes this remarkable cheesecake finds it impossible to tell it is a nondairy version of the popular dessert. What impressed our tasters when we tested this cheesecake was not only the wonderfully tart flavor of key lime, but the incredible creamy texture. And that delicious filling bakes in a prebaked graham cracker shell that had already filled the kitchen with the heavenly aroma of cinnamon and ginger. You can find most of the organic and vegetarian ingredients in your local supermarket now or in a gourmet or health food shop.

Crust:

1/2 cup plus 2 tablespoons Earth Balance margarine* at room temperature	1/2 cup plus 2 tablespoons natural brown sugar*
1 teaspoon ground cinnamon	1-1/2 cups graham cracker crumbs
1 teaspoon ground ginger	

Preheat the oven to 350 degrees. Combine the ingredients in a food processor fitted with the metal bade. Process until well combined. Press the mixture onto the bottom and about 1-1/2 inches up the sides of a 9-inch springform pan. Bake in the center of the oven for about 10 minutes, or until fragrant and firm. Remove from the oven and cool completely.

Key Lime Filling:

2 pounds soy cream cheese* at room temperature	1/2 cup plus 2 tablespoons key lime juice
2 cups sugar	1/2 cup egg replacer*

Preheat the oven to 350 degrees. Place a baking pan on the center rack of the oven.

Place all the ingredients in the workbowl of a food processor fitted with the metal blade. Process until smooth and well blended. Pour the filling into the cooled crust and place on the baking pan. Bake the cake for 45 to 50 minutes or until firm around the edge but still slightly soft to the touch in the middle. (It will still joggle a bit.) You do not want to overbake or it could become dry. Let cool to room temperature then cover lightly and refrigerate for several hours or overnight before cutting.

Makes 12 servings.

*Can be found in health food stores, gourmet shops, or in some supermarkets.

CULINARY TIPS AND TIDBITS

Over the years of doing research for books, columns, and articles, I began noting the interesting, informative, and sometimes amusing culinary tips and tidbits in many of the sources I waded through and studied. I began making notes of any worth remembering and/or repeating, and share some of them below. The first is one that could be the introduction to any cookbook!

1. A recipe is a series of step-by-step instructions for preparing ingredients you forgot to buy, in utensils you do not own, to make a dish even the dog won't eat!
2. Fish, to taste right, must swim three times—in water, in butter, and in wine. (An old Polish proverb.)
3. To make a great and easy rice pudding, prepare a 4-serving box of vanilla pudding, stir in about 1-1/2 cups (more or less is not crucial) leftover cooked rice, and flavor with a little cinnamon and nutmeg.
4. In the event you have wondered where the name *coleslaw* originated, it is from the Dutch who, in the eighteenth century, called cabbage cut into long, thin strips "koolsla." *Kool* is the word for "cabbage" and *sla* the word for "salad." You will still find the word incorrectly used as *cold slaw*.
5. The word *restaurant* derives from the French *restaurer*, "to restore." According to *Larousse Gastronomique*, the modern-day restaurant began around 1765 with a Parisian bouillon seller whose sign stated that he sold "restoratives fit for the gods" and incorporated a motto in dog Latin: "Venite ad me omnes qui stomacho/labaoretis, et ego restaurabo vos," which when translated means, "Come unto me, all you whose stomachs are aching, and I will restore you." Perhaps that is what today's restaurants aim to do, albeit more subtly.
6. Mushroom Trivia: In medieval Ireland, mushrooms were thought to be umbrellas for leprechauns; the English believed mushrooms had to be gathered under a full moon to be edible; and ancient Egyptians considered mushrooms the sons of gods, sent to earth riding on bolts of lightning.
7. A hostess must be like a duck—calm and unruffled on the surface, and paddling like hell underneath.
8. Whenever you buy grapes, remember this delightful remark by Brillat Savarin—that French magistrate, politician, and gastronome born in 1755—who, when offered grapes for dessert, said: "No thank you. I am not in the habit of taking my wine in pills."

9. If you want to get more vegetables (one-fourth serving) into your family without them suspecting, mix in a cup of grated carrots or zucchini for each pound of meat in your burgers.
10. In France, in the year 1680, a pastry cook in the kitchens of the Duke of Choiseul de Plessis-Pralin browned almonds in boiling sugar and discovered that they had an entrancing new flavor. This find made the duke's name immortal because *praline* (pronounced pra-lean-ay) has been used ever since to create delicious desserts.
11. You never know where or when you might pick up cooking tips. I overheard the following in the emergency waiting room of a hospital. One lady complained about the difficulties of cutting an acorn squash in half. Another gave the following advice: Put the squash, pointed end down, in the drain hole of your kitchen sink. It keeps the squash from rolling around. Cut it as far as you can straight through, then simply pop the remaining connective fibers apart. It works!
12. The most remarkable thing about my mother is that for thirty years she served the family nothing but leftovers. Though archaeologists were hired, the original meal has never been found.—Calvin Trillin
13. The first meat grinder is attributed to the chef to King Louis IX who is said to have invented a little wheel with cutting edges and a small tunnel through which one pushed food. (Refinements on that first meat grinder have kept the world in preground meats ever since.)
14. If you overcook vegetables, don't despair or discard. Puree them, stir in some butter or cream, reheat, and you have a delicious side dish. Or you could thin them further with cream or broth and turn out a tasty soup.
15. For a simple and tasty dessert, swirl slightly warmed crunchy peanut butter into softened vanilla or chocolate ice cream and refreeze. Serve in parfait glasses sprinkled with peanuts.
16. A few years ago, the *British Medical Journal* published a list of alcoholic beverages in the order in which they caused hangovers, from the least severe to the most. The list reads: vodka, gin, white wine, whiskey, rum, red wine, and brandy. Choose wisely!
17. Considering how tuned in we all are to eating right, exercising, etc., to prevent everything from aging to various diseases, this humorous information from a cookbook published in 1909 called *Things Worth Knowing* will amuse you. Called "How to Cure Aging": Steep the young leaves of periwinkle or creeping myrtle in fresh springwater until the latter has imbibed all the essence; a teacupful taken each day will slow the aging process; it quickens the mind and purifies the blood and prevents anxieties. Some find it quite beneficial to add a wineglassful of brandy." I've a feeling it's the last ingredient that helps in every case!

18. From an IACP quarterly food forum of facts complied during a project research came this interesting information: "Adults have ten thousand taste buds. Rabbits have seventeen thousand. Cows have twenty-five thousand. Idly, one wonders why."
19, In an old recipe for Indian pudding, molasses was measured this way: Let the molasses drip in as you sing one verse of "Nearer My God to Thee"; sing two verses in cold weather.
20. It takes four men to dress a salad, a wise man for the salt, a madman for the pepper, a miser for the vinegar, and a spendthrift for the oil. —Anonymous
21. For a finale: All cookbooks resemble each other like brothers. The best is the one that one writes himself.—Fernand Point

I have been involved with the development and literary end of food and recipes since the late 60's when I was Manager of the Harrington's of Vermont gourmet food and cookware shop in Greenwich, CT. I was recruited by the late Carl G. Sontheimer, father of the Cuisinart Food Processor, to direct the test kitchen, eventually becoming the editor of his magazine, The Pleasures of Cooking. In this position I helped promote the then new food processor, as well as conducted instructional classes, and handled promotional advertising and private seminars, one of which was to help Sontheimer introduce the food processor to the late Julia Childs. I worked with many well known chefs and food writers, including the late Julia Childs, James Beard and Roy Andres De Groot. In 1980 I wrote The Low-Cholesterol Food Processor Cook book (Doubleday).

After retiring from Cuisinarts in 1986 I moved to Florida with my husband. I was approached by the Tribune-owned Fort Lauderdale Sun-Sentinel newspaper to write special articles on cooking, which led to the weekly column, "You Asked For It". It invited readers to request recipes from well-known restaurants, past memories and lost family favorites as well as general and specific cooking information. Sixteen years later I retired and I moved to Louisiana to be near family and to enjoy having time to share some of those recipes with you.

INDEXES

GENERAL INDEX

A

A.1. Steak Sauce, 293
a la crecy, 78
alcoholic beverages, 396
Allen, Frank, 125
allspice, 373
almonds, browned. *See* praline
Annie's Naturals brand raspberry
    vinaigrette, 124
Asiago cheese, 281
Asiago cream sauce, 281-82

B

backfin crab, 47
Bahamian peas, 172-73
balsamic vinaigrette, 91-92
barley, 89. *See also* malted barley
basket cheese, 223
Beard, James, 71, 175, 289
beef cheeks, 237
beet, 54
Bert, Jean, 255, 325
Big Bear Brewing Company, 97, 305
Bimini Boatyard Bar and Grill, 253
Bisquick, 27
black bean salsa, 327-28
blackberry vinaigrette, 125-26
black walnuts, 379
Blanchard, Marjorie Page
    *Treasured Recipes from Early New
    England Kitchens*, 205
Boca Raton, Florida, 79, 143, 197, 301,
    327, 387
bordelaise sauce, 250-51

bouquet garni, 53
Bragg Liquid Aminos, 85
Brassiere Mon Ami, 197
braunschweiger, 22
Brennan, Patrick, 113
Brie, 39-40
British Medical Journal, 396
broccoli, 63, 176
Brooks Restaurant, 189
Brown Derby, 103
brussels sprouts, 193

C

Caesar salad, 113
California Prune Board, 329
Cap'n Crunch, 277
caramel frosting, 357-58
Cardini, Caesar, 113
Carson Pirie Scott, 163
cauliflower, 177
cayenne pepper, 53
Charcuterie Too, 95
Cheddar cheese, 19, 51, 157, 231
    sharp, 29, 186
cheese straws, 19
Child, Julia, 263, 289
chili, 269
chocolate chips, 139, 365, 387
Colby cheese, 221
coleslaw, 395
cookbooks, 397
Cooking Edge, The, 53, 381
cornmeal mush. *See* polenta
couscous, 97
Cracker Barrel, 221

Craye, Kie, 148
cream cheese, 18, 20, 23, 29, 47, 139, 287, 335, 365, 384, 390, 394
Creole mustard sauce, 277-79
cucina povera, 73
Cuisinarts Inc., 33, 148, 157, 216, 237, 289
culinary tips, 395-97

D

devil's soup, 269
Dorothee (Rosemarie's cousin), 81
double-cut pork chops, 241
Dragon Palace, 291

E

Egg Beaters, 99
eggplants, 37
eggs, raw, 99
en riant, 17
epazote, 58
Esau, 75

F

Family Bakery, 377
farina, plain, 148
Fetzer, 229
fish, 317, 395
Floden, Christine Swenson Person, 266
French Culinary Institute, 203
Fulvio (chef/restaurant owner), 309

G

Ganter, Hugh, 173
garden candy. *See* parsnip
Gardner's Markets, 275
garlic, 35
Gerin, Jean-Louis, 248
gingerbread cookie, 369-70

goat cheese, 25-26
Golden Delicious apples, 241
goosefoot. *See* epazote
Gourmet Cookbook, 24
Graham, Sylvester, 155
Graham flour, 155
Granny Smith apples, 60
Grant (chef), 295
grapes, 395
Greer, Anne, 225
grissini, 41
gulaschsuppe, 81
Gustafson, Annie, 227, 389

H

Harralson, Curtis, 179
Harrington's of Vermont, 105
heavy cream, 229
Herta (German neighbor), 81
hogie (hoagie) roll, 323
Holly, 153
hominy, 58
horseradish, 71, 101, 275
hostess, 395
House Beautiful, 216
Howe, Jon, 189, 237
"How to Cure Aging," 396
hummus, 44-45

I

Ivanie (baker), 161

J

Jack cheese, 35, 231, 335
Jen (aunt), 132, 357
Jerusalem oak pazote. *See* epazote
Jim Moran Heart Center, 375
Johannes (restaurant owner), 327
Jones, Suzanne

Low-Cholesterol Food Processor Cookbook, The, 75, 78, 99, 101
Joy of Cooking, The, 213

K

Kantzanelos, Sam, 37
Kelley, Annie, 143
key lime vinaigrette, 102-3
Kitchenetta, 351
kjottfars, 266
Koss, Mayburn, 157

L

lard, 82
Larousse Gastronomique, 395
leftovers, 213, 396
Lentils, 75
lima beans, 206
liverwurst, 22
Low-Cholesterol Food Processor Cookbook, The (Jones), 75, 78, 99, 101
Lucarella's, 223
Lutece restaurant, 203

M

malted barley, 147
mangos, 106
McCully, Helen, 216
meat grinder, 396
Mexican tea. *See* epazote
Minestrone, 73
mixtamal. *See* hominy
Moller, Jorgen, 331
Moller, Monica, 331
mushroom cream sauce, 333-34
mushrooms, 395
mustard, Pommery. *See* Pommery (Moutarde de Meaux) mustard

N

National Rice Month, 111
Nealon, Chris, 103

P

Papa Hughie. *See* Ganter, Hugh
papillote, 331
Parmesan cheese, 149, 177, 210, 305
parsnip, 383
pate, 33
pate a choux, 184
Pepin, Jacques, 30
Pepperidge Farm Company, 287
Perry, Belle, 159
Pete Rose Ballpark Café, 125
Pete's, 301
pigeon peas, 173
Pillsbury, 149
Pillsbury Bake-Off, 145
pistachios, 24
Pleasures of Cooking, The, 30, 363
plum, dried. *See* prunes
Point, Fernand, 189, 397
polenta, 219
Pommery (Moutarde de Meaux) mustard, 95
Powell, Jean, 207
pozole, 58
praline, 396
prunes, 329

R

Rapoport, Burt, 181
Rapoport, Ray, 54
raspberry vinegar, 108
recipe, 395
Recipes of the Month, 381
Reed (kitchen manager), 161
restaurant, 395

Restaurant de la Pyramid, 189
Restaurant Jean-Louis, 248
rice pudding, 395
Riverside Hotel, 161
Rosa's and Pasquale's, 285
Rosemarie (German friend), 81
Rossi, Rita, 163
Rudkin, Margaret, 141
rutabaga, 183

S

saffron threads, 326
Salisbury, J. H., 261
Salisbury, Marquis of, 261
Salisbury Steak, 261
salmon, 30
Saquella Café, 387
Savarin, Brillat, 395
Sax, Richard, 231
Seafood World Restaurant, 173
Sea Watch, 345
soft fry, 20
Soltner, Andre, 203
Sontheimer, Carl, 33
sour cream, 20, 23, 46, 95, 145, 219, 294
spaghetti, 219, 233
Sticky Buns, 133
Stouffer's, 163
Summers, Trish, 120
sun-dried tomato vinaigrette, 317
sweet potatoes, 181
Sweet Tomatoes, 167
Swiss cheese, 46, 120

T

tahini, 41
taste buds, 397
terrines, 33
Tex-Mex cuisine, 225
Things Worth Knowing, 396

Tolbert, Frank, 269
tomatoes, green, 372
Tony (chef), 79
Treasured Recipes from Early New England Kitchens (Blanchard), 205
Trillin, Calvin, 213, 396
turkey ham, 34
turnips, 183

V

veal hind shanks, 255
vegetables, 396
Verge, Roger, 184
vichyssoise, 60

W

Whale's Rib, 349
Whole Foods Market, 123, 195
whole wheat flour. *See* Graham flour
Willoughby, Bill, 67
Wolf, Oliver, 259
Wool, Fran, 366

Y

yellowtail snapper, 343

Z

zingara, 321

RECIPE INDEX

A

appetizers
  American Café Homemade Ketchup, 17
  Baked Chicken Nuggets with Hot and Sweet Mustard Sauce, 18
  Blue Cheese Cookies, 19
  Cheese and Chive Spread, 20
  Chicken Pate with Almonds, 21
  Corned Beef Pate, 22
  Cream Cheese and Vegetable Spread, 23
  Favorite Chopped Chicken Livers, 24
  Froggies La Tarte au Tomates et Fromages Chevres (Goat Cheese and Tomato Tart), 25-26
  Holiday (or Other) Ham Balls, 27
  Hot Cheese and Crab Dip, 29
  Jacques Pepin's Salmon Tartare, 30
  Lobster Fritters with Lemon Sauce, 31-32
  Low-fat (Holiday) Terrine, 33-34
  Max's Grille Spinach Artichoke Dip, 35-36
  Melitzanosalata (Greek Eggplant Dip), 37-38
  Pistachio Brie with Raspberry Sauce, 39-40
  Roasted Sweet Potato Dip, 41
  Seafood World Stuffed Mushrooms, 43
  Sesame Cheese Bread Sticks with Sundried Tomato Hummus, 44-45
  Swiss Onion Squares, 46
  Two Georges Crab Dip, 47

B

breads
  Apple Cream Coffee Cake, 131
  Bourbon-Pecan Bread, 132
  Buttery Caramel Quicks, 133
  Cereal Brunch Coffee Cake, 134-35
  Chili Bread, 137-38
  Chocolate Chip Coffee Cake, 139
  Chocolate Sticky Buns, 141-42
  Dried Cranberry/Nut Muffins, 144
  Easy Onion Casserole Bread, 145-46
  English Muffin Bread, 147-48
  Herbed Oatmeal Pan Bread, 149-50
  Hero Bread, 152
  Holly's Mystery Muffins, 153
  Honey Graham Crackers, 155
  Mayburn's Pepper Cheese Bread, 157
  Orange Juice Muffins with Honey Spread, 158
  Risen Biscuits, 160
  Riverside Hotel Brown Bread, 161-62
  Stouffer's Coffee Cake, 163-64
  Stuffing Bread, 165-66
  Sweet Tomatoes Tangy Lemon Muffins, 167-68
  Whole Wheat Biscotti, 169-70

C

casseroles and combinations
  Andre Soltner's Potato Pie, 203-4
  Baked Apples and Onions, 205
  Baked Lima Beans, 206
  Biscuits and Gravy, 207-8
  Browned White Rice Casserole, 209
  Casserole Carrots, 210
  Cassolette de Fruits de Mer (Seafood Casserole), 211-12
  Cooked Chicken or Turkey Loaf, 213
  Corn Relish, 214-15

Fish Soufflé with Mustard Sauce (An
   Elegant Aftermath), 216-17
Gorgonzola Polenta, 219
Ham and Mac Bake, 220
Hash Brown Casserole, 221
Italian Easter Pie (Pizza Rustica), 222-24
King Ranch Casserole, 225-26
Macaroni Croquettes, 227-28
"No Cream" Cream, 229
Onion Shortcake, 230
Richard Sax's Comforting
   Cafeteria-Style Macaroni and Cheese,
   231-32
Spaghetti Pizza Pie, 233

D

desserts
   Apple Pound Cake, 355-56
   Aunt Jen's Blackberry Jam Cake, 357-58
   Banana Cream Pie, 361
   Chocolate Almond Balls, 364
   Cream Cheese Chocolate Chip Pound
      Cake, 365
   Easy Rice Pudding, 366
   Frozen Fruit Yogurts, 368
   Frozen Key Lime-Ginger Pie, 369
   Green Tomato Fudge Cake, 372
   Guinness Fruitcake, 373-74
   Holy Cross Hospital Oatmeal Raisin
      Cookies, 375-76
   Marble Cake (a.k.a. Condo Cake), 378
   Mother-in-Law Apple Cake, 379-80
   Oatmeal Layered Brownies, 381-82
   Parsnip Tart, 383-84
   Potato Chip Cookies, 385
   Saquella Chocolate Espresso Cookies, 386-88
   Shortcut Gingersnaps, 389
   Sweet Potato Cheesecake, 390
   Tourtes de Blettes (Swiss Chard and
      Apple Pie), 391-92
   Vegetarian Key West Lime Cheesecake, 394

M

main dishes (poultry)
   Anthony's Chicken Al, 272-74
   Awesome Turkey Loaf, 276
   Cap'n Crunch Chicken with Creole
      Mustard Sauce, 279
   Chicken Asiago Pasta, 280-82
   Chicken San Remo, 284
   Chicken Silana, 285-86
   Chicken Wellington, 287-88
   Chicken with Forty Cloves of Garlic, 289
   Dragon Palace Mango Chicken, 290-92
   Easy, Easy Chicken, 293
   Ground Turkey Stroganoff, 294
   Henry's Coq Au Vin, 297
   Palm Chicken, 299
   Pete's Chicken Pecan, 302
   Potted Turkey Legs, 303-4
   Pretzel Chicken with Beurre Blanc
      Sauce, 307
   Stuffed Chicken Breasts, 310
   Tender Poached Chicken Breasts, 311
   Turkey Loaves with Apricot Glaze, 312-13
main dishes (red meat)
   Book's Veal Stew, 236-38
   Brandy Burgers, 239
   Burger Bundles, 240
   Double-Cut Pork Chops with Country
      Applesauce, 241-42
   Ham Patties, 243
   Henry's Beef Stroganoff, 247
   Jean-Louis' Lamb Stew, 248-49
   Meat Loaf, 250-51, 253
   Meat Loaf with Mushroom Sauce, 253
   Osso Buco, 256
   Reuben Croquettes, 257-58
   Rigatoni Bolognaise, 260
   Salisbury Steak with Mushroom Gravy,
      261-62
   Shepherd's Pie, 265
   Swedish Meatballs (Kjottbollar), 266-67

Texas Chili, 269-70
main dishes (seafood)
   Atlantic Salmon with Sun-Dried Tomato Vinaigrette, 316-18
   Baked Beer Batter Shrimp, 319
   Dolphin Zingara, 321-22
   Grilled Lobster Club Sandwich, 324
   La Coquille Shrimp Pasta, 326
   Mahi Mahi Mango Mango, 328
   Monkfish with Prunes, 329-30
   Out of Denmark Snapper en Papillote, 331-32
   Pan-Seared Scallops in Mushroom Cream Sauce, 333-34
   Salmon Quiche, 335
   Seafood Cakes, 336-37
   Seafood Newburg, 339-40
   Shrimp Mousse with Sole, 341-42
   Snapper Calypso, 344
   Stuffed Sole, 347
   Tuna Catania, 352
   Whale's Rib Baked Dolphin, The, 348

S

salads
   Barley and Sausage Salad, 89-90
   Chicken Pasta Salad, 93
   Chicken Salad with Grapes, 95
   Cold Lamb Salad, 96
   Couscous Salad, 97-98
   Egg White Only and No-Egg Mayonnaise, 99-100
   Fresh Cucumber Mousse, 101
   Grilled Chicken Cobb Salad with Key Lime Vinaigrette, 102-4
   Ham and Macaroni Salad, 105
   Mango Salad Dressing, 106
   Martha's Vineyard Salad with Raspberry-Maple Dressing, 107-8
   Molded Potato and Ham Salad (a.k.a. Cake), 109-10
   Oriental Rice Salad, 111-12
   Patrick's Caesar Salad, 113-14
   Roasted Three-Potato Salad, 115
   Shanghai Chicken Salad with Spicy Honey Mustard Dressing, 117-18
   Strawberry-Pretzel Salad, 119
   Trish's Hot Chicken Salad, 120-21
   Walnut and Watercress Salad, 122
   Who's On First Fresh Tuna Salad, 125-27
   Wild Rice Salad, 124

soups
   Baked Potato Soup, 50-52
   Butternut Squash Soup with Pears, 53
   Cabbage Borscht, 54-55
   Chicken and Escarole Soup, 56-57
   Chicken "Pozole," 58-59
   Chilled Apple Vichyssoise, 60
   Country-Style Tomato Soup, 62
   Cream of Broccoli Soup, 63-64
   Cream of Garlic Soup, 66
   Cream of Mushroom Soup, 67-68
   Cucumber and Dill Soup, 69
   Horseradish Soup, 71
   Nick's Minestrone Soup, 74
   Priest's Soup (Lentil Soup or Esau's Potage), 75
   Pumpkin Bisque, 77
   Puree Crecy (A Cold Carro/Potato Soup), 78
   Real Gulaschsuppe, The, 81-82
   Salmon-Tomato Bisque, 79-80
   Tomato Bleu Cheese Soup, 83
   Vegetarian Pumpkin Soup, 85
   Watercress Soup, 86

V

vegetables
   Bahamian Peas and Rice, 173
   Beer Batter Fried Asparagus, 175
   Broccoli Custard Bake, 176
   Cauliflower au Gratin, 177

Curtis' Broccoli Soufflé, 180
Henry's Sweet Potato Gratin, 182
Himmel und Erde (Heaven and Earth), 183
Light Corn Fritters, 184
Mashed Potato Puffs for Two, 185
Nutty Baked Cabbage, 186
Orange Glazed Carrots, 187
Ratatouille, 189-90
Roasted Garlic Bread Pudding, 191-92
Sautéed Brussels Sprouts with Nuts, 193
Spinach Rosemary Cakes, 194-95
Sweet Potato Mash, 197
Zucchini Soufflé, 199

Edwards Brothers, Inc.
Thorofare, NJ USA
September 8, 2011